EVERYTHING **MUST** CHANGE!

EVERYTHING MUST CHANGE!

The World After Covid-19

Edited by

Renata Ávila and Srećko Horvat

OR Books
New York · London

First edition published by OR Books, 2020

© 2021 Renata Ávila and Srećko Horvat

Published by OR Books, New York and London
Visit our website at www.orbooks.com

All rights information: rights@orbooks.com

First printing 2021

Cataloging-in-Publication data is available from the Library of Congress.
A catalog record for this book is available from the British Library.

Typeset by Lapiz Digital Services.

paperback ISBN 978-1-68219-305-1 • ebook ISBN 978-1-68219-271-9

Contents

Introduction: Everything Must Change, So That Nothing Remains the Same

Srećko Horvat

Since armies can reach each other regardless of the thousands of miles which lie between them, friends have to show that they are just as independent from spatial distances as enemies. So let's continue shooting our long distance missiles of friendship to each other in order to show those who are inventive only in order to destroy, that we are just as able to nullify space as they.

— Günther Anders to Claude Eatherly, 1959

In the famous novel of the mid-twentieth century *The Leopard*, Giuseppe Tomasi di Lampedusa chronicles the struggle of the Sicilian aristocracy to survive in the face of civil war and revolution, the so-called *Risorgimento*. One of the most famous sentences—later proclaimed by Alain Delon in Luchino Visconti's movie adaptation of the book—reads, "Everything must change, so that everything remains the same." In a similar way, forced by the Covid-19 crisis, our contemporary ruling class is well aware that a deep transformation is taking place and that the only way for things to remain the same is the emergence of a new social and political arrangement that can keep them in power. What other proof is needed of the deep tensions plaguing capitalism but the spiking of Jeff Bezos's fortune by $13 billion in a single day in July 2020,[1] as the Covid-19 crisis prioritizes the free movement of goods even higher than the free movement of people, while, at the same time, Amazon workers have been dying of Covid-19 and protesting their inhuman working conditions? What other proof than Elon Musk, the embodiment of the capitalist expansionist dream, who, when challenged with the claim that the United States coup against Evo Morales occurred to enable him to obtain Bolivia's lithium, simply answered, "We will coup whoever we want! Deal with it."[2] And this is not the first time that the ruling class has openly proclaimed that

1   https://www.telegraph.co.uk/technology/2020/07/21/jeff-bezos-adds-record-13bn-fortune-one-day/.

2   https://www.telesurenglish.net/news/elon-musk-confesses-to-lithium-coupin-bolivia-20200725-0010.html.

there is a class war going on. Remember Warren Buffet, another billionaire, who famously said, "There's class warfare, all right, but it's my class, the rich class, that's making war, and we're winning." With the Covid-19 crisis, which is exacerbating existing inequalities and enhancing the accumulation of profit for exactly those driving the planet toward mass extinction, it has never been so tangible that a brutal class war is happening. And they are, again, trying to win.

"Everything must change, so that everything remains the same," proclaims the ruling class once again, clinging to the hope that they will manage to stay in power and continue the vicious cycle of exploitation, extraction, and expansion—the three E's of the world system called capitalism. Instead of investing in the hospitals and schools that were already victims of decades of austerity and underfunding, they are, once again, bailing out the companies responsible for the climate crisis and global injustice. Instead of protecting workers' rights and using technology to abolish exploitation, the suffering of so-called essential (or "frontline") workers has only increased with the Covid-19 crisis, while the situation is being exploited for the expansion and acceleration of "surveillance capitalism." Instead of protecting the climate, further extraction of natural resources and destruction of habitats is leading to an age of pandemics, with even deadlier viruses than Covid-19 waiting just around the corner. Instead of defunding the police, almost everywhere police have responded to Covid-19 as to a war, transforming themselves into an army. As a recent commercial for the National Guard in the United States claimed, "Sometimes the front lines are right in our backyard." It seems the famous call of the Weather Underground to "Bring the war home!" has suddenly been realized, only its cause is not a social movement or a clandestine revolutionary party, but a virus. From Minneapolis to Portland, Budapest to Istanbul, and Santiago to Belgrade, the capitalist war has now, indeed, become a civil war. "I can't breathe"—repeated again and again by Eric Garner, George Floyd, and many other victims of structural racism—has become the predominant feeling of those suffering and dying from the suffocations of police brutality, air pollution, viruses, depression, anxiety, fear, and the myriad other symptoms of the expansion of capital into nature, animals, lungs, minds, and souls.

While the viruses of capitalism and racism ravage the world, this book itself is the product of a different kind of virus. Not only would this publication not have come to light without the Covid-19 coronavirus, but it is a product of the "viruses" of cooperation and internationalism that are aimed precisely at the virus of a world system that is driving us toward extinction. The plethora of critical voices that have emerged from "self-isolation" is a proof—bye-bye, Maggie Thatcher!—that *there is* such thing as society, even if we are often forced to behave and die as individuals. The project to document some of these voices, first in video conversations and then in this book, started in a room in Vienna in which I was confined to isolation in mid-March 2020, just as Europe became the epicenter of the Covid-19 pandemic and before it would severely hit the United States, Brazil, Mexico, and elsewhere. In those early days, states across Europe declared a "state of exception" with unprecedented restrictions on movement, and I was unable to return to my country, Croatia, for another two months. The only way to prevent myself from going crazy and falling into utter hopelessness consisted in hacking my way out of "self-isolation" by creating what we called "DiEM25 TV: The World After Coronavirus." For those of us in the Democracy in Europe Movement 2025, who are used to tirelessly traveling around the world, meeting people, and organizing on the ground, isolation was a new situation, as it was for every true internationalist. Suddenly, all that was left was the digital. And even this would soon be turned into what Naomi Klein called the "Screen New Deal": the penetration of surveillance capitalism into our brains and souls, the further exploitation of cognitive workers, and the extraction of our affects and even our unconscious.[3]

Yet, for a short time between mid-March and July 2020, which already seems like centuries ago, we succeeded in exploiting a crack in the "Screen New Deal" and launched an online "television" channel from our living rooms and places of self-isolation. Much more than just television, this was the creation of a common space, free to everyone, constructed by

3 https://theintercept.com/2020/05/08/andrew-cuomo-eric-schmidt-coronavirus-tech-shock-doctrine/

hundreds of activists and intellectuals from around the world. Rarely have so many people been connected through a single event like the Covid-19 pandemic, with billions around the world placed in some form of quarantine. Rarely have the people on this planet engaged in so much communication, and this despite widespread "social distancing"—for while there was physical distancing, the *social* resurged as never before. We have seen the worst of times and the best of times: on the one hand, a completely new situation of an unprecedented health crisis and, on the other, the necessity to connect and construct a world beyond the destructive notion of "progress" that dominates capitalist modernity. If the slogan of the World Social Forum was "Another world is possible," ours is that graffitied in Minneapolis after the brutal murder of George Floyd: "Another end of the world is possible." Over the course of 2020, it has become clear (even to those previously in denial) that the end of the world as we know it is everywhere. People are suffocating not just at the hands of a virus but of police brutality and a world system based on extraction, expansion, and exploitation. The climate crisis, the nuclear threat, pandemics, and racism: these are the four horsemen of global capitalism and its structural violence against nature, humans, and the future itself. If we want this to change, *nothing* can remain the same.

This book is intended as a collective message that transnational cooperation and resistance, precisely in times of global lockdowns and police states, not only remains possible, but becomes necessary. The list of people to thank, including both those whose conversations have been published and those whose haven't (simply because of a tight schedule and publishing constraints), is long and incomplete. If there is one person without whom DiEM25 TV would certainly have been impossible, it is Davide Castro: a brilliant comrade from Portugal who made our program live and alive in the first months of quarantine. Next are the human machines Yanis Varoufakis and Renata Ávila who, with their immense energy and critical thinking, led and organized many of the conversations; Judith Meyer, who was a true driving force in the shadows; and our brothers and sisters in arms from DiEM25: Ivana Nenadović, Erik Edman, Luis Martín, Mehran Khalili, Sissy Velissariou, Johannes Fehr, Simona Ferlini, Pawel Wargan, David

Adler, Claudia Trapp, Jordi Ayala Roqueta. A big thanks also to numerous DiEM25 volunteers: Andrea Chavez, Max Gede, Dilek Guncag, Esmé Flinders, Ioannis Theocharis, Jerome Bertrand, Julie Hamilton, Micah Jayne, Michael Giardino, Pim Schulte, Rodrigo Fiallega, Niels Wennekes, Matias Mulet, and many others.

Last but not least, in a world in which education and journalism, publishing and critical thinking, become not only a privilege but subversive acts in themselves, it is the courageous publishers—and readers!—who are in a race against time itself, not only preserving an archive for a future in which mass extinction is quickly becoming our only horizon, but disseminating the tools for a common struggle toward a world beyond the ceaseless expansion of capitalism and fascism. Thanks to the daring publisher Colin Robinson and our diligent editor Catherine Cumming, these conversations have truly become a sort of collective diary of the early weeks and months of Covid-19, a common endeavor that might one day serve to document that, even in dark times, to paraphrase Bertolt Brecht, there was singing. And the songs were not just about the dark times, but about friendship and love, solidarity and egalitarianism, mutual aid and resistance to the old world that is dying and kidnapping our future. Everything must change, so that nothing remains the same.

Nothing of the old system must stay, and everything of the beauty, humbleness, and determination of our common struggle—as heterogeneous and ambiguous it often appears—must be cherished as one thing that the old system will never be able to understand. It must be grasped as one of the key ingredients that will bring this system down. Other ingredients include, as we hope this book shows, lots of organization and introspection occurring at the same time; less work, more love; less monologue, more dialogue; less ego, more compassion—and, again, *lots* of organization! If they have missiles that can destroy entire countries thousands of miles away, let us, to paraphrase the great Günther Anders, never stop shooting our long-distance missiles of friendship to each other, in order to show those who are inventive only in order to destroy that we are not out to nullify space as they are—we are, unlike them, able to create *new* spaces and reinvent a future worth living for.

The Cost of Covid-19 Must Not Bankrupt the People

Vijay Prashad and Srećko Horvat

Srećko: As of today, India and the UK are under lockdown. The Olympic Games scheduled to take place in Tokyo are postponed until next year. We have witnessed Cuban doctors arriving in Italy, and Chinese doctors in Serbia, to fight Covid-19. Besides being beautiful gestures of solidarity, these developments also raise questions concerning the future of geopolitics, some of which I hope we can tackle together in our discussion, Vijay.

Vijay: As you said, the government of India has asked 1.4 billion people to self-isolate, and perhaps almost a billion of them will not be able to do so. This is one of the odd things about this time. Those who don't live in slums are able to feel the claustrophobia of entering their homes and shutting the door, but much of the planet is made up of day laborers, people who rely on a daily wage, and unless we change the system, those people are going to get obliterated, not only by this virus but of course by the many viruses that put pressure on their lives.

Srećko: When I look at my Twitter feed, I see so many people in Europe complaining about being in self-isolation, but from the perspective of people in India, Asia, and Latin America, this really looks like a luxury and a privilege. When the authorities instruct populations to "self-isolate," they don't speak about housing or any of the measures that must be implemented before it is possible for someone to self-isolate.

Vijay: Yes, but let's not exaggerate the privilege of those in Europe or the United States. Last year the US Federal Reserve did a survey of households and showed that 40 percent of American households cannot meet an emergency costing $400 or more.[1] Eurostat has a similar survey that showed that one in three Europeans is unable to meet an emergency expense.[2] This lockdown is of course an emergency expense. People don't have the money to pay their rents and mortgages, to pay for the virus tests, or to eat for more than a few days or weeks, depending on the size of their household. We are

---

1 https://www.federalreserve.gov/publications/2019-economic-well-being-of-us-households-in-2018-dealing-with-unexpected-expenses.htm.

2 https://ec.europa.eu/eurostat/web/products-eurostat-news/-/DDN-20181124-1?inheritRedirect=true&.

in the middle of a crisis that capitalism has produced—the conjuncture of this crisis is Covid-19. This virus has, in a sense, pushed over a system that has been very sick for a very long time. And I think this has shocked a lot of people. Many have been shocked by the inability of their governments to take care of them in a time of crisis and have begun to question the kinds of promises made to them by governments, the corporate media, and education institutions. These promises now seem so very empty.

Srećko: In many countries in Europe, a decade of austerity has ruined the public infrastructure that is so needed in this situation of crisis. But instead of simply analyzing the situation and demonstrating what is bad about it, we must also come up with some concrete proposals in terms of what can be done. You, Vijay, have worked on this question, together with your comrades and different organizations, to come up with sixteen very concrete points to guide us in terms of what can be done in this global pandemic. Could you elaborate on these?

Vijay: To give you some background, the International Assembly of the Peoples is a platform of about seven hundred organizations from over eighty countries. And we at the Tricontinental Institute for Social Research worked in collaboration with the Assembly to come up with what we think is a very rational plan.[3] Part of the point of elaborating the agenda was to show that we can't do things in a piecemeal fashion—a lockdown here, something else there. It doesn't instill confidence in anyone to see clownish characters like Boris Johnson one day saying one thing, another day saying something else. This is why we wanted to articulate the sixteen-point plan. The second broad point I want to make before going into detail is that one of the great victories of neoliberalism, this philosophy that capitalism has been pushing for almost a hundred years, is to suggest that the state and state institutions themselves are authoritarian or problematic and that it is the private sector, rather than the state, who should act. If the state is involved at all, the private sector should be a partner. The austerity we have experienced is actually the outcome of an ideological vacuum that has sought to destroy

3 https://www.thetricontinental.org/declaration-covid19/.

not only state institutions but also the concept of the state. According to this, it is all very well to have a police force and a military, but it's not good to have public health systems. In *The Road to Serfdom*, what Friedrich Hayek was arguing, essentially, is that the road to creating state institutions leads to the gulag. Against this, we are now seeing that it is countries with robust state institutions, whether it's China or South Korea, that have been able to tackle Covid-19 effectively. Another example is the small state of Kerala, in India, with a population of thirty-five million. Kerala has built and maintained state institutions against a lot of pressure from institutions such as the International Monetary Fund, which says, "Kill off your state!" My second broad point is, then, that we have to make an argument for the importance of public institutions, whether you call this the state or not. Covid-19 is not the last pandemic. This, now, is the beginning of a new period. We have to build not only more public health, but more public control of pharmaceutical companies, which, at the moment, deal largely to the ailments of the rich and have no incentive to invest in experimenting on potential public health problems. In elaborating the sixteen points, we talked directly about the need for more public institutions and the need for more pressure to be put on governments from below. At the moment the headlines are saying "Spain Nationalizing Hospitals," but I don't think they are nationalizing anything; it's a shell game. The more important question, though, is that if countries can nationalize hospitals and implement so-called socialist policies in a time of emergency, why not do so in times of "normality"? This is part of the demand people need to make from below. The other point I want to make here concerns the question of income. Over the course of the last thirty years, because of vast productivity gains and the shift of production to low-wage countries, we have seen large-scale structural unemployment and underemployment or "precarious" employment. Globally, increasing amounts of people, hundreds of millions, are unable to find proper full-time jobs. On the table for a long while has been the notion of a universal basic income, where households and individuals are provided with a certain amount of money by the government. This, as well as other demands such as the living wage and government-sponsored job programs, are now back on the agenda. However, what tends to happen in a crisis is that the capitalist class use the situation to their advantage, while social movements get outflanked. I recognize that this is partly because our movements are not strong enough. We need to put our demands back on the agenda and focus the work of our movements. The capitalist classes have used the concept of the universal basic income, for instance, in a very distorted way. Rather than paying social welfare, or spending money on public schools, education, health, parks, and transportation, they propose to give people a cash payment and then privatize all of these services so that people have to pay for them. The universal basic income should not be a substitute for public services, but a supplement. People may ask, "How will you fund all this?" Listen, [as of 2016] there is an estimated $36 trillion sitting in tax havens.[4] Another aspect of this, therefore, is capital controls that force people to keep capital within their tax jurisdiction. And we need to have a wealth tax. Rather than thanking Bill Gates for donating money to Covid-19 research, we should be demanding his taxes. It is not the philanthropy of billionaires we need, but their taxation. There are sufficient resources already existing in our societies: trillions spent on defense, trillions in tax havens. We need to accumulate these to produce a social, decent society, not this kind of criminal society where one virus is able to paralyze us.

Srećko: Let me return to the question of the state and the role of financial institutions today, around which you have developed a very interesting, concrete proposal. The present pandemic is forcing even the proponents of neoliberalism to realize the importance of the state. This kind of situation makes it obvious that we need transnational cooperation and massive infrastructure projects, and I'd like to share with you an idea that seemed completely crazy a few years ago: this is Frederic Jameson's proposal in *American Utopia*, which is that the US Army be used as an emancipatory institution, one that helps the population instead of waging wars over oil.

Vijay: We already have an example of an army that doesn't go to war but goes to heal, and that's the Cuban Army. Cuba has produced an army of doctors and medical practitioners and nurses, without which Ebola would

---

4   https://www.foreignaffairs.com/articles/panama/2016-04-12/taxing-tax-havens.

not have been contained. The US government claims credit for having sent people, but it was the Cubans who played a frontline role alongside African doctors in tackling Ebola. Today, Cuban doctors are once again on the front line. When Jair Bolsonaro came to power in Brazil, one of the first things he did was expel Cuban doctors, just as Jeanine Áñez did when she came to power through the coup in Bolivia. Today, the Brazilians want the Cuban doctors back, because they realize that Cuba has used its surplus not to produce an immense army that goes and bombs people, but an army of doctors and medical practitioners. There is also a debate occurring about whether the Chinese took sufficient action when Covid-19 first emerged. I have been talking to people in China about the sequence of events before the World Health Organization (WHO) was informed and, to my mind, there was no suppression. Everything happened extraordinarily fast: a sample taken from a patient was confirmed to contain a new kind of coronavirus on [December 27], and by [January 3], officials provided information to the WHO. The Trump administration is trying to use the fact that this virus apparently begins in Wuhan for geopolitical ends, but the truth is that it is the Chinese who are sending medical assistance and supplies to other countries around the world, whether in Italy, Serbia, or Greece. And it is Russian doctors who went to Venezuela. The Venezuelans asked the International Monetary Fund (IMF) for $5 billion to help them finance the import of machinery to tackle Covid-19, and the IMF, which had said that it had a trillion dollars available to help its membership, promptly denied them.[5] This is Washington denying Venezuela the Russian-sent doctors. We are in a different period now where it is possible to see who is heartless and which states have collapsed, against which states are attempting to be decent on the world stage.

Srećko: Covid-19 also demonstrates how the world is rapidly changing geopolitically, in the sense that those states who responded irresponsibly at the national level are also responding selfishly on an international level. Nations such as Iran continue to be sanctioned by the United States instead

---

5 https://peoplesdispatch.org/2020/03/19/imf-refuses-aid-to-venezuela-in-the-midst-of-the-coronavirus-crisis/.

of offered assistance. And the European response, the failure of certain countries to assist their neighbors in Italy and Spain, really demonstrates the lack of any kind of geopolitical vision within the European Union. Let me come to a question I have about one of your sixteen points, which concerns the suspension of the dollar as the international currency. Could you explain the thinking behind your demand for the United Nations to call for a new international currency?

Vijay: This is a very complicated issue but the bottom line is twofold. This issue is actually not just the dollar, but the dollar-denominated financial system, or what we call the "dollar–Wall Street complex." More than half the world's trade is denominated in dollars. For a country like Iran to trade with another country, let's say India, it often has to denominate the trade in dollars and use a financial wire system that is based in the European Union, known as SWIFT. Iran can't have an independent relationship with other countries, it has to go through the United States and Europe. In that sense, we don't have an international financial system, we have a financial system dominated by the North Atlantic. This financial system in which everything is denominated against the dollar must be transcended, because it allows the United States extraterritorial economic power immediately. The US can print money without fear of inflation because the money is used outside its boundaries and jurisdiction. The Indian rupee, for instance, is not used outside India but is constrained by its value against the dollar. The proposal we developed seeks to reopen the question of international currency, which is a very old debate. Why should Libya, for instance, hold dollars in its central bank? Why can't it hold an international currency? If Libya wants to trade with Italy, why does it have to convert its currency into the dollar and then to the euro? Why can't it trade directly and denominate the trade in its own language, its own currency?

Srećko: Yes, why not? Just before Gaddafi was overthrown by then secretary of state Hillary Clinton, as well as Nicolas Sarkozy, what did he want to introduce? A pan-African currency. And that posed a big problem because of the control exercised by the French National Bank in West Africa.

Vijay: Yes, in most francophone countries they still use the franc, and Gaddafi proposed the Afrique as the currency, which is an amazing idea. Why can't there be continental currencies? In fact, the Bolivarian movement in South America led by Hugo Chávez came up with the idea of having a currency for the continent, which was initially produced as a digital currency so that trades between Brazil and Venezuela, for instance, need not be dollar-denominated. It is actually a narrow demand within a much broader discussion to be had about the nature of sovereignty of parts of the world from the dollar–Wall Street complex. The Institute of International Finance has reported that since late January, almost $68 billion has fled the Global South for the North. As uncertainty develops, so-called emerging markets are hemorrhaging money. People are now concerned about what is going to happen to Wall Street and the London Stock Exchange, but what about these countries that are struggling with enormous dollar-denominated debts, which are not being forgiven? One of our central demands needs to be a debt jubilee where all debts are scrapped, right now. Let's start there.

Srećko: Historically, as David Graeber shows in relation to disasters in Egypt, for instance, debt jubilees were the first stage in a kind of restart of society.[6] They provided the poor with at least an opportunity to participate, again, in social and economic life. How is it possible, though, to implement measures such as debt jubilees, capital controls, the suspension of the dollar, or wealth taxation in the absence of some form of global government that is willing to do so?

Vijay: I am not in favor of a global government at this time; it's impossible. The United Nations, for instance, is relatively paralyzed at the moment. Yesterday, the UN secretary-general, I think quite rightly, called for a ceasefire in all wars, given the Covid-19 pandemic we are all facing.[7] It was a very important statement, but nobody is taking it seriously. What

6 David Graeber, *Debt: The First 5000 Years* (Brooklyn, NY: Melville House, 2011).

7 https://www.un.org/sg/en/content/sg/statement/2020-03-23/secretary-generals-appeal-for-global-ceasefire.

we need, in the very short term, is to fight to establish more sovereignty for countries over their economies, and we need more regionalism. For instance, I would like to see a West African country such as Senegal have sovereignty over its economy and not be subordinated to the French franc. And I would like to see the African Union have a much larger role in the continent. My first suggestion to governments would be to implement capital controls to stop this "hot money" coming in and out of their countries. This way, the wealthy cannot escape with their money and can be taxed. A common assumption is that if you tax the rich, economic activity stops. Let me ask you a question: Over the last couple of weeks, as these quarantines have taken place, economic activity has stopped, correct? And why has it stopped? Because labor has vanished. This crisis is proving the Marxist point that it's labor that creates value, not money. If labor goes on a state-imposed general strike, the whole of capitalism shudders to a halt. This shows that if states implement capital controls and tax the wealthy, economic activity is not going to stop. It will continue because labor will continue. The money obtained by taxing the wealthy can be used productively, for instance, to build public institutions in these societies. We are not looking for a global government, but to strengthen the sovereignty of regions. The African Union and the Bolivarian project in South America should each be allowed to grow, and the South Asian unity to take place. Why is it, if Europe is supposedly in favor of unity, that it always goes and attacks other people's attempts at unity? When the Bolivarians tried to create a project in South America, Europeans joined with the United States to undermine it, just as they undermined the project in the African Union. What is good for the goose should be good for the gander.

Srećko: Hungary recently received ten planes of masks, gloves, and other medical equipment from China. Do you think this is a signal that Viktor Orbán's connections with China have paid off where the European Union has failed?

Vijay: This is a question to ask Orbán and the Chinese government, but we have already seen that the Chinese have offered to send supplies to all kinds of countries—there is no litmus test, as far as I can see. China hasn't gone and asked, "Are you a country that has been pro-China before?" and on that basis offered help. China has said openly that it will provide assistance to any country that wants it. China and India, for example, don't have a very close relationship. China has been pursuing the Belt and Road Initiative (BRI), while India has joined with the US in the Indo–Pacific strategy, which the Trump administration developed to counter the BRI. And yet, the Chinese government has offered to send supplies to India. I am not convinced that these actions are entirely politically motivated. It could well be that the Chinese are viewing this as a "soft power" opportunity, but I don't think we should reduce it to that. I am not one to believe that everything happens cynically. I think that China is recognizing that this is a pandemic and, having been able to manage Covid-19 internally, are now offering to send surplus equipment elsewhere.

Srećko: You mentioned the Belt and Road Initiative, and I think many people are wondering what will happen to this "New Silk Road." How do you think the Covid-19 pandemic will impact Chinese infrastructure projects around the world in ensuing decades?

Vijay: This is a very important question. Firstly, I would like to say that I think that the Trump administration is being extraordinarily racist in branding this a "Chinese virus." It is racist because it obscures the nature of viruses. The Spanish flu didn't start in Spain. It is only called that because it was wartime and, unlike other countries, Spain didn't have a censorship so the media covered the flu outbreak. That particular flu apparently started in Kansas in a US military establishment, through chicken to human transmission, but we don't call it the "American flu" and say America should pay reparations. Of the people who died in the 1918–19 influenza epidemic, 60 percent were from India—should India now claim reparations from the United States? That is ridiculous, it doesn't work like that. Cholera came from my home state of West Bengal in India, where it was first discovered in 1817. That cholera lasted until 1923, a hundred-year cycle. At the time, we called it an "Asiatic cholera" in the same racist tones as Trump. In the 1830s, the French actually passed a resolution in the parliament declaring that cholera would not impact them because they were white and democratic, whereas the disease was an authoritarian, Asiatic problem. Of course, it devastated Paris, it obliterated populations. Viruses can begin anywhere, and we need to have a much more human understanding of this.

It is true, however, that this attempt to frame Covid-19 as a "Chinese virus" is likely to hurt China in the short term. When China says, "We're going to build a high-speed railway that goes all the way to Turkey," some people may say, "Let's rethink this, because do we want viruses to come that quickly from China into Italy again?" In the short term, the Belt and Road Initiative will suffer slightly in consequence of this ideological barrage, but let's face it, there is no other game in town. The Indo-Pacific strategy that the US government is pushing is so wildly underfunded because there are no state funds that can underwrite the American challenge to the BRI. What China is doing in building this infrastructure is looking for new markets. It is a new kind of international order and, for sure, China has an interest in it, but many of the countries it is investing in don't have the ability to raise funds to build their own infrastructure. So, yes, there will be a short-term effect on the BRI, but in time it will be back in business.

Srećko: In addition to the Spanish flu and cholera, there is of course the "Black Death," the plague. In thinking about the plague, I find your long-term, system theory perspective very fruitful. The plague also "came from" China, through the Silk Road, taking around ten years to arrive in Europe, in Venice and cities mainly in the Mediterranean. But it didn't really "come from" China, in the sense that, while it originated in China geographically, it was a consequence of the Mongolian Empire attacking China years before. The Mongolians created the foundations for the spread of the plague. In the same way that the "New Silk Road" is creating the foundations for the circulation of the virus, at that time, Mongolian warriors and traders were actually bringing the plague to Europe. I'm just amazed how it seems, as Hegel said, that if we learn anything from history, it is that we don't learn anything from history. These historical comparisons show that we need to have a long-term perspective looking toward the future. The current situation is bad and it will worsen in coming months, but we need, now, to be already constructing the world after Covid-19, the world to come in one or two years. I urge everyone to read the sixteen points set out by the Tricontinental and the International Assembly of the Peoples. Returning to the subject of Europe, one question that many people are asking is whether Italy will leave the European Union, or the euro, after the pandemic?

Vijay: This comes back to the question of "What is the European Union?" By which I mean, what is the "union" in the first place? What is the collectivity of peoples? If European countries are not able to help one another in a crisis, what is the point of being in a framework together? This is a question that the Italians may want to pose to Brussels directly. Greece could also have posed it in that way after the 2008 financial crisis, and Yanis Varoufakis did so when he was finance minister. If the Union is not going to negotiate humanely and in solidarity, then what is the point of Greece being in the eurozone? In my opinion, the real question to ask of any unity, whether you are part of a collective process, a unity of nations, or a unity within a nation, is "What is our unity for?" We need to ask, actually, in every country, "What is the state for?" If these institutions do not help us in times of crisis, then why should we belong to them? I think this is a very important question. For countries such as Italy, the real question that must be asked of Europe is, "Where were you at the time of the crisis?"

Srećko: Unfortunately, we are seeing that the role of many institutions in times of crisis reflects what Carl Schmitt described with "the state of exception." It is enough to look at Hungary to see how the situation is being used by those for whom this crisis appears as a kind of dream coming true. That is one perspective, but there is another, more hopeful perspective, which is what we are trying to develop. To leave Europe aside for the moment, it would be interesting to learn more about the situation in India. What is the Modi government potentially going to gain from this crisis, given that it is shutting down the massive protests that were taking place against him even before the Covid-19 pandemic? And has there been much mobilization of smaller-scale cooperative structures to battle the pandemic?

Vijay: It is hard to say what Modi's administration will gain, but one thing to remember is that Modi is able to produce popularity. He had a very silly idea on Sunday for people to go outside in public and make noise to thank the medical practitioners. What is the point of doing that if you're not, as the government, providing medical practitioners with the equipment they need? I find this a very dangerous kind of demagogic politics. Those on the frontline of this crisis need government support, they need gloves, masks, and all kinds of equipment. The government must stop producing garbage and start producing these items. They need to change lines of production, as China did (which is why it has an enormous supply of masks it can provide to others). The Modi government is, to my mind, useless, but it is able to manipulate public opinion in a very crafty way. In terms of the second question, my colleague Subin Dennis and I just published an article on the response of the left government in Kerala to Covid-19.[8] It is promoting these slogans such as "break the chain" and "physical isolation but social unity." Public action has been hugely important. What you have in a state like Kerala, with its thirty-five million people, is a highly organized and educated population with almost 100 percent literacy and strong trade unions, women's organizations, and cooperatives. There is a women's cooperative called Kudumbashree that has 4.5 million members. People are already highly involved and organized, and what this means is that public action is immediate. When the government announced the measures it would take to slow the spread of Covid-19, trade unions immediately mobilized to go to bus stations and erect sinks with hand sanitizer. The government didn't do this, the trade unions did. Kudumbashree started making masks on a mass scale. What I want to emphasize is that, as part of the evisceration of the state and equal to it has been the relative evisceration of social institutions in our countries. Trade unions have been wiped out, by and large. The fact of being in an organization is so fundamental to building a human society, but people have become individualized. As you mentioned earlier, you go on social media and people are bemoaning isolation in their homes. If these people were in a social organization, they would find a way to band together and do something productive in their societies. In Kerala, a very large number of the population are day laborers—how do you bring "break the chain" to

8 https://www.brasildefato.com.br/2020/04/14/kerala-is-a-model-state-in-the-covid-19-fight.

them? How do you bring cleanliness to the areas they live in? You construct open-air sinks, bring hand sanitizer to them, and give a public lecture on the importance of maintaining distance—because you are organized. Public action is crucial, but it cannot happen in a society where social organization is destroyed. We need to build social institutions alongside public state institutions.

Srećko: I see the role of technology similarly. What the Covid-19 crisis has showed is that despite social distancing, we have more social cooperation than ever. Obviously, it is not possible to take our politics to the streets anymore, but this is a fantastic opportunity for people to come together online. I am very grateful for the non-Western-centric perspective you are providing and, returning to the subject of Cuban internationalism, I am curious to know how you would respond to a critic who argues that Cuba is only sending its doctors abroad to earn foreign currency to trade with?

Vijay: Let me put it this way: I would take that criticism seriously if I saw doctors from countries such as Germany, the United States, Canada, and the United Kingdom going to places like, for instance, even Italy. If we saw doctors from these privileged countries traveling, then I think we could ask questions like, "Is Cuba just in it for foreign exchange?" It is a remarkable thing to even think that. We saw Cuban doctors in the Ebola crisis who went to work in West Africa, in Sierra Leone and different places. One of them contracted Ebola, went back to Cuba, healed, wrote about it, and then went back to work in the field. To impute to these doctors that they are merely instruments of foreign exchange I think is very disingenuous. I would say to the right-wingers who hold these views, "Well, why don't you go to the front lines and try to help people?" Why is it that we are only seeing socialist doctors helping? I think it was in early February that the Communist Party of China said that all Communist Party members have to be frontline workers in the Covid-19 crisis. An enormous number of Communist Party member doctors went to Wuhan as the front line. When that video circulated of the medical practitioners removing their masks, you could see that they wore Communist Party pins. They were told, "The reason you joined the Communist Party is to serve the people." They didn't want non-Communist doctors on the front line unless they wanted to be there. For those in the Party, it was an obligation, and I tip my hat to that kind of motivation. I would say to the right wing, "Let's see your doctors travel across the world and go into the slums to vaccinate people." I don't see them doing that and, therefore, I wouldn't take the question seriously.

Srećko: I think Cuba, besides showing what real solidarity means, is being smart in sending doctors, because once Covid-19 hits Cuba they will have gained experience in how to handle it. That is what the states and doctors of Europe could have done. The responsibility lies with states, not with doctors themselves. Indeed, we can see the terrible conditions faced by doctors all across Europe. In Spain, many of the doctors are infected, and in France the police have been smashing protests by the medical workers. For years, European governments have been suppressing working conditions, privatizing hospitals, and implementing austerity, and now the medical workers are struggling on the frontline. For me, the heroes are the doctors, the waste collectors, the shop assistants, and all those who are on the front line.

Vijay: In the last Tricontinental newsletter there was a line which said, "I'd prefer a planet of nurses to a planet of bankers." This is a battle of ideas and I would really welcome people to read the proposals on the Tricontinental website. This is not about putting out a platform and just watching it. We want to build a campaign, maintain the pressure, and deepen our understanding. We want to raise again the question "What is the program of action for a country?" I was so happy to see that yesterday, in the middle of the cruelty that they are experiencing (most recently with the International Monetary Fund denying their request for funds), the Venezuelan government said that all salaries will be paid 'till December 2020. It said that all healthcare will be maintained, and rents and utility bills will be completely forgiven. This is an economy that is in serious crisis, yet the government is putting people before the well-being of the economy. This is part of the battle of ideas and there is a lot to learn from such examples.

Conversation held on March 24, 2020

Hope and Humor in Times of Coronavirus

Larry Charles and Srećko Horvat

Srećko: The other day, Larry Charles and I were joking that this series of conversations should be called "The Light in the Middle of the Tunnel," because, as German playwright Bertolt Brecht said: "In the dark times, will there also be singing? Yes, there will also be singing about the dark times." We are, perhaps, in dark times, but there is no better person than you, Larry, to tell us why jokes and humor are so important in a moment like today's.

Larry: My first thought as you were saying that was, *When have there been light times?* I look at the history of civilization, and I'm hard-pressed to think of a really light time. Even when we think of eras that are often characterized as being positive, like the Renaissance or post–World War II America, there were always oppressed people, those who were sick, poor, and not taken care of, and there was always power inequity. Humans are often plunging themselves into dark times that we could have done something about and didn't, and here we are, it's another dark time. Humor is a natural human antidote to bleakness, a way to survive bleakness that is as important, in my view, as water or food. If you lose your sense of humor, you lose your humanity and your ability to feel compassion toward others.

Srećko: Let me tell you a joke from Zagreb, Croatia. This Sunday, Zagreb was already in confinement, like most cities in the world, when something tragic happened. The worst earthquake in more than 140 years hit Zagreb. Just at the very moment when people are requested by the authorities to stay at home, they wake up at six o'clock in the morning to a 5.3 earthquake, and suddenly the authorities are saying, "Hurry, get out on the streets!—but maintain social distance!" This is the kind of complex situation we are in. A good friend of mine from Bosnia said, "Imagine you are watching a movie about a global pandemic, and then an earthquake hits—it would get the poorest ratings ever!" The people of Zagreb, as you suggested, do give the same importance to jokes as food and water. So my friend thought, *Okay, a pandemic happened, an earthquake happened, what is next?* and immediately someone organized a virtual "waiting for Godzilla" the next day in Zagreb!

Larry: It's very much like a monster movie. Normally, in the first two acts of the movie the monster does a lot of damage, and then about two-thirds of the way through, the scientists find out the weakness, for instance, that Godzilla doesn't like electricity, and the rest of the movie is figuring out how to attack the monster's weakness and destroy it. At times, we are lulled into a sense of complacency that things are going to be okay, that we have some control over our environment and over our destiny, but then these disasters come in waves that we have no control of, and it humbles us as humans to realize that there are no guarantees; you can have a pandemic and an earthquake happening at the same time, and it doesn't mean something else won't happen, too. This is where humor steps in to buffer that sense of bleakness and hopelessness. When you start to see the larger reality and it's overwhelming, your humorous perception of it can help you to find your way through it.

Srećko: You know what you are talking about. I and many of my friends were addicted to *Seinfeld* in the '90s after the collapse of Yugoslavia. When I look at it retrospectively, it is interesting to note that *Seinfeld* (and also *Curb Your Enthusiasm*) touched on some of the most interesting phenomena of the Covid-19 crisis: hand-washing and toilet paper. I still remember the episode where Jerry Seinfeld is in the toilet at a restaurant and a man enters, pisses, and then doesn't wash his hands. Jerry returns to his seat and the waiter comes offering a pizza, and he is the same man from the bathroom. Jerry thinks, *I cannot eat this pizza*, because he remembers that the waiter's hands were not washed.

Larry: Yes, you could do a great "pandemic supercut" of *Seinfeld* because Larry David and Jerry Seinfeld were both very germophobic people long before it became trendy—that's why there are so many toilet-paper and hand-washing stories, cleanliness and hygiene stories.

Srećko: Another famous one is "I Don't Have a Square to Spare," the episode where Elaine steals all the toilet paper.

Larry: Yes, that's one that I wrote actually! The idea that someone wouldn't share their toilet paper struck me as a funny idea, but now we see that people *are* very possessive of their toilet paper, to the extent that its being hoarded and people are fighting over it in the supermarkets.

Srećko: How do you explain this, that toilet paper is currently the most precious commodity? Is it because people shit a lot? Or that they copy the actions of other people? Or is toilet paper really so precious?

Larry: You are tapping into something very interesting. In the travels that I did for my documentary television series, *Larry Charles' Dangerous World of Comedy*, I came to realize that paper is a precious commodity in most parts of the world. In certain places, you go to a hotel and they give you a tissue, and that's supposed to be your napkin, your toilet paper, and serve all your purposes. We in America have become very spoiled and complacent. You go to the supermarket and there are forty-two different brands of toilet paper, and they're all comfortable and soft, they have lotion if you want—whatever you want! But we take it for granted, what it takes to get that toilet paper up our assess. Maybe this pandemic and its ability to shine a light on things like this will make us more aware of how we use and waste things, and possibly change our behavior also, and then that *Seinfeld* episode will become a kind of a quaint artifact of a previous time.

Srećko: The panic at the supermarket that we are seeing also highlights our unstoppable consumerism. We've seen these photos of empty supermarket shelves in Venezuela or some Latin American country with captions like "This is the proof that socialism doesn't work," but what about capitalism? There are so many empty shelves at the moment, how can capitalism not produce enough toilet paper? And where does this human desire for toilet paper come from?

Larry: It becomes a metaphor, doesn't it? It's almost like we are trying to protect our asses. We are so scared and our ass is our most vulnerable place, in a way, and so everybody sort of retreats to that primal fear, which comes to life, is embodied by, this toilet-paper hoarding and the fear of not being able to wipe your ass. Toilet paper, as you probably know, is a relatively recent phenomenon. For most of civilization, people did not use toilet paper, and yet today people can't imagine living without it. It is interesting because, who knows, we may have to live without it again someday in future.

Srećko: People in many parts of the world already live without it and are probably more hygienic than people in the "Western world."

Larry: Yes, because Americans are lazy so they use toilet paper instead of the hard work of cleaning their asses.

Srećko: When I listen to you, it's impossible not to remind myself of a certain philosopher, one who didn't appreciate *Seinfeld*, and that's Jacques Derrida. In 2002, Derrida was asked by a journalist, "What do you think about sitcoms, and do you think that *Seinfeld* is a sort of deconstruction?" Derrida basically said, "If you want to do deconstruction don't watch sitcoms, read books and do your homework." I can tell you what I felt when I saw that: I was really disappointed in Jacques Derrida, because what I found in *Seinfeld* was precisely a sort of deconstruction. There is that scene, for instance, with Kramer, George, and Jerry where Jerry is talking about his hands, and then he has a self-ironic comment about how "these are not manual hands."

Larry: Absolutely; you would think that it would be Derrida's favorite TV show because it is all about deconstructing every aspect of itself from the structure of the show and the structure of sitcoms that we've gotten used to. The characters themselves are self-aware and self-conscious in a way that was quite new, and then you have the dialogue itself, which is constantly being torn apart and put back together again in different ways to experiment with language.

Srećko: I want to come now to your most recent project, *Larry Charles' Dangerous World of Comedy*, in relation to the current Covid-19 crisis. You traveled to really dangerous, war-torn countries across the globe, such as Somalia, and, in most places you visited, you discovered jokes and dark humor in the ways people coped with their situations. Compared to the experiences you had in these places you visited, how do you see the Covid-19 crisis that now confronts us? Is it an unprecedented historic event? Did you see any jokes coming already? Is it possible to joke?

Larry: One of the things that has struck me is that I had to get various vaccines to go to all those countries, like Liberia and Somalia, and I didn't get a cold or anything. It is here, back in my house in Los Angeles, that I may wind up catching something and having it kill me. More importantly, I was in Liberia in the post-Ebola period and what all the comedians and actors that I met there told me was that the comedy industry, such as it is in Liberia, was born out of the Ebola crisis. There, at their nadir as a society, with the Ebola crisis wiping them out, humor was one of the masts of the sinking ship that people held on to. They discovered the humor that was inside of them when they were faced with this bleak future. Everybody I met there before the Ebola crisis was just trying to get by, but afterwards, they started picking up their cellphones and cameras and started shooting videos and using social media to talk to each other. It really became a lifeboat for the society. It can't be underestimated, the power of humor.

Srećko: What are some of the most ridiculous, absurd things you have seen happening in the Covid-19 crisis?

Larry: The one that pops into my head because it's a daily event is the Trump news conference. The daily Trump press briefings are like the three stooges in a pandemic: it's frighteningly inept, it's sociopathic, its weirdly awkward, it's everything it's not supposed to be, to the point that it crosses the line into absurdity, even though all this is going on while people are dying. We've come to accept Trump's briefings and normalize them, but if you listen to what he says and the way he says it, and even his presentation, it is absolutely mind-bending that he is in charge of anything. The daily exposure to that is almost like watching some kind of apocalyptic sitcom.

Srećko: When I stopped worrying (to paraphrase Kubrick) and started to love coronavirus was the moment I realized that Covid-19 is really unmasking the populist leaders who are, so often, bullshitting us. Trump is one of them, another is certainly Bolsonaro in Brazil, and another one is Vučić in Serbia, who was initially saying, "Oh, this is nothing, it is no more dangerous than the flu." At one point, he even suggested to the Serbian people to drink rakija, which we in the Balkans love to do—can you imagine a leader suggesting this in a global health crisis? One good outcome of this, though, is that perhaps more than ever, people are finally starting to listen to scientists and doctors, who are appearing more in the media (as much as the media itself is complicit in the populist rise). There is a small shift in our attention because everyone now feels that their lives are in danger and, if you listen to Trump, Bolsonaro, and Orbán, for instance, you might end up without your life. What do you think—do you see the Covid-19 crisis as an opportunity for more progressive politics?

Larry: I absolutely do, but just to add humor to the conversation, the polls today show that Trump's popularity has actually increased, so you have a further fissure in society here between the people who are craving truth, science, and medicine, and those who are craving magic. You can never underestimate the amount of people who want to believe in magic, whether it's Jesus, or the resurrection—Trump is trying to combine Easter and the end of this virus, by the way, and that's not an accident; he wants to tap into people's fears, anxieties, and false hopes. There are people, like you and I, and most people that we know, who are seeking answers, and then there are people who just want to put faith in Trump's magical solutions—such as injecting disinfectant or bringing sunlight "inside the body"—or whoever it is that is making these crazy, completely illogical promises. The frightening part is that there are millions of people who are completely buying it.

Srećko: How can we make humor in this time of crisis accessible and unifying, and can we make it classless?

Larry: I think it already is—humor is a classless act. Humor transcends political systems, ideologies, and economies, and that's what makes it so universal. There is comedy everywhere in the world, from the poorest countries to the wealthiest. The issue is that capitalism needs to possess, own, and commodify, and it has taken comedy and made it into a product that can be sold, very successfully, around the world. Capitalism needs comedy because it's profitable, but comedy doesn't need capitalism and will survive long after capitalism disappears.

Srećko: You mentioned that Trump is rising in the polls, as though the more stupid he is, the more popular he becomes. What do you think about the cooperation between the DNC establishment and the media in attacking Bernie Sanders?

Larry: I am absolutely disgusted by the DNC's behavior toward Bernie Sanders. He has clearly been thwarted by his own party once again. The pandemic aside, there was a desperate need on the part of the Democratic Party, the Democratic establishment, and the Democratic donors who really drive it to stop Bernie Sanders from being the candidate. That was very clear when you looked at the media coverage—not only the lack of content on Sanders, but the way the narratives framed him as some sort of rabble rouser, as opposed to being a US senator and congressman for forty years. On the other hand, Trump is on TV every single day, and that is why, I think, his ratings are going up—whether he's stupid or not, whether you want it or not, he's there, for two hours every day, on every channel.

Srećko: There haven't been many victories lately for the left. But what I find interesting is how the Covid-19 crisis suddenly makes everything seem possible. I woke up this morning and Britney Spears was talking about wealth distribution and a general strike! Did you see that?

Larry: There is the definition of comedy in the time of coronavirus: Britney Spears is now a socialist.

Srećko: There is another moment I'd like to mention, which goes a bit deeper into the political economy of global capitalism. When Jeremy Corbyn's Labour Party was running for the UK elections in December 2019, it was advocating the nationalization of the railways. The establishment was claiming that this was dangerous radical socialism, and so on, and then Covid-19 came along, and Boris Johnson announced the temporary nationalization of the railways. It's not the same thing, of course, but it shows that it is possible. Similarly, Trump is now announcing some sort of universal basic income, when only a few weeks ago Andrew Yang suggested it and everyone laughed about it. Suddenly, what seems impossible is becoming possible. Do you think there is hope in this? That we might use this moment?

Larry: I have a certain innate optimism that people can seize these sorts of black swans and turn them into something very positive in our societies. My fear is that as long as Trump and others are giving lip service to some of these measures, people will become complacent and accept quick fixes, rather than pushing for structural change. People like Boris Johnson and Trump want to bring things back to "normal" as quickly as possible. What's important is that the positive changes that have been instituted are retained, and that we approach life in a fundamentally different way. My fear is that people are not willing to do the hard work, they are willing to accept magic rather than reality, and once this is over we will have social amnesia and return things to the way they were as quickly as possible, only to face something worse the next time. How's that for humor?

Srećko: That was very hopeful! Is there a danger, do you think, of too much humor making people take things less seriously—for instance, policies that affect their lives?

Larry: Yes, I think there is a danger in that, and I've seen it in America and other countries. There are two kinds of humor: the humor that makes you want to forget, and the humor that makes you want to remember. There is humor used in many societies, including fascistic and totalitarian societies, to placate the masses. There is that danger at all times. Factors like who is speaking, how much freedom people have, and how much censorship exists in the culture will dictate how prominent that kind of humor is. But in a lot of places around the world, the voice of humorous, comedic dissent is still very strong.

Srećko: If we put Kramer into the Covid-19 crisis, what would be his philosophy, how would he react? Could you perhaps imagine it?

Larry: He knew it was coming all along and he's been hoarding for years! And, if you finally go into his apartment, you will see that it is stacked with boxes of stuff—he's ready, he's got the bunker all ready in that apartment.

Srećko: Yes, I remember in one episode of *Seinfeld*, Kramer is on the street with his car packed full of stuff and Jerry comes along and asks, "What is all this?" and it turns out Kramer is just panic buying. And that was thirty years ago!

Larry: Yes, he's the original survivalist.

Srećko: Another character you are connected to is, of course, Borat. What would Borat do in this situation?

Larry: I think Borat would be oblivious to the virus. He'd be kissing people and touching things and horrifying people on the street by not believing in it. Don't forget that the dominant religions in Kazakhstan believe in the hawk. They are very magical thinkers. Borat would probably blame the Jews and think it was a hoax and be touching everything and horrifying people. He would actually destroy civilization himself, probably.

Srećko: Borat would be the best friend of the coronavirus.

Larry: The least socially distant person you could imagine.

Srećko: I hope that this conversation might be comforting for some people. Since Sunday, when the earthquake hit Zagreb, I've felt utterly helpless. I'm not in Croatia at the moment and I cannot go there because borders are closed. My family is there and my father is seventy-one with health issues, so he's at risk. To be honest, these conversations, where we connect, share thoughts, and organize, give me a reason to wake up. Without them, I had the feeling that everything had stopped, even my psychological life went into a kind of PTSD. I think we need these kind of spaces, definitely.

Larry: I hear what you're saying. We feel hopeless and overwhelmed and we're looking for something to bring us back to reality. Let us land the reality in the present moment where we do have a little bit of control over it, because the rest of it is pretty much out of control, but we can control our moments as best we can. It bothers me to hear you feeling so bleak, because when I think about you, I think about your book, *Poetry from the Future*, and that's who you are: a person who believes in poetry for the future. It reminds me of Stanley Kubrick, whom you mentioned before. When he made *The Shining*, he told people that it was an optimistic movie, and people said to him, "How could you say *The Shining* is an optimistic movie?" He said because the premise is that there are ghosts, there is something after death, and that's an optimistic scenario. Similarly, I see you as a very darkly optimistic person. Do not let go! I am counting on you! It's very hard. My parents both died recently and I spoke to my brother and we both agreed that, in a strange way, we were grateful that they died before being in nursing homes. I hate the idea of being glad that my parents are dead because it means they have avoided worse pains. This is the kind of stuff that we're now thinking about that we didn't before.

Srećko: This point worries me when thinking of my father, because if this crisis gets longer and deeper, we might have the Italian scenario where funerals are canceled and we cannot visit people who are sick. In that way, I understand your feelings about your parents. Although, to be honest, my father doesn't seem to care much about the pandemic. I called him the other day and could hear that he was on the street. I said, "Where are you? On the street?," and he said, "Going to the supermarket!" I thought, *No, Dad! This is precisely the kind of thing you shouldn't be doing.* There is something with old people where they just don't listen, and I think it is because they have survived so much and are fed up with people telling them what to do.

Larry: You're tapping into our perception of death and how we face it. People like your dad or my dad, who was a soldier in World War II and whose family was wiped out by the Holocaust, have seen a lot of shit in their lives. Maybe you reach a point where you know that you're going to die, that there is an ending, and you are okay with it. The American ego does not really acknowledge death. There is a kind of assumption that "there's gonna be a way out." I think the current pandemic is going to force people to be more honest with themselves about their anxieties about death, and with accepting the fact that there is an end to each human life. If we could somehow figure out a philosophy of death, like the Buddhists have done (or like your dad has done, perhaps), then that could be a positive change in society.

Srećko: I completely agree. There is a famous essay by Michel de Montaigne, in which he describes the tradition among the Egyptians in times of death, where they would bring a skull to a big celebratory feast, and that was the origin of the *memento mori*. The best times of your life are when you remember that you are mortal and, unfortunately, I think Trump, Bolsonaro, Orbán, and the rest haven't realized that yet—they think that they are immortal.

Larry: Someone like Trump, who's never really had any adversity, may be among the last people to be able to labor under the delusion that they are immortal. The concept of immortality, which we've carried with us from the beginning of time, may—returning to the matter of deconstruction—finally be fragmented and demythologized properly, which is possibly what we need to go forward into a more realistic and better future.

Conversation held on March 25, 2020

Covid-19: What Is at Stake?

Noam Chomsky and Srećko Horvat

Srećko: Noam Chomsky, a hero for many generations, was born in 1928 and wrote his first essay at just ten years old, which was on the Spanish Civil War. It was written just after the fall of Barcelona in 1938, which seems very long ago, at least to my generation. Noam, you witnessed the Second World War, the bombing of Hiroshima, and many important historic events from the Vietnam War, the 1973 oil crisis, Chernobyl, the fall of the Berlin Wall, 9/11, and, more recently, the financial crash of 2007–8. In terms of your background in being a witness and protagonist in major historical processes, how do you see the current Covid-19 crisis? Is it an unprecedented historical event? Is it something that surprised you?

Noam: My earliest memories, which are haunting me now, are from the 1930s. The article you mentioned on the fall of Barcelona was mainly about the apparently inexorable spread of the fascist plague across Europe. Much later, when internal documents came out, I discovered that United States government analysts at the time, and in the years following, expected that the war would end with the world divided into a US-dominated region and a German-dominated region. So my childhood fears were not entirely out of place. These memories have been returning to me lately. I can recall, when I was a young child, listening to Hitler's Nuremberg Rallies over the radio. Though I couldn't understand the words, it was easy to understand the mood and the threat, and, I have to say, when I listen to Donald Trump's rallies today, it resonates. It's not that he's a fascist—he doesn't have that much of an ideology, he's just a sociopath, an individual concerned with himself—but the mood and the fear is similar, and the idea that the fate of the country and the world is in the hands of a sociopathic buffoon is shocking. Covid-19 is serious enough, but it's worth recalling that there is a much greater horror approaching. We are racing to the edge of disaster, far worse than anything that's happened in human history, and Trump and his minions are in the lead in racing to the abyss. In fact, there are two immense threats that we are facing. One is the growing threat of nuclear war, which has been exacerbated by the tearing apart of what's left of the arms control regime, and the other is of course the growing threat of global warming. Both threats can be dealt with, but there isn't a lot of time. Covid-19 is horrible and can have terrifying consequences, but there will be recovery. As for the other threats, there won't be recovery. If we don't deal with them, we're done. And so the childhood memories are coming back to haunt me, but in a different dimension. As for the threat of nuclear war, you can get a sense of where the world really is by looking at the Doomsday Clock, which is set every year with the minute hand a certain distance from midnight, which means termination. Ever since Trump was elected, the minute hand has been moving closer and closer to midnight. Last year, it was two minutes to midnight. This year, the analysts dispensed with minutes and moved to seconds. It is now one hundred seconds to midnight, the closest it has ever been. This is because of three things, according to the scientists: the threat of nuclear war, the threat of global warming, and the deterioration of democracy, which, at first, doesn't seem to quite belong with the others. However, then you realize that, actually, it does, because it is the one main hope that we have for overcoming the crises facing us: an informed, involved public taking control of their fate. If that doesn't happen, we are doomed. If we leave our fate to sociopathic buffoons, we're finished. Trump is the worst, but that's because of the power of the United States, which is overwhelming. People are speculating about US decline, but, if you just look at the world, you don't see that happening. When the US imposes sanctions—murderous, devastating sanctions—it is the only country that can do that. Everyone else has to follow. Others may not like it—Europe, in fact, hates the sanctions on Iran—but they have to follow the master or get kicked out of the international financial system. In the case of Europe, this is not a law of nature, but a decision to be subordinate to the master in Washington. Other countries don't even have the choice. To return to the subject of Covid-19, one of the most shocking, harsh aspects of it is the use of sanctions by the powerful to maximize the pain of others, and perfectly consciously. Iran has its own enormous internal problems, but they are worsened by the stranglehold of tightening sanctions, which are openly designed to make them suffer, and now bitterly. Cuba has been suffering from sanctions from the moment it gained independence. It's astonishing that they survived and stayed resilient, and one of the most ironic elements of today's virus is that Cuba is helping Europe. This is so shocking that we don't know how to describe it—a situation where Germany can't help Greece, but Cuba can help the European countries. If you stop to think about what that means, words fail, just as when you see thousands of people dying in the Mediterranean, fleeing from countries that Europe has devastated for centuries, you don't know what words to use. The civilizational crisis of the West at this point is devastating to think about, and it does bring up childhood memories of listening to Hitler raving on the radio to raucous crowds at the Nuremberg rallies. It makes you wonder if this species is even viable.

Srećko: You mentioned the crisis of democracy. At this moment we find ourselves, in many ways, in a historically unprecedented situation. Almost two billion people are, in one way or the other, confined at home. At the same time, European countries and many others have closed their borders. There is a state of exception almost everywhere, which means curfew in places such as France, Serbia, Spain, and Italy, and, in other countries, armies on the streets. And I want to ask you, as a linguist, about the language that is now in circulation. Political figures including Trump, Macron, and others constantly use the language of war. The media, too, speaks of doctors who are on the "front line" and the virus is framed as the "enemy." This discourse reminded me of a book written by Victor Klemperer during the rise of Nazism—*Lingua tertii imperii*, which is about the language of the Third Reich and its utility in building the Nazi ideology. From your perspective, what does the current discourse of "war" tell us, and why is the virus being presented as an "enemy"? Is it simply to legitimize the new state of exception or is there something deeper here?

Noam: In this case, I don't think the language is exaggerated; it has some significance. It communicates the message that, if we want to deal with the crisis, we have to implement something like wartime mobilization. If you take a rich country like the United States, it has the resources to overcome the immediate economic issues. The mobilization for the Second World War led the country into far greater debt than it is contemplated today and it was a very successful mobilization: it practically quadrupled the US manufacturing and ended the Depression. It left the country with an enormous debt, but a capacity to grow. Today, we aren't facing a world war and resources probably don't need to be mobilized on that scale. However, we need the mentality of a social mobilization to try and overcome the short-run crisis, which is severe. Here, we can also recall the swine flu epidemic of 2009, which originated in the US and killed a couple of hundred thousand people in the first year. And the situation in poor countries is of course far worse. What happens when an Indian who lives hand to mouth is isolated? They starve to death. In a civilized world, the rich countries would be giving assistance to those who are in need, instead of strangling them as they are currently, and particularly India. We have to bear in mind that, assuming current climate tendencies persist, South Asia will be unlivable in a few decades. The temperature reached fifty degrees Celsius in Rajasthan this summer and it's increasing. The water is running out and this will likely worsen. There are two nuclear powers and they are going to be fighting over restricting reduced water supplies. Covid-19 is very serious and we can't underestimate it, but we have to remember that it is a small fraction of major crises that are coming our way and will disrupt life to the point of making the species unsurvivable in the not so distant future. We have many problems to deal with—immediate ones, such as Covid-19, and vastly larger ones that are looming: a civilizational crisis. One possible good outcome of the Covid-19 crisis is that it might bring people to think about what kind of a world we want. Do we want the kind of world that leads to this? We should think about the origins of this pandemic and why it emerged. It is a colossal market failure that goes right back to the essence of markets, exacerbated by the savage neoliberal intensification of deep socioeconomic problems. It was known for a long time prior to the present outbreak that pandemics were very likely to arise, and, further, that they were likely to be coronavirus pandemics, slight modifications of the SARS epidemic of fifteen years ago. That time, the virus was overcome; it was identified, sequenced, and vaccines were available. Between then and now, labs around the world could have been working on developing protection for potential coronavirus pandemics. Why didn't they? The market signals were wrong. We have handed over our fate to private tyrannies, corporations that are unaccountable to the public—in this case, big pharma. For them, making new body creams is more profitable than finding a vaccine to protect people from total destruction. It would have been possible for the government to step in. Polio, I can remember very well, was a terrifying threat and it was ended through the discovery of the Salk vaccine by a government institution set up by the Roosevelt administration. There were no patents; it was available to everyone. This time, the neoliberal plague has blocked governments from intervening. We are living under an ideology, which economists have worked to legitimize, that comes from the corporate sector. It is typified by Ronald Reagan, with his sunny smile, reading the script handed to him by his corporate masters: "Government is the problem, let's get rid of government." This of course means, "Let's hand over decisions to private tyrannies that are unaccountable to the public." On the other side of the Atlantic, Thatcher was instructing us that there is no such thing as society, just individuals thrown into the market to survive somehow, and, furthermore, that there is no alternative. The world has been suffering under this ideology for years and we are now at the point where actions that could be taken, like direct government intervention on the scale of the invention of the Salk vaccine, are blocked by the neoliberal plague. My point is that the present coronavirus pandemic could have been prevented. The information was available in October 2019, when a high-level simulation of a pandemic was conducted in the United States in order to assess the impact. It showed that the next severe pandemic would cause huge loss of life and trigger major economic and societal consequences. No actions were taken. On December 31, China informed the World Health Organization of pneumonia-like symptoms with unknown etiology. A week later, some Chinese scientists identified it as a coronavirus and, furthermore, sequenced it and gave the information to the world. At that stage, virologists and others who bothered to read World Health Organization reports knew that there was a coronavirus and knew how to deal with it. Did they do anything? Some did. China, South Korea, Taiwan, and Singapore began to act and have now, it seems, contained at least the first surge of the disease. To some extent, this also happened in Europe. Germany, which just managed to save its hospital system from neoliberalism, did have spare diagnostic capacity and was able to act in a highly selfish fashion, ensuring a reasonable containment of the outbreak within its borders. Other countries just ignored it, among the worst of them being the United Kingdom. The worst of all is the United States, which happens to be led by a sociopathic lunatic who one day says that there is no crisis, it's just like the flu, then says that there is a terrible crisis and he knew it all along, and the next day says that we must get back to business because he has to win the election. The fact that the world is in these hands is shocking. But the point is, again, that the pandemic started with a colossal market failure that points to fundamental problems in the socioeconomic order exacerbated by the neoliberal plague, and it continues because of the collapse of the kinds of institutional structures that could deal with it. These are topics that we ought to be thinking seriously about, for they raise the question of what kind of world we want to live in. If we overcome this pandemic somehow, there will be options ranging from the installation of highly authoritarian states to the radical reconstruction of society on terms concerned with human needs, not private profit. We should bear in mind that highly authoritarian, vicious states are quite compatible with neoliberalism. In fact, the gurus of neoliberalism, from Ludwig von Mises to Friedrich Hayek and others, were perfectly happy with massive state violence, as long as it supported what they called "sound economics." We shouldn't forget that neoliberalism has its origins in von Mises's seminar in 1920s Vienna, in which he could barely contain his delight when the proto-fascists of the Austrian state smashed the labor unions and Austrian social democracy and joined the early proto-fascist government. He praised fascism, in fact, because it was protecting sound economics. When Pinochet installed a murderous, brutal dictatorship in Chile, von Mises, Hayek, and Friedman loved it; they all wanted to help realize this marvelous miracle that was bringing sound economics to Chile, and great profit for foreign interests and a small part of the population. It's not outlandish to think that, today, a savage neoliberal system might be re-installed by self-proclaimed libertarians with the use of powerful state violence. That is one nightmare that might come about. But it is not necessary. There is the possibility that people will organize, become engaged, as many are doing, and bring about a much better world that can also confront the enormous threats of nuclear war and environmental catastrophe, from which there is no recovery. It is a critical moment of human history and not just because of Covid-19, although this should bring us to an awareness of the profound flaws and dysfunctional characteristics of the whole socioeconomic system, which has to dramatically change if there is going to be a survivable future.

Srećko: Many of us who have been active in social movements and organization for decades, central to which are physical and social closeness among people, are now suddenly getting accustomed to what is being called "social distancing" and "isolation" in our homes. What do you think the future holds in terms of social resistance in these times of social distancing, which will last at least a few more months, if not years? What would be your advice to progressives around the world—activists, intellectuals, students, and workers—on how to organize in this new situation? And could you perhaps tell us whether you are hopeful that, instead of increased authoritarianism, this open-ended situation might herald a radical transformation of the world, which would be green, equal, just, and built on solidarity?

Noam: First of all, we should bear in mind that prior to the pandemic, there already existed forms of social isolation that are very damaging. Go into any McDonald's and take a look at a bunch of teenagers sitting around the table having hamburgers—what you'll see is two conversations going on. One is a normally quite shallow discussion among the group and the other is the one that each of them is having on their cellphone, with some remote individual. This has atomized and isolated people to an extraordinary extent. The Thatcher principle that "there is no such thing as society" has escalated with the misuse of social media, which has turned people into very isolated creatures. In the United States, there are actually plaques in the footpaths of university campuses now which read "Look up," because the students are walking around glued to their cellphones. This is a form of self-induced social isolation that is very harmful. We are now in a situation of externally imposed social isolation and it has to be overcome by recreating social bonds in whatever way we can: helping people in need, developing organizations, making existing ones functional, planning for the future, and coming together on the internet to consult one another, deliberate, and find answers to the problems that we face. Face-to-face communication is essential for human beings, but if we are to be deprived of this for a while, we can find other ways to continue and, in fact, extend and deepen our activities. It won't be easy, but humans have faced worse problems in the past.

Srećko: Did I just hear a parrot squawking from somewhere in the house as you were talking?

Noam: Yes, a bilingual parrot. It can say "Sovereignty to all the people" in Portuguese. That's better wisdom than we hear from Washington.

Conversation held on March 25, 2020

The Flames of Truth: Julian Assange

John Shipton and Srećko Horvat

Srećko: The last time John Shipton and I saw each other was in London, when we took a train together to visit Julian Assange. Could you tell us, John, when was the last time you saw Julian and how is the prison situation at the moment?

John: I saw Julian about two weeks ago. He asked me to take extra precautions so I wouldn't get Covid-19, and we parted knowing that we wouldn't see each other for a month or so while the virus raged. The jail has now stopped social visits. Under the present circumstances in the jail, Julian is still brought to the meeting hall through a series of controlled moves. He is moved from his cell to a holding cell, where he waits until all of the corridors to the meeting room are empty, so that he doesn't meet anybody on the way. To get into the meeting room as a visitor, you have to go through four double portals: a dog-smelling portal, a portal to take your fingerprints, an X-ray portal, and another fingerprinting portal. Your clothes are searched, shoes and belt taken off, pockets emptied. It is a mission to get into this monstrous jail. You're issued with an ID card and allowed to take in £20, which you can use to buy Julian a cup of coffee. In the meeting room itself, there are high-definition cameras and high-fidelity audio recording.

Srećko: It was in some sense a fortunate situation that you, and also Julian's lawyers and other visitors, could at least visit him, but now the situation has changed. According to the data, there are around 11 million people in the world who are in prison at this moment. The United Nations' High Commissioner for Human Rights and the World Health Organization are urging governments to protect the prisoners, including by releasing them. Could you tell us what happened yesterday at the UK court and why Julian has been denied bail?

John: The oppression of the judiciary by the United States is continuous and has been demonstrated in the seven court appearances Julian has now had. I wait for the penny to drop on the magistrates in the extradition court that they are being used and manipulated into rejecting every humanitarian obligation that the court has, and the United Kingdom has, in order to service the judicial abduction of Julian to the United States. The court hearing yesterday was for a bail application to allow Julian to come and live with me and his partner, or just one of us. His situation is secure in as much as there's nowhere for Julian to go with all the airports shut down, but the application was rejected. The United States prosecutor said that the human rights obligations of the United Kingdom don't apply to Julian. They don't apply to a remand prisoner who has committed no crime in the United Kingdom and who is in danger of catching Covid-19 in a maximum-security prison. It's just disgraceful.

Srećko: It's a scandal. It has become so obvious that it's an erosion of democracy and of human rights. Clearly, this is an attempt to further isolate and silence Julian. I have done some research about various viruses on WikiLeaks, and I was surprised to see how much WikiLeaks published on swine flu, Ebola, and the avian flu, which the Polish government infected homeless people with in order to test the vaccine. In the present situation, if anyone's voice is missing it is definitely Julian's. Perhaps you can tell us how was he doing when you last saw him?

John: The European Council issued a request that Julian be freed, and the extradition not go ahead, and the UN—under two of its auspices, the Rapporteur of Torture and the Working Group on Arbitrary Detention—has made several declarations, backed by factual information, that the extradition must be stopped.[1] Julian has been in arbitrary detention now for ten years now, seven of which were spent in the Ecuadorian Embassy. For the last eleven months, he's been in maximum-security prison. Julian has committed no crimes. The Swedish case was abandoned three times. In the United Kingdom's case, there was a documented conspiracy between the Crown prosecuting service and the Swedish prosecuting authority.[2] This is

---

1   Resolution 2317, Parliamentary Assembly Council of Europe (PACE) http://semantic-pace.net/tools/pdf.aspx?doc=aHR0cDovL2Fzc2VtYmx5LmNvZS5pbn-QvbncveGlsLlhSZWYvWDJILURXLWV4dHIuYXNwP2ZpbGVpZD0yODUwOCZ-sYW5nPUVO&xsl=aHR0cDovL3NlbWFudGljcGFjZS5uZXQvWHNsdC9QZGYvW-FJlZi1XRClBVClYTUwyUERGLnhzbA==&xsltparams=ZmlsZWlkPTI4NTA4.

2   United Nations Special Rapporteur on Torture Nils Melzer's letter to the Swedish Government, September 12, 2019, p. 9–10, https://spcommreports.ohchr.org/TMResultsBase/DownLoadPublicCommunicationFile?gId=24838. See also, https://www.repubblica.it/esteri/2018/02/13/news/few_documents_many_mysteries_how_our_foia_case_is_unveiling_the_questionable_handling_of_the_julian_assange_case-188758273/.

an ongoing injustice which has brought shame and disgrace to the British and the Swedish services of justice. The English peoples made a great gift to civilization throughout the world when, 790 years ago, they placed a shield between the sovereign and the people. This shield, which works both ways, has been progressively abandoned in the case of Julian Assange. It is a great tragedy.

Srećko: There is a deep conspiracy and injustice happening to Julian. In terms of the court decision yesterday, what can you reveal about the next steps? Is the legal team going to appeal? Is it going to a higher court? What will happen to the extradition hearing planned for the end of May/June? The witnesses from the US obviously cannot come to UK at the moment.

John: I expect that there will be an appeal through judicial review in the High Court, which should be more cognizant of what is just, humane, and appropriate. The High Court has the stature to assert the rights of justice without fear of being contradicted by a higher court. I expect that Julian will be able to come home to his family and be able to join you and I—if we sit six feet apart.

Srećko: I keep thinking about the fact that Julian continues to go through the isolation that we are now experiencing, but in a much worse form. When he was in the Ecuadorian Embassy, he couldn't even walk around. I first heard about the technology we are using now, Zoom, from Julian. He used it from isolation to act on and influence the outside world. Could you perhaps tell us what shaped Julian's understanding of technology and geopolitics, from when he was in Australia to moving to Europe, and how he came to found WikiLeaks?

John: Honestly, I don't really know. He called me one day and said that he wanted to start WikiLeaks, using Tor to protect people's anonymity if they wished to make leaks. We always chatted about the shape and form of the world, but we didn't have access to the sort of information that was in the cables. That information gave the world an insight into the geopolitical world, and how those within it were bribed, bullied, and seduced into serving the United States' interests. Though, in his hacking days, Julian did discover targeting procedures used by generals in the United States Army, including the phrase "the Iraqi people must feel the pressure of war." This meant, in the case of Baghdad, the blowing up of a shelter that killed 356 women and children. Julian had a very powerful sense of world justice, and his determination has enabled justice for many people. An example is the Mauritius Islanders who, with the help of the cables, won a case in the international court of justice against the United Kingdom for the dispossession of their homes.[3] Another example is the dumping of toxic waste off the coast of Africa by Trafigura, which ruined the lives of coastal villagers.[4] Julian and WikiLeaks brought that to our attention and enabled the pursuit of those who committed these crimes. The awful irony is, of course, that Julian himself has not been able to have justice.

Srećko: I found a document on WikiLeaks from 2009, which describes the United States wanting to import the genomes of viruses such as Ebola and Marburg.[5] As Slavoj Žižek recently remarked, what we need at this moment is a Chinese Julian Assange who can provide leaks about what is actually happening with Covid-19, who is exploiting the present situation, and to what ends. What do you think the role of propaganda is in terms of the Covid-19 pandemic?

John: It seems that Covid-19 has driven us to communicate and read voraciously over the internet to sort out what is believable against what is simply propaganda. Every day, I read various reports on the internet to attempt to make sense of what is best to do, whether it is good to meet people, to wash your hands, or to get in a stock of chloroquine. I feel that we will begin to further abandon the legacy media.

Srećko: Once, at the Ecuadorian Embassy, when it was still possible to visit Julian, he described how he felt intellectually isolated in the vast land of

3 https://www.theguardian.com/world/2019/feb/25/un-court-rejects-uk-claim-to-sovereignty-over-chagos-islands https://www.theguardian.com/politics/2010/dec/03/wikileaks-cables-diego-garcia-uk.

4 https://www.theguardian.com/world/2009/sep/16/trafigura-african-pollution-disaster.

5 https://wikileaks.org/plusd/cables/09BERLIN1588_a.html.

Australia, and so he "hacked his way out" through the internet. This was in the '80s; Julian understood the internet as a possible emancipatory tool very early. Edward Snowden's recent memoir similarly talks about how, in the early years of the internet, everything seemed possible. Do you think, in this current moment, we might rediscover the potentialities of the internet?

John: The internet is a wonderful engineering marvel and it has facilitated the means whereby people all over the world can exchange ideas. The administration of social media companies, though, has been poor. In Australia, there are privacy protections but they are not enforced, and Google harvests massive amounts of data. The administration of the internet is a deficiency in our government which can be rectified quite simply: we just need to insist that our data is ours. In Israel and in Singapore, cellphones are being used to track people's locations and Covid-19 infections. These administrative regulations allow the state extraordinary insight into our doings. Every move you make and relationship you have is recorded in time and space and the state can use it for whatever they wish. It's becoming common for even PR firms to harvest data so they can perceive people's habits and stimulate them in a certain direction. These are the problems we face in the future. My current job is really quite narrow: to do everything I can to ensure that Julian comes home. In order to do my job, I have a certain understanding, which is that the United States has three avenues of action. The first is the oppression and intimidation of publishers, publications, and journalists. The second is the judicial abduction of people who have technical capacities that the United States wants—for instance, Meng Wanzhou from Huawei, Ola Bini from Ecuador, and Michael Lynch from the United Kingdom. The third avenue, to make it plain, is the extra-judicial assassination of people, the last great example being General Soleimani, but that's not isolated. During Obama's eight-year tenure, there were over 400 people assassinated extra-judicially on the kill list.[6] My job is to point out to the Europeans that it is in their own interests to unify against the intimi-

---

6 The Bureau of Investigative Journalism's estimate is much higher, putting the number of *civilians* killed between 384 and 807, and thousands of people in total. See: https://www.thebureauinvestigates.com/stories/2017-01-17/obamas-covert-drone-war-in-numbers-ten-times-more-strikes-than-bush.

dation of publications and journalists, to insist against the plunder of their technical knowledge, and to ensure that the extra-judicial assassinations stop. The technical aspects of the internet's movements into and shaping of society is out of my remit, except to say that I take Heidegger's analysis of the effect of technics upon society: that it gives rise to pathological social arrangements and mediated, distanced conversation instead of the warmth and feel of people gathered together. My remit is to remind people that Julian is banged up, that it's an injustice, and that it's in their interests to ensure that Julian is free and that no other journalist suffers in the way he has.

Srećko: In Heidegger's last interview, published in the *Spiegel* after his death, he was asked a question about whether people can influence technology as a "network of inevitabilities," and his answer was, "Only a god can still save us."[7] Today, there are many supporters of Julian who want to know how can they practically help.

John: Converse with each other, in person and on forums, and read widely so that you can analyze and understand the actual situation. Donations are very important. There are over a hundred lawyers and one hundred thousand people worldwide working on this, in four jurisdictions. Please give, it helps a lot. Support the DEA in England, and the Assange Campaign in Australia who, for instance, prepare letters to parliamentarians. So far, ten thousand individual emails have gone to Foreign Minister Marise Payne of Australia. This seems simple but it mounts up; a lake is full of raindrops.

Srećko: Why do you think the press failed so much in the past, when it comes to defending Julian Assange and his freedom?

John: The governments of the United Kingdom, Sweden, the United States, and, to some extent, Australia, brought about a campaign. Newspapers have two functions, generally. One is to garner public unity behind policy positions. This is a really important aspect of governments' administration. If the people don't support policy, the organization capacity of the state is reduced.

---

7 https://lacan.com/heidespie.

Newspapers obey, to a certain extent, what governments want, and that was the destruction of Julian Assange. They did that through calumny and lies, to the extent that the *Guardian* in the UK printed outright lies on its front page.[8] However, journalists throughout the world now realize that they can be un-judicially abducted, and Julian is an icon of that. If they protect Julian, then they protect themselves; if they can't, they become cyphers. That's how I see it.

Srećko: There has been a change over the past year in the support for Julian, with many more people awakening to the struggle and joining in. At the last big protest in London, I had never seen so many people on the streets for Julian—thousands of them. Respected global institutions such as Amnesty International and Reporters without Borders are now standing in Julian's defense. Although we find ourselves in this new and complex situation, where people cannot travel and must isolate at home, the support network has never been bigger. It is a brilliant time to dig into WikiLeaks, to visit the DEA campaign and the Courage Foundation.

John: The support for Julian has been a wonderful up-worlding from the masses, a historical realization that this is a monumental injustice. If we are sincere and our observations hold true, we articulate the up-world-ing of support for Julian right across Europe among every man and among parliamentarians, journalists, and bureaucrats. It's powerful, and I feel that we will succeed.

Conversation held on March 26, 2020

---

8 https://theintercept.com/2019/01/02/five-weeks-after-the-guardians-viral-blockbuster-assangemanafort-scoop-no-evidence-has-emerged-just-stonewalling/.

Is This the Beginning of a Possibility?

Saskia Sassen and Srećko Horvat

Saskia: I will start by saying that, to me, what we are experiencing now is not simply a virus, but a call for us to be on alert. Something foundational has happened, it's partial, but it's quite foundational in that it really reduces the weight of power. We know that the powerful will do better than the poor in this crisis, but, at the same time, the powerful are also getting hit; it is not just the disadvantaged poor who are being affected. I do find this coronavirus event a telling event. It enters the picture at a moment when we already had quite a few unsettlements. The second point I want to make is that we in the West have really messed up with a lot of our initiatives. The question of climate change, which many of the younger generations are really gathering around, is something that we elders have never taken very seriously, but we are also being pulled in now, because we realize something has changed. And one way of thinking about that something that has changed is that we have crossed the limits of a system. With one foot, we have stepped out—and it's just a bit too much. We are dealing with systematicities that can't quite fully narrate themselves, whether that's people or events. I want to take that seriously, that this is no longer just us, the people. I want to look at this microbe as an invitation for us to sit down and think. This invisible microbe that is without smell, without sound, invites us to do that; it is a call to attention to things that we hadn't thought about. We are confronted continuously with big things, big sounds, big initiatives and here is this invisible—in vast quantities, evidently—that is creating a new landscape as it moves, and as we stop moving. It is navigating across all the barriers that we have—the necessity for passport controls? None of that; it navigates at another level. It's not that I am enamored or intrigued, or that there is too much to be said about this microbe, but it is interesting, for me, to capture that side of it. It can navigate above all that we have done, it has its own modalities and capabilities, it doesn't ask anything from us (except, every now and then, a bit of blood, or whatever it is that it eats), it doesn't need to threaten us, it is powerful in its own way. It can enter anything—our houses, our noses—and it has a certain fluidity in the world that is interesting in terms of many situations that confront us. I am not trying to invoke internationalism or globalism, but just the navigational aspect of diseases (or of storms, for instance; it's not just this particular microbe). To me, there is a tale to be produced collectively that asks, "What can we learn from this?" We can't just talk about the microbe itself, but what tale, if we were elders of another time and place, we would use to narrate this experience. Covid-19 has affected everybody, more or less. This is something particular, and it's not the American army, that has entered into many parts of the world. The second issue I want to raise is much more pedestrian, not as elusive, and that is how we have constructed our economies and the systems that protect and nourish us, and the capacities involved in this. There are so many hungry people in the world, so many villages that have been destroyed in the name of "modernization." We have destroyed, across the world, instantiations of something productive and helpful: villages of local people who moved the land and plants, who knew when the water comes and when it stops. We have just entered these with plantations and mining and eliminated a vast amount of knowledge about local conditions. In the end, our big world is a collection of localities. We need the local knowledges and we're losing them. That is a second major issue that Covid-19 inevitably brings to mind. I can imagine a play in which this virus figures as a signal; it is not simply a negative. It is not the enemy. We humans are the enemy, maybe. Moving away from these very imminent issues and toward more familiar ones, I am interested in the question of how it is possible, with all the mobilizations that have happened across a century and more, that it is so difficult to deliver even a small degree of social justice for those who are disadvantaged, treated improperly, abused, suffering, and never enabled—probably half of the world's population, if not more. We have the knowledge, capabilities, and machines, but we are failing, and the question is why? I do not think the solution lies with one big actor to solve it all, but with multiple localities. In a way, these multiple localities are found in much of Europe, which has localized its production of food and basic goods. In the United States, our food often comes from places like Australia. This is totally unnecessary. We urgently need to address food production and distribution, but how do we re-localize what has been internationalized?

Srećko: I love how poetically you frame your perspective. It does seem that we need a form of poetry to understand the Covid-19 pandemic, because it goes beyond our understanding and immediate experience. What do you think the outcomes of this pandemic might be? Will it reinforce an even worse version of global capitalism, or might it spur deeper changes resulting in societies with more empathy, solidarity, and equality?

Saskia: I'm not at all religious, but one way of interpreting this event is to evoke images and possibilities that are not part of daily life. We are confronting something that we were not ready for. Supposedly, we have all these machines, capabilities, and brilliant people, but the virus, invisible and without smell, won. The victory was the victory of the virus. This tells us a couple of things. The first is that with our culture of selfishness, consumption, and accumulation, somehow, we forgot something. I haven't quite decided what the name of this virus is, or what it represents in our daily lives. We can call it "the virus," but it is also, separately, an actor in our lives. It is a virus, but it has also *functioned* in a very particular way. If it had arrived three hundred years ago, it wouldn't have functioned in this same way. Our mode of dealing with it—to hide from it, withdraw from it, and kill it—is very particular. Secondly, the virus is not just in one place, it is all over. It is simply the superior actor. We are not. When you see how people are beginning to take care of others, you can already see that this virus is—the old Greeks might say—a new type of god. It is not a god in the sense of an agent who has almighty powers, but in the sense of a capability to alter. The virus is teaching us something, enabling us to recognize our flaws and the poverty of our endeavors. In this way, it is an alert. There are many versions of this event that will emerge, and these versions will not simply be about the narrow meaning of Covid-19, but will be narratives like those we have had historically, where there were gods, good and bad, that taught us something. I can imagine a collective project emerging from this that would look at whether, if this virus had encountered a different mode of human society and production, it would have had a different impact on us. If we had dealt with Mother Earth differently, would this virus also be different? These are speculative elements, ways of finding our version of history.

Srećko: I think the most uncanny aspect of this tiny organism is precisely the fact that it's asymptomatic—that you can have it without knowing that you have it, you can spread it to someone without knowing you have spread it—and it challenges you to completely redefine not only your daily life but also the future. In terms of narratives, I'm still struggling with the fact that there are not many treatments of the Spanish flu in literature, for instance, unlike the Black Death. Walter Benjamin, Franz Kafka, and many famous historical writers were affected by the Spanish flu, but they didn't write much about it. The question today is how can we create a more progressive narrative that would, on the one hand, be very localized—in the sense that we have these daily microforms of solidarity, such as helping others with supermarket shopping—but, at the same time, would be internationalist. There is already a certain narrative being shaped, a hegemonic narrative, that does not admit that the prevailing political economy has failed utterly.

Saskia: Yes, we have a whole series of experts who are working very hard to keep this virus under control and save lives, and then they find out that there aren't enough face masks, for instance, and a whole series of little things they needed. These are not grand elements, but very simple things, and there aren't enough. That then mobilizes all kinds of people, so that we have grandmas making masks for their communities. One could almost say that this situation is an indicator of our arrogance: we never even considered that these little things would be important or necessary. There are these little lessons to be taken from the present situation, these juxtapositions of powerful actors with the little things that they didn't have, because they hadn't seriously considered that something like a pandemic could happen. There's a whole variety of these juxtapositions and I find them quite ironic. I just stand back and think, *How could we (the West) miss so many little things? What is it in our culture that doesn't see them?* Of course, nobody saw the crisis coming, but the little fact that we didn't have enough masks is an image that you just want to play with and create a bit of a drama about. This virus is creating a return to elements, by which I mean things that have standing, if you like, vis-à-vis a profession. And these include things we would not have called "elements" before. A little mask that grandmas can sew—that is now an element, it has standing, though we didn't notice it before. This little virus that we cannot see or smell has mobilized all these materialities that we had forgotten about. It really makes us work very hard, even if we are not directly affected by it, because it invites us to think about all the little things we have taken for granted, as well as the people who make those things. I want to register those elements; I think they tell a tale.

Srećko: You mentioned the importance of local knowledges earlier. How do we capture all of the many knowledges produced, including online, and transform them into something tangible?

Saskia: Well, that is clearly a collective project in the sense of multiple collectivities. It cannot just be one collectivity as it is now, wherein we think we know, more or less, what we need to know. We have to recognize that there are so many knowledges, including those in Africa and parts of Asia, which are very different kinds of knowledge from our Western knowledge. Some of our current knowledges are critical to us, but we have destroyed older knowledges in the process of building them. When I was a child growing up in Latin America, the older grandmothers had knowledges that my parents' generation didn't because they were already too modernized. I always think about how, in some countries in Europe, the pharmacies have a large variety of natural medicines, whereas in the United States everything is more or less chemical. We need to go back to those natural medicines, and we can, the knowledges are still there. Those are just little examples. On a totally different note, part of what we need to think and confront is the relationships among major powers. In its response to Covid-19, China conducted itself in a much more serious and adult way than Donald Trump, who kept calling it the "Chinese virus." We can't have political classes that are as stupid and childish as Trump. I am hoping that one thing we learn from this event is that it really matters who our political classes are and that we need particular knowledge to be present in them, even if that means changing the notion that anybody can run for president. We need expertise, and the range of expertise that we need is expanding enormously. But that is just one level. The people's level is, in my reading, far more significant. It is the people who can make the difference and can innovate, and this has been shown across centuries. There are always some individuals who are creative and innovative, but the important question is how to collaborate. Every city has a whole range of forms of knowledge that partly comes from other parts of the world.

The knowledge function needs to be part of the story we use to talk about Covid-19. The fact that so many people died in the early weeks of the virus was in part a function of a lack of recognition of the power of an invisible *something*, in a context where we (the West) think we have the most advanced medical knowledge. I want to see a discourse emerging from many different voices about these pieces of reality that have been thrown up, realities that were there but that we (in the West) didn't see.

Srećko: That's how I see it, too. Following the pandemic closely, as I have since mid-January, gives you a kind of comparative possibility. You are stuck in one country and you can see what other countries are doing or not doing, how their healthcare systems are affected. And you notice the differences in very little things, as you say. My local supermarket here in Vienna has no entry restrictions, so it has basically become a disco club, a place for socializing. On the other hand, I hear from my parents in Zagreb, for example, that there is a limit of just five people in the supermarket at one time. When people share this kind of information, they can see how competent or incompetent certain national governments are. This is working on many levels of society that are now being unmasked, so to speak.

Saskia: Exactly. The virus is an invitation for us to rethink things, to recognize, to hear, to listen, to pay attention, to want to discuss with others. It has that quality, I think, because it is so invisible and so powerful and these two qualities just don't fit.

Srećko: One topic you address in numerous books is public space. With the Covid-19 pandemic, we are seeing private places becoming public as people must stay at home to work and communicate. Do you think this phenomenon has the potential to reverse the privatization of what is public?

Saskia: This question will take a bit of decoding, but I hope that it can make that kind of difference. When it comes to so-called public space, we know that much of what is presented as public space is actually private space. There is such a lack of transparency in so many of the situations we face in this modernity of ours. This is a modernity marked by representations that are often illusions, they are not real, and the reality is far more brutal than the representations. This invisible little virus brought us down to earth again, showing us that any piece of food matters, that your neighbor matters. It really is an invitation to think.

Srećko: At the same time, precisely because it's invisible, it creates a fear, not only among theoreticians but ordinary people, that we will lose many civil liberties and end up in a sort of normalization of the state of exception. Even if it is necessary to be careful at the moment and have restrictions on mobility, one of the questions on everyone's lips is: What if these measures remain and allow the dreams of the populist leaders to come true? After this crisis is somehow solved—or the tiny organism decides to leave, or to live with us without killing us—what form will these measures take? The powers that be have the means to force people back to "business as usual" and even worse. How can we stop this?

Saskia: Yes, in the United States the corporations already have a whole program that they are forcing on us and which Trump is very open to. This is the ambiguity we must address. Every war generates possibilities for both good and bad. The baddies, in this case, are very powerful and very smart; they know what they want and they usually get it. We have to be on full alert. I do want to emphasize again, though, that this virus has also generalized something. Besides the arrogance of those with power, there is also the possibility for the powerless to experience this as an opening, as an "aha" moment. It is a spectrum, there are openings. It doesn't all belong to them.

Conversation held on March 27, 2020

Love in the Time of Coronavirus

Gael García Bernal and Srećko Horvat

Srećko: In this conversation, we will show you how dreams are prepared. Many people think it is a very simple and easy process, but our minds need to mix up a whole range of things to produce dreams: songs, music, random thoughts, love, relationships, friendships, all those ships. And if there is one person who knows a lot about all those ships, it's Gael García Bernal.

Gael: I've been sleeping and dreaming a lot recently, with all of these monothematic conversations we are having with our friends, family, and everyone. The point of departure, in a way, is to say how privileged we are to be able to talk about all these things from our home, from a place that harbors us, that we're able to isolate ourselves in. This has been a crazy time, both in dreams and in reality, with reality being more real than ever before. I have to mention that a couple of days ago, a dear colleague of mine, a friend and actor called Mark Blum, died from Covid-19 complications in New York. One wakes up from the dream space and we are faced with good things—with life, with birds, with the clean air—but, at the same time, with this reality that hits us very hard, with the passing of a very dear friend, or real economic and social complications that span beyond health, or being stranded in a foreign country, like yourself.

Srećko: I agree. It's a total privilege to be able to talk to you and it's thanks to the coronavirus, actually, that we are doing so. I am in Vienna and the situation here is serious. I've been in isolation for fourteen days now. The whole country is in lockdown, borders are closed, and I and others cannot return to our countries. Can you perhaps tell us what the situation looks like in Mexico?

Gael: That is a very complex thing to talk about. In a recent interview with representatives of the World Health Organization here in Mexico, they were saying that, obviously, there is no perfect solution to this pandemic. Yes, there are great examples of places that have managed to interact positively with their context and actually achieve some goals. Italy is an extreme example of action being taken long after—from what I've heard or read—the spread of the virus was known about. Compared to that approach, Mexico is taking action earlier. Mexico's response is closer to, but not the same as, what South

Korea is doing, aside from the testing. We should take into account that Latin America, as a whole, is more used to things like disasters and viruses than perhaps other places are. I'm not bragging about it, but I think it gives us a certain kind of approach, a resilient approach that forces us to engage with the context in a much more thorough way. We are trying not to panic at the beginning. Of course we feel the fear, everybody is afraid, but with communication and information we've managed to understand the situation a little bit more. The approach of Latin America and that of the Western world can be seen as two extremes. Mexico's approach is that there is no point in testing and, instead, let's act like we all have it, or we all could get it, and just stay home. Some advocate testing to find out where the hotspots are, but the most direct action is to say, "Okay, let's all go home for the moment." Another example is Argentina, which is taking very strict measures to lock up the country, including not even allowing entry to Argentinians, which leaves many people stranded. It is quite an unusual, extreme situation to experience: your own country not letting you in. Then there is the example of leaders such as Boris Johnson, Donald Trump, and Jair Bolsonaro. What they are doing is kind of ridiculous. It brings to mind a Miss Universe pageant, where they ask, "How would you achieve world peace?" and the answers—although, they are immediately much more thorough and interesting than what Johnson, Trump, or Bolsonaro would say—are quite shortsighted, stupid, and, if it wasn't such a dramatic topic, comical. I've heard a lot about how doctors are having to make the most horrendous, tragic, and cruel decisions on who lives and who doesn't. But this is something that happens naturally in hospitals most of the time, no? Also, this difficult and cruel decision is not far from the reality of the kinds of decisions that take place on the political level. The social approach toward this crisis is something that definitely needs to be tackled. Decisions are having to be made about whether, for instance, it is better to allow one chunk of the population to get sick so as to prevent others from dying of hunger and poverty. It is a tremendous decision but, then again, the whole world is in this situation. What this virus has enabled is for us to see how fragile everything is, how fragile the forms of organization that we've decided to live in are. This invisible virus is like the little drop of water that finally spills the full glass!

Srećko: I like this Latin American perspective that you gave, this idea that people have been through so much shit already that they are resilient. My family and friends are based in Zagreb, and last Sunday, when they were already in lockdown because of the virus, an earthquake hit, the strongest in 140 years. The people of Zagreb reacted in a very funny way, because what is there to do but to make jokes about such a situation? When I told the news to my friend from Guatemala, I told her it wasn't one earthquake, but thirty tremors in total, and she said, "Oh, you know, we in Guatemala live with earthquakes every day, we've gotten used to it." I'm not downplaying the tragedy of what happened in Zagreb, but it also shows that, for many, self-isolation is not such a bad or unusual thing. My big fear, though, is that once Covid-19 starts spreading in Latin America—even with the resilience you guys have—it will hit hard, because after hundreds of years of colonialism, decades of Chicago-boys' ideology, austerity, privatization, and so on, the system itself is perhaps not so well prepared. Recently, you have been filming in Cuba; perhaps you could tell us something about how it has come to happen that it is Cuban doctors who are showing international solidarity, who are equipped with the necessary knowledge, and who are reacting effectively to the pandemic?

Gael: It is, again, reality hitting very hard, because the reality is that there is a very strong medical system in Cuba, and a lot of doctors from Cuba live in many different parts of the world, working for public or private institutions. These people have dedicated their lives to health and solving illnesses, and that is something that is incredibly real and incredibly generous, and it is, also, a definite triumph of the Cuban Revolution. The established narrative doesn't allow that fact to have importance, because we still have a horrendous, ridiculous, tragic embargo implemented by the United States that has killed more people, or will kill more people, in Cuba than Covid-19. But I find it incredibly generous and moving that people from one part of the world are helping others elsewhere. Chinese doctors are doing the same. People that have already been through this, with their own special point of view, are supporting others, and this is what also throws us into this reality that we are talking about all the time now. I find myself, in every conversation I have, speaking as though there has been a kind of a paradigm shift, where I now speak from the world—I speak in first person as the world. I start from there and then I go into my context, my problems. It is crazy, I've never experienced it before.

Srećko: You mentioned the Cuban Revolution, so let me ask you a question connected to that, because everyone knows that you played Ernesto (Che) Guevara in *Motorcycle Diaries*. There is this beautiful scene on the boat when Guevara has an asthma attack, and I understand that you are also asthmatic. My question is, on the one hand, what can Che Guevara teach us about how to cope with a near-death experience? And also, what is your experience with this? Perhaps you could connect your answer to the current global pandemic, a time when everyone has to protect their lungs and take care.

Gael: Fortunately, I only had asthma as a kid and it went away. Definitely, though, when portraying Ernesto, I felt I understood it. I understood, a little bit, how the asthma attacks became a place for him to grab strength from, to read, to study, to intellectualize certain thoughts, and then afterward, when he was feeling better, he would go out and take action. Similarly, right now we are grabbing strength and getting everything into shape in order to emerge from this stronger. Our bodies are naturally doing that as well. So, what would Ernesto think about these times? Well, he thought something that I definitely wouldn't agree with today, which is that the armed way is the only way out. I understand why he thought that, and maybe if I had been born in that moment I would have felt the same. I understand what he saw in the communist context, and how destiny put him in hotspots all the time, how it brought him to meet Fidel Castro here in Mexico City. Those series of consequences led him to think what he thought and to try and act on it. When we were doing the film, we were asking Alberto Granado, one of Ernesto's friends, a lot of questions about his journey, and he said what is perhaps the most modern thing anyone has ever told me—modern because it was incredibly futuristic and generous. He said, "Don't try to imitate our voices, use your own voices to describe your journey, play yourselves, 'cause you have much more information and much more of a sense of the world and of Latin America then we did." That, ultimately, was what *Motorcycle*

Diaries was for me. It made me, and all the people who participated in the film, immediately feel so much bigger, and feel that the place we are from is so much bigger. Ever since then, whenever I am in Latin America, I feel I am where I am supposed to be.

Srećko: I would love to say that as well, but I was actually planning to travel to Mexico and this global pandemic stopped me. Che Guevara and other revolutionaries—if they were real revolutionaries—were always dreaming about internationalism, and today we at least have the possibility of internationalism and it is more important than ever. To make one short historical parallel, unlike with the Spanish flu in 1918, where someone in Germany or Mexico didn't really know what was going on, not just because of censorship but also technology, today, I sense that a global awareness is rising. More than two billion people today are, in one way or the other, in confinement and most of them are going to sleep and waking up with the same thought: "the coronavirus." From there, the thought expands in many other directions, developing into an assessment or criticism of your government's response, or a criticism of the political economy of global capitalism, which ruined the healthcare systems and doesn't appreciate care workers, shop assistants, waste collectors, and so on. We can see that there is a struggle going on for what kind of world will rise out of this.

Gael: Yes, and our strategy for making it through day by day is, perhaps, to be a little bit optimistic. There is a general certainty that we will not go back to the horror we were living before. That horror can mean different things for different people, but we can agree on certain things. There is an optimism and certainty that we need a public health structure that is strong enough to tackle events like this. This is something on which everybody, I think, is starting to agree. No matter what political perspective they have, they know that this is important because they can now see how fragile the system is, and how a health crisis can affect so many aspects of their lives. I've always had existentialist crises, questioning everything, but they're usually hypothetical or abstract. The issues that storm my head are normally "Who do I want to be?" and these kinds of long-term questions. But now we are questioning what's going to happen in a couple of weeks, wondering about jobs, what to do, where to go, who we can help. The existential crisis, in a way, has become much more short-term. At the same time, with the calm of the night, or in the morning, we start to ponder about the kinds of optimistic outlooks that will hopefully come out of this. Obviously, sometimes, I have pessimistic thoughts. I wouldn't say I've been depressed, because depression often involves a feeling of being the only person who is living this, and a small consolation in this crisis is that we are all living it, so you don't feel alone. But I sometimes feel incredibly scared and anxious, wanting the horror not to become a reality.

Srećko: I notice similar things with myself as well. For instance, one week ago, I woke up expecting all of the bad news about Covid-19 and I got a message from my sister with photos of Zagreb in debris and I thought, *What the fuck, what's happening now? An earthquake? What's next?* Everyone is waking up with that sense of anxiety and you're completely right that the way we count time has changed. I used to schedule things months, even years, ahead, but now I don't even count time in weeks or days; it is becoming hours. When I was watching some of your movies, I realized that most of them are, in one way or another, connected to a sort of disaster. In *Science of Sleep* you play Stéphane, who is making a calendar of disasterology, and recently you told me that you were in Chicago filming a TV series about a global pandemic called *Station 11*. What happened to that? Did you finish it? Is it going to be aired? Is there any lesson we can take from science fiction? Does science fiction have a lesson anymore?

Gael: It is based on a book that I'm sure many people have read. It deals with a lot of the consequences of a global pandemic, but it's also a little bit on the edge of the future, looking at what happens to human relationships afterward—on the premise that the institutions of the world have collapsed, and nothing is what we thought it was before—and how this sense of spirituality blossoms in this situation. We managed to shoot some of it, and we are going to pick it up again sometime soon. In terms of entertainment, I've been finding myself very distracted. I can't concentrate on films and series and they just numb me. Instead, I've been connected to something which elementally throws me into a very strong sense of being, which is playing the guitar. I'm very bad at it but I love it; it has given me an immense sense of meaning. I've been finding the expression of love in the strangest combinations, in all sorts of artistic consequences, be it cooking or just the contemplation of the outside world, and also in science and scientific language. I have a friend who is a biologist, and he always talks in these two terms of science and art. What he does as a biologist has very strong artistic consequences and he's always argued the point of encounter between science and art. I've been finding a lot of solace there; how about you?

Srećko: For me, the first days of lockdown were quite traumatic, thinking, *Can I return home? When will I see my family?* Then, out of this feeling of utter helplessness, we created DiEM TV, and, to be honest, it gives me a reason to wake up, to have a shower, even, because otherwise what would be the point? To see people like you and read the comments from our audience is wonderful, because we're in a very interesting situation in which public spaces don't operate anymore, and we are increasingly using these online spaces as public spaces. Through these spaces I have also come to the realization of what you call love—in the sense of people from many different places and time zones all coming together in this, sharing our thoughts, fears, and hopes. I've also noticed, since the global pandemic started, the huge amount of phone calls and emails I've had from people I love, just saying, "How are you?" "Is there any way I can help you?" "Do you need money?" Even, "Do you need an apartment?" This kind of solidarity is growing. That keeps me from sinking into depression.

Gael: I think there is a strong relationship between this discovery and time—as well as there being a strong relation between time and being confined. It is "the best of time" in a sense. Maybe one of the main lessons that we can take from all of this concerns time. For example, it's always been said how The Beatles were confined to a place in Hamburg for one year, playing five or six nights every week, practicing all the time. They were extremely talented and gifted, but it was this practice that helped them evolve into the kind of musicians that they became. This is something that time makes, and it is what we are experiencing right now. I found myself wanting to be incredibly productive as soon as this whole thing started. I failed, of course, to keep to my schedule. But my daughter established a calendar for the whole family, and one of the periods of time she made was called "time for peace," which means, basically, time to do whatever you want without anybody telling you, "Hey, you have to do this or that." Maybe we all need that. Hopefully, some of these things are going to be retained. I'm definitely going to give myself more time to do things and try to stop this crazy notion that I could be in any part of the world at any time. I'm not going to go back to that because it was affecting me, hurting me, even, and I found myself dry, with nothing to talk about anymore, like I wasn't living.

Srećko: I fully agree. Thinking of your daughter's "time for peace," my friend recently told me that some parents are complaining, saying, "We cannot do this anymore, we are constantly with our kids in the apartment, this is hell, can I sell my kid on eBay?" And one of my younger friends said, "If my parents told me as a child that I had to stay at home playing video games, I would have thought I'd died and gone to heaven!" So, there are good sides to this, at least from children's perspectives. There is also a philosophical point that you are pointing to. Walter Benjamin, in his "Theses on the Philosophy of History," has this nice image of French revolutionaries shooting at the clocktowers. That was the first thing they were doing after the revolution: shooting at time. And if you go back to the Middle Ages, you can see that there is a direct link between the clock-time universe and schedules and capitalist realism, where everything is measured by the hour and we end up, as you said, dry, without time for meaningful things. Changing our sense of time would definitely be a good outcome of the crisis. And what advice would you give to the youth regarding love in the time of coronavirus?

Gael: Well, I was a kid when, all of a sudden, we heard about the AIDS pandemic. The first thing we learned, and this was before we had learned sexual education, was that it was sexually transmitted. Obviously, it was something that, as kids, we were naturally very curious about. The whole of humanity was deeply scared of the transmission of this thing and of how little they knew about it. They came up with this notion that, in Mexico, was called "solo con tu pareja," or "only with your partner." At a certain point, I was like, "Shit, this is my sexual awakening and I'm stuck!"

I remember thinking that the older guys had the chance to fuck all they want, and now I'm in this situation where it's impossible to even know what is right and what is wrong. The lack of information back then was huge, and institutions like the church instilled fear in people, with messages like, "You're going to die if you touch!" My advice to young people would be that we were born into something much more frightening, and something much more connected with an integral part of being young, which is sexual awakening. And we understood it and resisted it, in a way, and changed the dynamics of the situation through information, eliminating the stigma that existed with AIDS. Medicine made huge advances in this as well, and now we know what AIDS is. With Covid-19, we know what it is, and that makes a huge difference. With AIDS, people like Ronald Reagan were trying to hush it and were stigmatizing homosexuality and Africans, and it was terrible. Information is a way out, definitely.

Srećko: Art and cinema play an important role in any crisis as well. European cinema productions have, for the moment, stopped. What do you think will happen with the global industry and when will production resume? Do you think this is an opportunity for national cinema? And do you think cinema will change after the Covid-19 pandemic?

Gael: In most parts of the world, production has halted from independent films to big international movies and local TV productions. It's going to recover, of course, but not with the same hype, not with the same kind of drive for "content," that horrendous word. What will happen, I think, is that the things we will be able to create will arise from what is in our own hands. We won't depend on third-party studios or big corporations to say yes or no. This gives us an advantage, because we can talk about things that haven't been talked about or are no longer terms of discussion. Actors no longer talk about an "artistic journey"; that is something from another time. The situation after Covid-19 will not be about "creating content" but about an artistic journey, because the consequences of the virus will not be glamorous or extreme. It's going to be production that you can have in your own hands. This connects to what Bong Joon Ho said about *Parasite*. He said he wanted to do a film about South Korea, about Seoul, about two particular neighborhoods, and then he realized, with the huge global reaction to the film, that we all live in the same country, which is capitalism. It has been said many times: if you want to be universal, be local. We have to engage with our contexts because we have so many things to say. I have a lot of things to say in my language; this is where I expand. I don't want to waste my time trying to follow the route of somebody else. I want to work from my own place, because I want to have an artistic journey and I want my life to have artistic consequences. I think that is where things are heading and maybe films will be much more personal after this. We will want to know what a person from Sarajevo feels in this whole craziness, rather than knowing what a superhero feels about it, because we can't come up with dialogues for superheroes right now.

Srećko: This idea that we all live in one country called capitalism also reminds me of your movie *Chicuarotes*. It is set against an earthquake and it deals with people who are in the excluded, exploited, and forgotten parts of society, showing how resilient they actually are. On that note, what are your thoughts on how Covid-19 is affecting poor people in Mexico, the ones who can't quarantine?

Gael: This is something that the government in Mexico has been trying to talk about. Some of the houses in Mexico are not good places to be quarantined in. The elemental social necessities are not there, one of them being love, for example. Maybe we need to think of love as something that is a privilege to have. It is something that we think of as an accident, but often it doesn't exist; home is sometimes a very violent place to be. I'm speaking from a place of privilege, and I do not assume that I know exactly what is going on, but I think love is a very interesting concept to take into account, in terms of how to deal with this pandemic socially. Fortunately, the Mexican government and many governments in Latin America, with the exception of Brazil, have talked about the extra, difficult consequences that a pandemic can lead to, such as men not doing their share of domestic work, for example, and people living in violent surroundings. Scientists, professionals, and doctors are among those talking about this. The recipe for what Europe, in general, needs and what Mexico or Latin America needs is not the same. It's a whole different thing.

Srećko: Rimbaud famously said that love has to be reinvented. Do you think that this global crisis will lead, also, to our reinvention of love?

Gael: In a very elemental and straightforward way, love can also be interpreted as work, as you mention in your book, *Radicality of Love*, bringing in Alexandra Kollontai. The idea that love is work is something that we are all extremely familiar with at the moment. We may be isolating with a person we love and having a great time, but we are also finding that it is a test that involves a lot of emotional and manual work. Many people are experiencing this on its maximum level at the moment. I think our conceptions of love will definitely change. Before the pandemic, love used to be this kind of immediate thing that was either there or it wasn't. But work was not included in that whole idea, or maybe only in more overt forms, like couples' therapy or self-help sessions, but right now we are really feeling the difficulty of it. In a way, it is fantastic, because it puts love to the test and it puts us to the test. Right now, we have to deal with our love consequences and the hard work that love is. What do you think Kollontai would have thought about this time?

Srećko: That is a tough question and I'm pleasantly surprised that you brought Alexandra Kollontai into this. No one would have expected the two of us to discuss Kollontai in connection with a virus! I think you put it beautifully. Kollontai was warning against the commodification of love, where love becomes a kind of product on the free market and the invisible hand will somehow bring you to the perfect partner. Today, love is, firstly, work at home, because we are spending more time with our loved ones than usual, which can create problems, as you touched on, and the figures of rising domestic violence are very worrying. On the other hand, Kollontai also wrote about the function of love in society. Those who are saving our lives at the moment show a sort of unconditional love—the doctors, medical assistants, postmen, waste collectors, and shop assistants. I am not saying that they necessarily love their jobs; they do it to survive. But this work is a work of care for the rest of society, and it is a kind of love for society as a whole. I hope that we will redefine love.

Conversation held on March 28, 2020

Corona-Neo-Fascism:
A Deadly Combination

Ece Temelkuran and Srećko Horvat

Srećko: Just one month ago, I actually saw you physically, Ece, in Vienna, where I am currently in "self-isolation." You brought hand sanitizer and we were laughing at ourselves, thinking perhaps we were being paranoid. Within a month, the situation has changed rapidly. Borders are closed and public events are no longer possible. Let's start with a seemingly simple question: How are you, Ece? What has happened in the month since we last saw each other?

Ece: I am trying to keep my spirits up. The world has been expecting of us contradictory things. Covid-19 demands that we stay at home, but recently Zagreb experienced an earthquake and we were all told to leave our houses and get out on the streets. People were walking around like headless chickens, nobody knew what to do. I am alone in Zagreb, as all my friends are in their summer houses in Croatia or Turkey. Living in solitude does not make things easier; although, considering that when quarantine ended in China there was a flood of divorces, perhaps it's better that way. I wouldn't say I am optimistic about the situation, but there is an atmosphere of people finding humor in despair. There is a new trend, for instance, of people recording videos of themselves gradually going crazy. I think there will come a time when we won't feel like making these videos anymore, to say the least.

Srećko: In one of our earlier conversations, you raised the subject of what you called the deadly combination of Covid-19 and neofascism. Could you explain your ideas around this? Your most recent book, *How to Lose a Country: The 7 Steps from Democracy to Dictatorship*, examines the processes that lead from democracy to dictatorship, and I am wondering whether, instead of "dictatorship in one country," we are now facing a dictatorship that spans the whole planet?

Ece: What strikes me is that the present pandemic is asking of us exactly the same things that fascism would: isolation, restrictions, atomization, and social distancing. The virus creates an environment that is perfect for the flourishing of right-wing populism, authoritarian regimes, and fascism in general. In [the] coming months, the surveillance measures being implemented now to track the virus and exert control over individuals will become normalized and legitimized. That is frightening, to say the least. We are being asked to rewire our brains, our mental and emotional being, as well as our physical behavior, and to do so very quickly because of the coronavirus. And we are performing very well, considering that not touching the face goes against our neurological system, and that social distancing is impossible because we rely on solidarity, sociality, and the care of others to get through crises. Within five or six days of "self-isolation," I was watching a movie that showed two people kissing and immediately thought, *Don't do it!* Fear is very effective; it can transform your thinking and lifelong habits in just a few days. We already knew this about fascism, but we are now learning it through the pandemic as well. And there are two sides to the coin here: we are simultaneously going through the worst of times and the best of times. They are the worst not only because of the immediate crisis and those on the horizon, and not only because we have the worst possible leaders in power, but also because solidarity is becoming impossible. We must reinvent solidarity very quickly, and DiEM TV is one contribution to this. When we are afraid, we feel an urge to act and to connect with one another, but we are reinventing the means by which this can be done. In terms of the "best" of the present situation, there is a general feeling that "it cannot go on like this." People who read and are politicized already knew, prior to the pandemic, that capitalism and democracy are in crisis. Now, however, even those who are not politically active are voicing demands for a better, fairer, and more equal world.

Srećko: Like comrade Britney Spears, who is calling for a general strike.[1]

Ece: Exactly. It shows that even the most apolitical person is capable of political thinking when he or she really needs to; it is activated when the time is right, when the conditions are mature. This courage and urge to speak up is taking shape very fast; it's as contagious as Covid-19. Another positive development is that those people who were not, before, convinced that right-wing populism is really political insanity are now seeing very clearly that our clownish leaders are completely incapable of dealing with real problems. Another observation I have made is that fewer and fewer people are talking about "post-truth." After four or five years of popularity, suddenly that

---

1   https://www.theguardian.com/music/2020/mar/25/comrade-britney-spears-star-calls-for-strike-and-wealth-redistribution.

topic is off the table, because we are now painfully aware that we need facts and we need the truth. Nobody now wants to be deceived by the fake news manufactured and multiplied by the troll farms. Almost as a reflex, people are turning to science, which has been discredited for so long. Issues that we have been grappling with for years have, within a month, been brought to the fore and addressed—all thanks to a virus. Where our criticisms of the "post-truth" world have failed, reality has succeeded. Another positive aspect of what we are currently experiencing is that, for the first time in generations, we have time on our hands to think. The world has come to a halt and we now have time to imagine a new world, and collectively, thanks to communication technologies. The political vacuum is now very apparent, and it should be filled by grassroots progressive movements. We can learn from Bernie Sanders's approach in no longer focusing on elections but on joining and building grassroots movements that have sprung up in response to Covid-19. I have been thinking about how we might conceptualize politics in times of constant crisis—because of course other crises, such as climate and economic crises, are expected to follow Covid-19—and I want to suggest the term "portable politics." This refers to the reality of a politics that does not take place inside political institutions but is carried to where the action is. This is not a completely novel idea, but I believe it might inspire people who are trying to build new ties of solidarity going forward. The Covid-19 crisis is not the first time that history has required us to reinvent solidarity, but it is the first time, perhaps, that it has required us to invent it so quickly. I am interested in how we might practically achieve this, given that we cannot be with each other and are restricted to a digital environment. Rather than obsessively reading news updates on the virus, we should study this question. The overlapping of the crisis of capitalism and the Covid-19 crisis is both a horrifying and wonderful thing, because it made it visible that the present world order is simply idiotic. I have been thinking about Beirut lately, which is the crib of crisis. I was there in 2006 the day after the Israeli bombardment of southern Beirut. The very next day after the attack, the Buddha Bar was full, people were dancing, and there was a new cocktail named after the bomb used by the Israelis. I learned, too, that the caipirinha cocktail was invented during the Spanish flu. Brazilians were told that they should drink lemon, so they thought why not add cachaça? In times of fear we laugh and make jokes at the same time as we are terrified and depressed—we have several emotional reactions at once, and from them we build solidarity ties. When the worst of times is over, though, we tend to forget the fear along with the solidarity that we built. During the Gezi uprising in Turkey, incredible, organic, and completely spontaneous solidarity was built, but only one proper permanent organization survived from that period, Oy ve Ötesi (Vote and Beyond), and it became a country-wide network to monitor the ballot boxes against election fraud, which is huge in Turkey. This time, we need to make the solidarity ties permanent. We need them to survive Covid-19 and become a platform for the coming crises. A few months ago, I was on a plane and an elderly lady was sitting next to me, dripping in Louis Vuitton. The plane went into turbulence, and she started shaking with fear. She grabbed my hand and was soon holding it with both hands. As soon as we landed, she let go, fixed herself, and started walking. Then she turned toward me, said, "thank you," and walked away. I don't think it was rudeness that made her act this way, but the fear of feeling humiliated because she was afraid. We should learn to adapt to fear—and unfortunately, we will likely have no choice. If we manage to do that, to relax in fear, we might not be embarrassed about the ways we behave when we are scared and we can broaden and deepen the solidarity ties that we build during crises beyond them.

Srećko: You've mentioned two crucial concepts: fear and solidarity. Right from the start of this pandemic, before it arrived in Italy from China, we have seen precisely this kind of fear that you describe, and it is interwoven with neofascism. The vice president of the senate of Italy went so far as to claim that the only protection from Covid-19 is to widely adopt the Roman salute in place of the handshake.[2] Indeed, it is very interesting to see why the fascist salute was introduced in the first place—it wasn't just because Mussolini was so much obsessed with the Roman empire and wanted to recreate it (in the same way that Hitler wanted to recreate the great German myths), but also because of hygiene. What makes our situation today even

2   https://www.archyde.com/the-vice-president-of-the-italian-senate-recommends-using-the-fascist-salute-to-avoid-getting-the-coronavirus/.

more dangerous is that we don't have an external enemy, for instance, another nation, but an invisible enemy that is everywhere. As you described with reference to the earthquake in Zagreb, we are facing contradictory threats in an immediate sense; but the longer-term democratic threat is contradictory, too. For instance, most of us are respecting, as much as we can, the restrictions on mobility and surveillance measures being implemented. At the same time, those of us who care about democracy are terrified about the potential directions in which these measures might develop within a kind of permanent "state of exception." To combat this fear, we have, as you mentioned, solidarity. Things that used to seem completely impossible now seem possible and there is a recreation of spaces of potentiality.

Ece: I don't know about you, but I first became politically aware when I was four or five years old and I thought that poor kids should not be humiliated just because they were poor. I later learned that this sense of justice is one of the basics of democratic socialism. At first, though, it was a moral stand, innate, so to speak. When we see someone like Britney Spears advocating wealth redistribution this is not because she suddenly decided, because of Covid-19, to dive into political literature and read Marx, but because it is common sense. In the 1950s, ideas of equality and social justice were associated with dangerous communists; in the 1980s, they were simply naïve; and in the 1990s, people were more concerned with cultural criticism. Finally, these ideas are again becoming normal. Speaking of a "return to normal," I do not think there will be one after the pandemic recedes. Instead, there will be a new normal, which is shaping now. And if progressive movements do not seize this process and guide it, the far right will. To give an inspiring example, progressive figures in Turkey, including the mayors of Ankara, İzmir, and Istanbul, have become extremely important political figures thanks to Covid-19. All of a sudden, there is a re-centering of politics back to the level of city-states. These mayors started voicing new proposals, building new solidarity ties, and implementing amazing programs. We are seeing similarly bold actions being taken by mayors in certain cities in the US. This kind of politics is not easy to forget when things return to "normal." Perhaps the new normal will, on the administrative level, be centered around city-states.

Srećko: This concept of municipalism and city-states is important. As we have seen in some Italian regions, for instance, more local forms of power are often more effective in dealing with Covid-19. In Croatia, the city-state of Dubrovnik, the Republic of Ragusa, was the first city in Europe to introduce a maritime quarantine and it was rather successful for the four centuries of the Republic's existence, even if outbreaks of plague would return. This was due to the very organized city-state model of Dubrovnik, which had public healthcare and very successful diplomacy. I completely agree that there might be a return to local politics, which I do not fetishize, because I always think it has to be scaled up.

Ece: Yes, perhaps we need to think about smaller self-sufficient political entities when it comes to mobilizing people or building solidarity ties. I just remembered something else, though, about the earthquake in Zagreb, which was the first in 140 years and arrived at the same time as Covid-19. I went through the 1999 earthquake in Turkey that was of a 7.3 magnitude, so I knew what to do in Zagreb: I drank a cup of coffee, went down on the street, and was able to calm my panicked neighbors. In Turkey, we are used to crises, sometimes three in one day. When the bombardment of crises began in Turkey around 2009, not many people were aware that the country was heading in a very dangerous direction and that we were already "losing it," so to speak (like the Brits lost their country during Brexit, and the Americans during Trump's election). In Turkey, we went through the political and moral madness earlier. And I remember one of my friends saying, "You know what? This is too tiring, let's shut down the country. We have cheese, tomatoes, and bread, the basics of Turkish cuisine, let's eat that for a year and think about what we are going to do." Stop everything and think. One week before the Covid-19 crisis began, we were talking about Syria and a possible Third World War—NATO was locking horns with Putin. Perhaps, nature itself has now given us a time to eat cheese, tomatoes, and bread and think about what we are going to do next. This is, really, a precious time—if we manage not to get depressed and to stay focused, neither of which is easy.

Srećko: Thank you also for the very concrete suggestion that, if an earthquake hits, first drink a cup of coffee, because you will need it, there will be another earthquake. How would you assess the short- and medium-term situation in Turkey in the face of the Covid-19 crisis?

Ece: In *How to Lose a Country*, I wrote about how right-wing populism operates the same way, in seven stages, in every country despite all their differences. I don't make predictions and I am not an optimist, but I do think Turkey has a chance after Covid-19. The mayors I mentioned from İzmir, Ankara, and Istanbul have shown people what a political leader should be, something we had forgotten after eighteen years of the AKP regime. People will likely hold on to that in coming months and use it to demand more justice. Otherwise, what I am seeing right now is a lot of political humor, which is great, but after a while it operates as a paralyzing tool.

Srećko: Yes, humor can be subversive, but it can also be very impotent.

Ece: Exactly. It creates an illusion of political engagement as well as a certain cynicism or fatalism, both of which are really dangerous. People are trying to keep their spirits up, understandably, but things are very serious right now and, as my book makes clear, you lose your country when you are living in it, not because you are exiled or made external to it in a physical sense. The feeling of being a citizen or belonging to a country is no longer there, and this is not only due to the right-wing populist leaders, but a combination of several things, the most important being a lack of solidarity. Turkey now seems to be relearning solidarity again, through Covid-19, which I find inspiring.

Srećko: I think it's about time to rename your book *How to Lose a World*. Many of the questions you tackle in your book come back to the question of citizenship, but what does this mean today? We both, and thousands of others, are presently in a country that we are not citizens of.

Ece: We actually need to prepare a list of urgent demands for the months ahead, chief among them being open borders. If the borders remain closed, we know that this will be used as an excuse to bar refugees and exiles long after the pandemic recedes. As we said at the start of our conversation, these kinds of measures provide the perfect environment for fascism to flourish. Imagine how easy it is to run a country without people—this is what is happening right now. Several political leaders have these "perfect" countries where nobody can move, nobody can speak up, and that's why we urgently need to reinvent solidarity. Speaking of which, the present situation of lockdown and isolation is really against our nature. A friend of mine lives in Madrid and in front of her building there is a care home for elderly people. She cried all day yesterday because there were body bags rolled from the building and the carers who are working there are locked down with the elderly. It's a horrible situation and I told her not to watch it, because watching atrocities like this unfold when you are unable to act or help in any way is the worst torture that the human soul can endure. This is not the first time that we are watching and are feeling helpless. We have to reinvent solidarity, again.

Srećko: In terms of concrete demands, I can see this already happening in different parts of the world. DiEM25 is just one of these trends and movements, and we published recently a three-point plan for what the European institutions, including the European Central Bank, should actually be doing instead of what they are currently doing.[3] Yesterday, we received the good news that Portugal has temporarily granted all migrants and asylum seekers in the country full citizenship rights, granting them immediate access to healthcare during the Covid-19 outbreak.[4] I think many other countries could follow in that direction.

Ece: Morally and philosophically, we are going to go through some sort of transformation. Here in Croatia, in order to enter a pharmacy you have to prove your identity so they can check if you are supposed to be in isolation or not. I went to the pharmacy but, since I don't know Croatian, I didn't know about the identity issue and the pharmacist couldn't let me in. It was so awkward. She wanted to help me because not doing so was inhumane, absurd, and idiotic, so she asked me what I wanted, told me to wait at the door, and went in and brought the things out for me. And I thought, *This is what is going to happen on a large scale.* People will realize, finally, that

3 https://diem25.org/diem25-presents-covid-19-economic-response-plan-and-green-recovery-investment-program/.

4 https://www.euronews.com/2020/03/29/coronavirus-portugal-grants-temporary-citizenship-rights-to-migrants.

what capitalism imposes on them—making them behave in evil, selfish, and self-centered ways—actually wastes a lot of energy, because moving toward good is actually innate in human beings, and in order to be evil you have to make an effort. For many people, this logic of selfishness will seem completely absurd after Covid-19.

Srećko: On the one hand, I see in the present situation the possibility of a far worse world, with fewer civil liberties, constant fear, and a permanent "state of exception." But, on the other hand, there is this evident kind of historical vacuum that you mentioned, this open historical situation where the relevance of mutual aid and of solidarity is primary. Even those who subscribe to capitalism's "evil" selfish individualism cannot operate in the same way that they did before, because even evil idiots get infected. Connectedness has become so visible. On another note, do you think Covid-19 will prompt a ghettoization of dirtiness?

Ece: I do think that parts of the world will be ghettoed, yes. I can imagine the European Union making a statement in coming months that bans people entering from Turkey, for instance, or whichever eastern or Southern countries are still, conveniently, contaminated. I brought up the border issue for a reason. There should be demands in place already to negate this, one of which should be open borders. Even before Covid-19 Europe was a ghetto, in a way: a white, rather clean ghetto.

Srećko: And what are the opportunities for antifascists in this moment?

Ece: They are already evident. In such times when people are afraid and confused, and when everything is uncertain, the certainty and determination offered by people like Bernie Sanders, the mayors in Turkey, and numerous leaders elsewhere, really makes a huge difference when viewed alongside the inaction of the right-wing populist leaders, who so blatantly do not care about rescuing people, but only capital. The big opportunity for progressive political movements at this moment is to say out loud, "We are on your side and we are going to beat this together."

Conversation held on March 29, 2020

Why We Must Save Julian Assange

Stefania Maurizi and Ivana Nenadović

Ivana: Like many around the world, I am in self-isolation here in Belgrade, Serbia, where we are under curfew and in a state of exception, with further harsh measures being threatened every day. One really pertinent thing I would like to ask you, Stefania, is how do we distinguish fake news from the facts these days? Why should we believe our governments now, when we know that they weren't providing us with correct information before? And what is the importance of whistleblowers? Of all the measures now being implemented under the veil of the protection and safety of the public, how many of them will be withdrawn once Covid-19 has passed?

Stefania: I have more than a decade of experience in dealing with the secret documents of high-profile whistleblowers, and with distinguishing what is true from what is false. And the question of how to cope with fake news is a crucial matter, especially at a time when we are literally struggling to survive. We are confined to our homes and we know that we have limited possibilities to verify what is true. I work in the mainstream media, and we have to fight this battle to establish what is true and false every single day. It is really hard, especially now that there are huge interests manipulating information, from major corporations and governments to military organizations and intelligence services. My first piece of advice is to find and read original documents. This is necessary to understand what is really going on underneath the masses of propaganda. And the most important documents are those that governments don't want you accessing; that is why whistleblowers are so important. I really value the WikiLeaks documents because they are based on particular facts that you can go through by yourself and double-check. You can understand how the journalists are spinning the facts and verify whether they are exaggerating or censoring information. I have huge respect for the whistleblowers who provide documents to WikiLeaks and to the journalists at huge risk to themselves, as well as for the media organizations that are brave enough to publish these documents. This is why Julian Assange is currently in prison: because he had the guts to publish what probably no one else did.

Ivana: We can all now relate, to a small degree, to Julian's situation: the awful feeling of being isolated and confined. Julian was confined in the Ecuadorian embassy in London for seven years, at times without internet, and is now in Belmarsh Prison. Julian's father, John Shipton, recently recounted for us the surreal experience of entering the prison through a series of portals, equipped with high-resolution cameras and microphones. This surveillance equipment that is already present in our societies is now being used to extract personal data, track people's locations, and to target those, for instance, who are supposed to be in quarantine. In Serbia, the government is now tracking arrivals from abroad to monitor their movements. All of this now appears reasonable. Where does this lead us?

Stefania: First of all, I would like to use this conversation to impress upon people the extent of the hardship Julian has experienced in the last ten years. We have been confined at home for the last four or five weeks, and we now realize how oppressive it is to stay inside twenty-four hours a day with restrictions on going outside for essential things like food and medicine. Julian spent an entire decade in confinement, initially under house arrest, and then seven years in a tiny room in an embassy. We give an hour outdoors to some of the worst criminals who have committed all sorts of horrific acts. Julian was not allowed to go outside for seven years. He was not allowed to go to the hospital when he needed treatment. Now that we are confined at home, we can start to understand how this must feel. I would have gone mad after seven months, let alone seven years. Now, Julian is in a high-security prison at risk of contracting and dying of Covid-19. I don't think many people realize how cruelly Julian has been abused. Nor do they realize how the United Kingdom authorities have acted on the United States' behalf. Julian knew from the beginning that if he left the embassy he would be arrested and extradited. Nobody believed him, but he was absolutely right. The UK authorities are absolutely determined to extradite him. Often people ask me, "Do you think they will kill Julian if he gets extradited to the US?" What they must realize is: they are already killing him. There are two different ways to kill a person: you can cut off their head, the blood spills everywhere, they die on the spot—or, you can kill them slowly, little by little, one drop of blood after another. That way, no one gets upset. There is no event. There is no public concern. But the person is dying in any case. This is what has been happening to Julian Assange for the last ten years. It is a win–win situation for the authorities: they will either drive him mad, or they will extradite him and imprison him for the rest of his life. Either way, he is broken. I want to use this unique situation, where we are confined at home, to help people realize this.

Ivana: Before this corona craziness absorbed all of our attention, journalists and media outlets that were previously not so interested in Julian's case started reporting on it, and some new organizations joined the effort to free him. Do you think this is a signal of hope for his situation? Is it even possible to pursue his extradition with the borders closed and flights canceled? What human rights are we talking about if a man who's committed no crime, and who already has fragile health, cannot be released from prison even temporarily to protect him from dying, as you rightly described, "little by little"?

Stefania: I hope there will be an appeal against judge Vanessa Baraitser's decision to refuse Julian bail.[1] But I'm not optimistic, and this is because I have spent the last five years trying to access documents relating to the case. I succeeded in reading some of these documents and have seen how absolutely cruel the UK authorities' stance is toward Julian. They are not interested at all in keeping him healthy and will do all they can to break him. They have tremendously assisted the US authorities in this way, when they could have handled things completely differently. They could have assisted Julian when he was in the embassy, and they could have assisted him with the Swedish investigation. Instead, although it was perfectly possible for Julian to be questioned in the UK, they specifically advised the Swedish prosecutors not to do this.[2] They have denied Julian safe passage, which we would expect a person to have in this situation because asylum is an international human right. They could have given him the opportunity to receive medical treatment. Instead, they have determined to extradite

---

1   https://uk.reuters.com/article/uk-health-coronavirus-britain-assange/wikileaks-founder-julian-assange-denied-bail-by-london-court-idUKKBN21C26G.

2   https://www.repubblica.it/esteri/2018/02/13/news/few_documents_many_mysteries_how_our_foia_case_is_unveiling_the_questionable_handling_of_the_julian_assange_case-188758273/.

him and have done absolutely all they can to make his life as miserable as possible. I have very little hope in the London courts, because I have seen how his case has been handled in a manner that is, quite frankly, highly unusual, distorted, and weird. It is completely incompatible with the freedom of the press in our democratic societies. And the complete lack of integrity by the media is a serious concern for me. In 2015, after Julian had been under investigation by the Swedish prosecutor for five years, no one had yet tried to get the documents. I asked colleagues about the facts on this case and no one had any clear understanding of it—everything was speculation and rumor. It was at that point that I realized that I needed to get access to the documents of the case myself. It was fortunate that I did, because otherwise we would have no understanding of what happened. Now, thanks to these documents, we have evidence of the UK authorities meddling in the Swedish case in order to assist the US to extradite Julian Assange—and not for Russiagate, but just for revealing US war crimes and tortures. This is really alarming. And let's not forget that if the US is able to extradite Julian Assange, then WikiLeaks editors like Sarah Harrison, Kristinn Hrafnsson, and Joseph Farrell will be next. Journalists like myself have a duty to speak out.

Ivana: Thank you for speaking out, Stefania, for so many years. I know you are not optimistic, but do you think Julian will have the right to appeal his case in an international court? Is it possible for him to avoid prosecution? And what is the future of investigative journalism after Covid-19, especially if some of the surveillance measures being implemented are here to stay?

Stefania: Yes, fortunately Julian does have the option to appeal in international courts and to bodies like the United Nations. I have huge respect for what the UN has done thus far for Julian. The UN Working Group on Arbitrary Detention had the courage to establish that Julian has been arbitrarily detained since 2010, and that the UK and Sweden were responsible for this.[3] You can imagine the huge pressure exerted on the

---

3   https://www.ohchr.org/EN/NewsEvents/Pages/DisplayNews.aspx?NewsID
    =17012&LangID=E.

members of this working group. Further, the UN Special Rapporteur on Torture, Nils Melzer, had the courage to announce publicly that Julian Assange has been tortured psychologically, and holding the UK, US, and Swedish authorities responsible.[4] If there is a hope for Julian's case, it lies in international bodies like the UN or the European Court of Human Rights, which Julian can appeal to. The problem is how long these processes take, because many of us are very concerned about his health. He is currently in a high-security prison at risk of contracting Covid-19, and it remains to be seen how much more abuse he can withstand. As for the future after Covid-19, of course I am concerned about the potential for supposedly temporary or exceptional digital surveillance measures to remain in place long-term, as they did after 9/11. Even the Snowden revelations were not sufficient to remove the measures implemented after 9/11. This new wave of surveillance concerns our movements, credit cards, and health data—some of the most precious information about us. And this massive collection of data being used to inform health systems will likely be performed by Silicon Valley companies. Palantir, the secretive company that in 2010 helped to plan a disinformation war to destroy WikiLeaks, has been engaged by the UK's National Health System to fight Covid-19.[5] Of course they will exploit the data. They claim it is anonymous, but it can be deanonymized. It is difficult to convey to people why I am so concerned. People tend to think that if countries like South Korea are using digital tracing to try and stop the spread of Covid-19, why shouldn't we? First of all, we don't have any evidence, any scientific, peer-reviewed studies, that demonstrate that such an approach is effective. Up until now, the tech companies have data on our movements and spending habits, but not on our health. Now, they have an opportunity to get this too, and we need to be very careful.

4   https://www.ohchr.org/EN/NewsEvents/Pages/DisplayNews.aspx?NewsID=
    24665&LangID=E.

5   https://www.computerweekly.com/news/252482365/Privacy-International-puts-
    Palantir-in-the-dock-for-NHS-data-analysis-work.

Ivana: It is really hard to avoid the feeling that Covid-19 is similar to 9/11 in terms of the "state of exception" being used to erode privacy and civil rights. What can we do from our homes in order to help Julian Assange?

Stefania: It is important to take to the streets physically, so the authorities realize how many people support Julian. But while we are confined to our homes, it is really important to inform ourselves. Also, try to exert pressure on the media. Email mainstream news outlets and help them realize how poor their coverage is, how many of them are not reporting on Julian's case at all, or are only focusing on very minor aspects of it. With Covid-19 likely to spread horribly in prisons, it is a good time to remind the media that there is a journalist who has exposed crucial information in the public interest who is arbitrarily detained in a high-security prison and in grave danger.

Ivana: And, in a way, Julian's situation serves as a symbol of the global problem that is the vulnerability of prisoners in the time of Covid-19.

Stefania: Yes, absolutely. In terms of Julian's case, though, it is unbelievable that he is in prison and has no chance of getting bail even though he never committed a violent crime. On the contrary, he is in prison for exposing violent crimes. Of course, he is a kind of symbol.

Ivana: Is there anything that can stop Julian from being extradited to the United States?

Stefania: Public pressure. What the UK and US authorities have done, essentially, is destroyed Julian as a person. He has undergone a real demonization campaign in the media that sought to make people completely indifferent to him and his fate. People have come to accept some notion that Julian must have put lives at risk, that maybe he's a rapist, or perhaps he's a Russian asset. Let's not forget the *Guardian* editorials that claimed that there was no such threat of extradition, that Julian was in the embassy because he wanted to be, because he was a paranoid or strange human being. If people don't take to the street to protest, or pressure the media to properly cover the case, the US will succeed in extraditing him.

Ivana: Covid-19 is another instance where we have various sources of information and statistics that can be presented to serve particular interests. Could you perhaps tell us what is happening with this in Italy?

Stefania: In Italy, we have had something like eleven thousand deaths, and many more that are not recorded. We have inadequate supplies of medical equipment, and doctors are at risk because they don't have masks and PPE. We have to ask ourselves how such a situation is possible. Since 9/11, we have been told that we are under threat from all sorts of chemical, biological, possibly nuclear, and definitely ideological attacks, and that the authorities therefore need to access our data and communications and pass special laws. Yet, now that we face a massive health crisis, we realize that these same authorities did absolutely nothing to prepare for it. They could have stockpiled medical equipment years in advance for very little cost. They could have trained doctors. Why didn't they? Instead, in Italy there has been massive military expenditure on F-35 stealth planes and weapons because we are part of NATO. Serious priorities were completely disregarded, and we are unable to address the Covid-19 crisis for that reason. Politicians, at both local and national levels, should be held accountable for this. And we should try to establish whether there was anyone trying to alert the public to these kinds of risks.

Ivana: We are in a contradictory space at the moment where we want to obey the rules because they are saving lives, but, at the same time, we are aware of the need to resist surveillance measures that might stick and become oppressive. We need to monitor these measures and find out where they are heading. A couple of months ago, we in Serbia were concerned about Huawei implementing three thousand face recognition cameras in Belgrade. But China has helped Serbia, as well as Italy, to access much-needed medical equipment to battle Covid-19, when we were denied help from the EU. We have to weigh our criticism of Chinese involvement carefully. It is concerning, though, that the doctor who sounded the alarm on Covid-19 in Wuhan was arrested, and it raises again the problem of the suppression of information and how to determine what is true and what is false in the media.

Stefania: As I said, original documents and whistleblowers are crucial, now more than ever. Thanks to my work with WikiLeaks, I have been able to get training in encryption, which has been so useful when working from home. I cannot meet sensitive sources in person, but I can still have safe and secure communications with them. Many journalists don't even have these basic techniques and tools. I still have hope for whistleblowers. That's why I defend and speak up for high-profile sources like Chelsea Manning, who spent eight years in prison and has tried to commit suicide three times. She is one of the most important journalistic sources of our times. Now, more than ever, we need people who have the courage to reveal and publish information, because our freedoms are at risk with digital giants seeking to access our health data. We are at risk of passively entering a new totalitarian system wherein the very same companies that provide our internet and phone services also have information on our health and movements and cooperate with the CIA's drone program. There is so much being kept secret about this present crisis and about how those in power plan to use it.

Conversation held on March 30, 2020

Communism or Barbarism,
It's That Simple

Slavoj Žižek and Renata Ávila

Renata: I'm thrilled to be joined by Slavoj Žižek, who is joining us from—where are you now, Slavoj?

Slavoj: I am at home in Ljubljana, I am isolated and fully aware—one should emphasize this again and again—that we who are able to isolate ourselves are, up to a point, the privileged ones. Just think a little bit about how many things have to function so that we can be, more or less, safely isolated: electricity, water, garbage collection, delivery services, pharmacies, doctors, the list goes on. I get furious when people say that we are now all in lockdown and isolation. No, we are not. It is a minority of us who are isolated.

Renata: Precisely. We are witnessing a kind of lockdown apartheid that divides those who can be sacrificed by the system and those who have the luxury of staying at home. We are also seeing a speedy authoritarianism happening in many countries. What is the situation in Slovenia?

Slavoj: In all countries, the problem is to what extent you can trust the data, the official statistics. For example, it may appear that one of my favorite countries in the world, Iceland, is in terrible trouble. The whole country has only around 360,000 inhabitants, and there are more than 1,200 people infected. Do you know why? Because they have tested an incredible amount of people. The extent to which we can trust the statistics depends on how much testing is done and how reliable the testing is. There are a lot of cover ups already. That's why I always repeat: we need Julian Assange. I take him now as a metaphor, or a certain attitude, more than ever. It is obvious that many governments are manipulating information and not telling us the real story. They say the situation is under control, while on the ground we are in chaos. My good friend Joan Copjec, from New York, whose husband, Michael Sorkin, died a couple of days ago from Covid-19, told me that while the official line is that everybody over sixty can get easily tested, she hasn't been able to. Why Assange today? Because on one level, it is obvious that we need, at least temporarily, these measures of isolation and controlled movement. And, this may surprise you, but I'm not terribly afraid of these measures. Some leftists, Agamben and others, claim that those in power are using the Covid-19 crisis to keep us under control, introduce a permanent state of emergency, and so on—that they like us in a panic. My counterpoint to this is that, of course, there is a temptation for governments to exploit the crisis. For example, how are we conversing right now? Through Zoom, through the internet. And the internet doesn't function by itself. If the state decides, together with a given company, they can disconnect us. However, the true state of affairs is not just that government is seeding panic and imposing control—isn't it clear that those in power are also in a panic? Never forget this. If there is something evident in all the various, often contradictory information we are given, isn't it that those in power are those who are really in a panic? They don't control the situation.

Renata: On that point, I would like to push back. I come from a "banana republic," a very limited country with a very corrupt elite, but all countries are, now, increasingly resembling my country: Guatemala. What is happening everywhere is that the elites—yes, they are panicking, but they are protecting their own kind. With our privatized healthcare systems failing to cope with Covid-19, we thought (at least at the beginning of the pandemic) that we were "all in the same boat," but I am increasingly getting the impression that there are many boats, that they are more divided than ever, and that the little boats of the Global South are sinking very rapidly. Different countries may be "united by the same threat," but they have very different tools to fight it. As an example, the Central African Republic, with a population of 4.6 million, has three ventilators.[1] Who will these be reserved for? Obviously the elites.

Slavoj: Yes, but the situation you describe in the Central African Republic isn't so different from that in the United States, where the elite have similarly provided for themselves. For weeks in the beginning, the message from the rich and powerful was "Don't panic," when they were already clearly panicking. They were already, for example, hiring private planes to escape to remote islands, or to the Rocky Mountain ex–Cold War bunkers where they

---

1 https://www.nrc.no/news/2020/march/just-three-ventilators-to-cope-with-covid-19-in-central-african-republic/.

can survive for a year without any external contact. Nevertheless, I would insist that in China and in the West, those in power are desperate. When you see those in power so obviously disoriented, not knowing what to do, and, as you said, just saving their skin, they may retain all the privileges in the world, but some basic trust is broken. We may be critical of the state, but don't underestimate the extent to which we still counted on it, up until now—it may be evil and corrupted, but we take it for granted that, somehow, the state guarantees that things work. Now, hospitals are approaching a state of panic. Whenever revolutions happen—think, for instance, of the Iran revolution, or when Ceaușescu fell in Romania—even while those in power are still in power, there is a moment, a kind of symbolic break, where people simply no longer take them seriously and simply ignore them. They can still use all the terror they want but, somehow, they know the game is over. For example, in Iran, when Khomeini overthrew Shah Mohammad Reza Pahlavi, there was a big demonstration in Jaleh Square in Tehran, in which police were killing demonstrators, and, although the Shah remained in power for two more months from that point, everybody knew, at that moment, that it was over. I think that something at this level is already happening today.

Renata: Now is different, because today we cannot demonstrate in the square without risking the lives of others—at least, that is what we are told by the authorities. So how can we use the fear that the elites have in this moment to our advantage? How can we seize this space if we cannot mobilize in the streets?

Slavoj: Yes, I see the danger and I'm not a naïve optimist. I am not saying that we have before us a chance for communism. And there is a great irony in how those in power themselves are responding to the emergency with some kind of primitive idea of communism. Who would have imagined, half a year ago, that Boris Johnson would nationalize the British Railways (even if temporarily)? Who would have thought that Donald Trump himself would evoke the Cold War Act so that he could directly control private companies and determine what they produce? It is a cruel irony that they are now acting, but not radically enough, as communists. And when you say we are alone, isolated, I disagree. Again, maybe "we," the privileged few who are confined to indoors, are somewhat alone. It was a beautiful moment when recently the British government made a call-out for volunteers, and over half a million people responded immediately. They still need our cooperation. And they know very well that if they do not maintain some kind of order, by maintaining people's trust, then (and I see this is quite a serious option) some kind of global disorder may explode. For example, it seems quite possible that in the United States, in some of these Bible Belt backward states, local militias will take over to "protect" people from the virus. What is happening in Europe is horrible, but the much greater threat is, on the one hand, in the United States, and, on the other, in so-called Third World countries. The very idea of isolation is absurd in a country like India. And about refugees and migrants, how can they isolate? It's clear, even to those in power, that in order to control the present situation the state is not sufficient. It has to not only allow but solicit the local mobilization of thousands, if not hundreds of thousands, of people in communities to take care of those who are sick, old, and alone. Not only does the government have to act as an almost communist state, taking over and violating the market, but this crisis will not even be minimally controlled without the mobilization of local people. Another thing that is clear is that, if anything, Bernie Sanders wasn't radical enough. It is not just universal healthcare for the United States that is necessary, but actually some kind of global healthcare system. We need mechanisms to follow epidemics all around the world, and to enable states to act in a coordinated, international way to prevent them. I recently learned that viruses are part of our bodily existence in daily life, and they are not only not all bad, but can even be very good. To process food normally, we need a tremendous amount of viruses and bacteria in our stomachs. And I learned that viruses similar to Covid-19 are always circulating quite harmlessly. Viruses need to be controlled, and at a worldwide level. So I think this idea of isolation doesn't work, it's not realistic, though I know this is the dream of those in power. For example, David Geffen, the movie producer, posted on Facebook to say that he's "isolated" on a gigantic yacht in the Atlantic, where he swims and enjoys life. He can enjoy this for a month or two, but

I don't believe that the rich can succeed in surviving in this isolated way for any real length of time. For them to survive, hundreds of thousands, millions of others, have to be working and risking their lives. Even Trump is using this kind of anti-elitist language, arguing that it's all very well for New York intellectuals, professors, and journalists to isolate themselves, but what about ordinary working people? In one sense, Trump is right, but the issue is that those "ordinary people" are now in such danger, are unprotected from Covid-19, precisely because of Trump's policies. He not only curtailed affordable healthcare but disbanded the National Security Council office that focused on pandemics. This is the disgusting strategy of Trump: first, he puts ordinary people into a very precarious situation, and then he poses as the savior of ordinary people, urging the nation back to work and so on. Trump is well aware that it's because of his politics that millions of ordinary people are in such a desperate position that they have to weigh going to work to feed their families against the risk of contracting a deadly virus. That's the horror of the situation.

Renata: I saw the horror of the situation in the UK last weekend as well, when the royals, celebrities, and masses of people were clapping like seals to celebrate NHS workers—the very same NHS workers who they decided they wanted out of the country when they voted for Brexit. There is this double-think where people are celebrating the heroes who risk their lives to help the nation through this crisis, while not taking responsibility for defunding and undermining the healthcare system.

Slavoj: I totally agree. It is the most disgusting thing, this collective thanking of all the workers who still have to go out on the streets. It is as if the ruling class is applauding the ordinary people who work for them, who take risks for them. That's why I think the solution is some kind of one-time communism. In Germany, the idea has already been proposed to establish a list of people who have survived Covid-19 and are, more or less, immune to it. We need measures like this. It seems crucial today to have a list of people on whom we can rely, and who perhaps should be ruthlessly mobilized. We are out of the economy of money, of the market, and are entering something else.

Renata: I'm in Berlin at the moment, and I can totally see something like that happening here, with Germany's strong rule of law. But just the idea of creating lists of people in a country like Brazil, for instance, which could end up in the hands of a psychopath like Bolsonaro, gives me the chills. It risks opening the door not merely to a humanized brutalism, but to an actual genocide. Measures that are deployed now in this war against the virus may have permanent and unexpected effects.

Slavoj: Of course we should be careful that these types of mobilizations are not misused. However, my point is that the rich cannot simply survive in isolation, they need us. Let's imagine that the rich try and control things from afar when/if things return to some kind of totally new normality. The rich still seem to think that the crisis will last two or three months and that they can wait it out on their islands, yachts, and resorts until things "return to normal." However, it will not be as simple as that, because it will not be the same normality. And at that point, I don't think that the ruling class will be able to survive. If they do, it will only be through direct barbarism. I cannot imagine capitalism surviving in its present form. There will have to be radical changes. And I'm not simply a communist optimist. More brutal direct dictatorship is one option, and another is chaotic barbarism, where local militias or gangs take over. I don't think that the ruling class will necessarily *want* to survive this crisis. As the philosopher of so-called assemblages, Bruno Latour, recently wrote, the Covid-19 crisis is just a dress rehearsal for the forthcoming ecological crisis.[2] I find it ridiculous when I read in the media these statements that the Olympics will be delayed until October, and then until next year, as if we are talking about a brief nightmare that will only last a few months, before life returns to normal. No—the whole financial structure of capitalism will be ruined; normality will not return. And there I see an opportunity. Those in power will not be able to pretend, now, that things return to a normal. If it is not this epidemic, it will be a different, possibly harsher one, or it will combine with ecological and other crises. Do you know that in North Eastern Africa and the Arab Peninsula, as well as Pakistan—and probably, soon, China—there is currently a giant

2 https://critinq.wordpress.com/2020/03/26/is-this-a-dress-rehearsal/.

locust invasion?[3] Do you know the extent of the hunger and catastrophe this could trigger? Clearly, some type of communism is, today, a matter of survival. By communism, I don't mean a Soviet Union model where central committees rule, but simply these three things: a relatively efficient state, which has the power to violate market rules, organize healthcare, and keep people alive, supplemented, on the top, with strong, active international cooperation, and, on the bottom, with local mobilization. It will soon become clear to everyone that we need this, and not as the result of some kind of utopian communist ideal, but of the urgency of life. These figures from Trump to Boris Johnson—even some well-meaning ones like Macron or Giuseppe Conte, the Italian prime minister—still talk in these terms of this being a two- or three-month crisis and, if we just follow their orders, things will soon return to normal. No, things will not return to normal. And that's the political moment.

Renata: The problem is that there's a particular group of people who are not talking in such terms, but are, instead, very much thinking ahead, and they are the technology giants. They love the idea of the dystopia continuing indefinitely, and they're already preparing "solutions" that will create a certain kind of normality in the dystopia that we are heading toward. I am very concerned about the formation of a techno-barbarism where total control is concentrated in the hands of a few technocrats. Many are fascinated with the way that South Korea and China have controlled Covid-19 with the help of magical technological solutions. Do you think there is a power shift occurring here? And what might be the reconfiguration of power in the near future if we do not activate this new form of communism?

Slavoj: I agree with you on this idea of technological barbarism. There will be brutal rules installed—and not only in the future, it is already happening. In hospitals in various cities around the world, doctors are already having to make brutal decisions on who lives and dies, who is deserving of a respirator. Nonetheless, I don't think that the big technology companies can simply impose on us some kind of a permanent technocratic dictatorship. If

3 https://www.theguardian.com/world/2020/may/25/many-will-starve-locusts-devour-crops-and-livelihoods-in-pakistan.

nothing else, don't underestimate another antagonism here, namely, scientists and other tech creators. Today, science is needed more than ever and scientists are already rendering problematic the mechanisms and operation of power. And it is too simplistic to think of technology companies as a unified, evil block against ordinary people. What I fear more is that the rule of barbarian technocracy will combine with a new brutal populism. The United States is already speaking in this brutal Darwinian language wherein, ultimately, this crisis is conceived as being beneficial to society by ridding it of the old, ill, weak, and burdensome, enabling only the "fittest" to survive. Hitler practiced this logic. That is why the Nazis didn't just kill just Jews and Roma, but also the mentally disabled, the elderly, and others deemed weak. Such a vision is not impossible, but I still think it is overly simple and paranoiac. At a certain point, politicization will reemerge. The problem will be, as I call it, the process of renormalization. When things return to normal, what kind of normality will it be? I agree with you that one option is a technocratic normality, where governments will demand that, if we want to live in safety, we must concede to total surveillance and control. Another option is direct barbarism. But these are not the only options. For one thing, I don't think that the technocratic elite will succeed in this simple way of legitimizing their rule by perpetuating the crisis. The problem with this is that I don't see how it can fit within the logic of existing capitalism. This type of permanent state of emergency would entail a tremendous change in our economic system. We would no longer have the global consumerist capitalism that we had before—Covid-19 has shut down more than half of our industries worldwide. We would have to reconstruct our daily lives entirely.

Renata: What do you think about these huge bailouts happening, the millions and trillions given to corporations?

Slavoj: I always like these moments when all of us are able to see that the state can do things that are officially considered impossible. According to traditional economic wisdom, these bailouts are a disaster, they cannot be done. We all know that they totally violate market logic, and that, when they occur, we are already entering a different system. At a certain point,

I claim, when you hand out trillions of dollars, money no longer functions in the old capitalist way. It's a simple means of allocation, no longer surplus exploitation. Marx thought that money would function like this in the first stages of socialism. But Trump's bailouts are very targeted and only protect companies. What we need is a totally irrational (from the market's standpoint) payout of trillions of dollars that is distributed socially. The crucial thing is that capitalism as we knew it is in its final stage here. The state is doing things that it has never done before, even in the worst crisis, the Great Depression, or, for example, in the financial crisis of 2008. The bailouts of 2008 were different, they were clearly a gift to the banks to keep the economy functioning. Now, something much more radical is happening. It no longer fits the capitalist logic. At the same time, it is clear that the system cannot survive through just printing trillions of dollars— somebody has to work. Problems are still ahead of us, but I think a space for struggle will open up.

Renata: I'm usually a pessimist, but lately I have seen three things that give me a little bit of hope. First are the gangs in favelas in Rio de Janeiro and in Central America. They declared a ceasefire and decided to respect the lockdown and help communities.[4] The most barbaric, disliked elements of society are acting in a more rational manner than the authorities. The second thing is strikes. Workers in the United States, in warehouses and precarious gig economy industries, are getting organized and striking. They are leveraging this moment in which we, those of us in isolation, are particularly dependent on them, and they are refusing to be abandoned in the present crisis.

Slavoj: Sorry to interrupt, but I know how the system will answer to this; it will say, "Oh, you don't want to help the suffering? Our survival relies on you." But, as you point out, the system cannot function without ordinary workers, and these workers can leverage this and strike. I think that the majority of people will support these strikes because they can see that the workers are not the spoiled "labor aristocracy," as Lenin put it, but are those

---

4 https://theconversation.com/coronavirus-narco-gangs-could-see-big-popularity-boost-from-helping-residents-in-latin-america-139613.

risking their lives so that some of us can live safely in isolation. What is the third thing that gives you hope?

Renata: It is very interesting to see even the most naïve popstars, as well as many ordinary people, starting to voice their demands in a language that is not that of the market, nor that of technocrats, which have been imposed on us for so long. For instance, comrade Britney Spears, who has called for strike and wealth redistribution.[5]

Slavoj: I don't trust these celebrities much, because this is an old imperialist strategy. There is a difficult situation, a war, for instance, and the rich and famous are always ready to adopt the language of solidarity, this idea that "we are all in the same boat," as you said at the beginning. But then again, the crucial political moment will not be when the crisis is over. It will never be over. The question has to be what kind of new normality will we construct—that will be the crucial political moment. And I claim that there is no return to the old. I see progressive potentials. In other words, I don't agree with some of my leftist friends who claim that this is not a political moment, it's just a crisis that we have to go through before normality is restored. Do you know who else I radically don't agree with? Those idiots who try to give a cheap, new age anti-consumerist spin to the situation, saying, "Now we have time to reflect on the really crucial things in our lives and realize that we really don't need to be consumerists." I hate this. What right do we have to criticize ordinary workers for their consumerism? I don't believe this idea that crises sober us, help us to acquire some wisdom. There will be no greater wisdom.

Renata: That is a point I fully agree with. Revolutions of the past, like the Cuban one or the Zapatista uprising, took advantage of quiet time to think about and plan strategies to realize the future that they wanted. How can we begin to organize today? Surely, when we are more connected than ever, we can do it in a very sophisticated way.

5　https://www.theguardian.com/music/2020/mar/25/comrade-britney-spears-star-calls-for-strike-and-wealth-redistribution.

Slavoj: Yes, I don't agree with those leftists who claim that isolation isolates us. We may be singularly isolated, but, as you point out, we are more connected than ever. This is one paradox that people should remember. The first stage of political thinking is when people become aware that, to even confront the present crisis, we need vast international links. When we leftists talked about this level of cooperation before Covid-19, people claimed this was not possible or utopian, that people are normally egotists. But now we see that precisely in order to survive as an egotist, you have to think globally. That's why I support DiEM25, which criticizes the financial politics of the European Union, but nonetheless emphasizes European unity. And DiEM25 is right to emphasize the case of Julian Assange, too. The only way to prevent, or at least control, the horror of this new technocratic barbarism that you describe is more Assanges. We need many more whistleblowers who work for the tech companies. Wouldn't it be nice to hear from a Chinese Assange now, to tell us what really happened in the beginnings of Covid-19?

Renata: There are some stories already circulating that document something that the mainstream media doesn't tell us: that it was community networks, the solidarity and resilience of grassroots Chinese, that enabled them to overcome the chaos in the cities.

Slavoj: We all, I hope, like horror movies. George Monbiot, who occasionally writes in the *Guardian,* made a wonderful comment today.[6] He said that, typically, when we see epidemics in horror movies, people turn into zombies, they eat each other's flesh. Now, we are seeing that epidemics can also do the opposite, spurring new forms of solidarity. And once we have this, it will not be so easy for the powerful to impose a technocratic barbarism. But we do need whistleblowers, or spies for the people, as Assange defined himself.

Conversation held on March 31, 2020

---

6 https://www.theguardian.com/commentisfree/2020/mar/31/virus-neighbours-covid-19.

Digital Colonialism and Covid-19

Renata Ávila and Saša Savanović

Saša: In the last few weeks and months, we have seen unprecedented use of surveillance and monitoring technologies, and data extraction and exploitation. We have also seen privacy laws being suspended indefinitely and, in recent days, very worrying developments that governments are considering collaborating with very murky surveillance companies. Welcome, Renata, I hope you can help us to understand some of the technological implications of the Covid-19 crisis.

Renata: As you say, we are seeing an unprecedented invasion of technology into every aspect of our lives. However, I want to be careful in how we frame this, because this conversation, recorded on Zoom and broadcast on YouTube for everyone to watch, wouldn't be possible without a level of collaboration among market forces and technological infrastructures supporting our ability to be connected. We are in different countries and we are able to communicate powerful ideas, many of which are criticisms of precisely those companies hosting us and their business models. We shouldn't take this lightly. The internet is no longer only a way to communicate, but, increasingly, a way of doing everything from organizing deliveries of basic items to schooling and many more essential daily activities. And that set off alarm bells for me as soon as this health crisis started. With earlier pandemics like the Black Death, people in Latin America would pray and make sacrifices to the gods, looking to them for solutions or for mercy, for something to make it stop. This was not an appeal to logic but to faith. It seems to me that this faith that we once had in the gods we now we have in tech companies, expecting them to find a magic solution that will solve everything. Instead of looking to multiple institutions, many are arguing that it is through strict surveillance measures, enforced through a magic app on your phone, that we will be able to get out of this crisis. This blind faith in apps, drones, and platforms to solve complex social problems is very worrying.

Saša: Now, more than ever, with millions of people confined to their homes, we are completely dependent on digital platforms for every aspect of our lives. We don't have a choice but to rely on giant corporations to communicate, to order food, to understand the reality outside. Can we talk about digital solidarity in this type of situation, and what the path might be toward a sort of digital sovereignty, which is currently completely missing?

Renata: Technology doesn't operate alone, but in combination with many other factors. One of these is the way that global trade is configured. In the last twenty years, states have paved the way for a system that punishes citizens' innovation and sacrifices technological sovereignty in order to preserve certain markets for certain actors. A system of very strict patents has tied our hands for finding solutions. At the moment, for instance, medical equipment is crucial to saving the lives of people everywhere. We are facing shortages of ventilators and basic medical equipment like masks, yet the solution is in our hands. Recently, starting in Barcelona and other cities in Spain, creative, committed people in labs and "maker spaces" that are equipped with 3D printers started printing components of ventilators according to do-it-yourself blueprints.[1] These people have the ability to provide solutions to communities that desperately need ventilators. It was a not-for-profit, very logical action to take. These are the new civics of the twenty-first century: you have a 3D printer, an intelligent mind, a good education, and you collaborate to save the lives of others. It's beautiful. But what happened? The makers were threatened with lawsuits. And the same thing will happen the moment we find an effective and cheap way to test for Covid-19—patents and big pharma will quickly make a takeover to ensure that the solution is not divorced from the privatization and commodification of health and of innovation. We are now seeing the crude realities of the privatization of public goods. How colonized must Europe be that it is impeding the power of innovation in its own citizens, and that the willingness of citizens to help each other is not supported or celebrated but threatened.

Saša: Yes. Let's return, quickly, to the issue of surveillance and private data. The focus of our attention in European media has been the Chinese social credit system through which the government is monitoring citizens, which everyone claims is a very big problem. At the same time, we seem totally

---

1 https://www.makery.info/en/2020/06/17/english-spanish-makers-ongoing-fight-against-covid-19/.

unaware that we are also monitored and surveilled, or perhaps we are simply accepting this as an unpleasant but necessary aspect of the technology we are using. Governments can, as we are now seeing, use this data, request it and mobilize it, when they feel it is necessary. Perhaps today this is necessary, but we are not sure how long these measures will remain in place or if they will ever end. In Israel, for example, the ministry of defense is collaborating with NSO Group to devise a system through which people will be given a score from one to ten that ranks their coronavirus "infectability."[2] Isn't this also a kind of "social credit system"? I am concerned about the potential combining of various sorts of data, not only geolocation data, but also health and other types of data. What are the consequences of all these developments?

Renata: Do you know what is concerning to me, that no one seems to be mentioning? Seven years ago, in 2013, Edward Snowden revealed to us the very sophisticated surveillance and control system of the United States, which extended not only over its own citizens but around the world. It is now probably at least seven times more powerful than it was, and I do not believe for a second that governments are not using those capacities to surveil and monitor people right now. This makes me even more angry at the slowness and incompetence of governments' responses to Covid-19. In all likelihood, governments already have the data that they need to address the pandemic effectively. They already have the ability to massively surveil populations. Such powers were not limited after the Snowden revelations, at least not in Europe. On the contrary, many of the national security agencies validated many of the US's data-sharing practices by passing legal reforms. Now, again, governments are seeking further validation for the private sector to access and share our data. Governments in Europe are using Covid-19 as a historical opportunity to relax attitudes toward privacy on the basis that citizens' health is essential and they must protect and save lives. It is the perfect justification when there's a data race going on between the US and China in which

2   https://www.amnesty.org/en/latest/news/2020/01/israel-nso-spyware-revoke-export-license/

Europe has been left behind. I would love for my personal data, during an emergency, with public health authorities taking a proportionate and reasonable attitude, to contribute to saving lives. I would volunteer my data. But the problem is that trust has been eroded and there have not been efforts to restore it. After Snowden's revelations, governments continue to allow massive breaches of privacy and the sharing of sensitive data with the US, which was left with total impunity. Trust has not been restored between citizens and governments, or between Silicon Valley and those using its services. In the same way that I blame much of the current health crisis on privatization and free-trade agreements that have undermined public interests, I blame the reluctance of citizens to share their data on the failure of governments to restore trust. The General Data Protection Regulation (GDPR) is not enough. There are too many exceptions. I like exceptions when they concern rights that we want to preserve and strengthen, but this is not the case here. This is the moment we need to fight back, mobilize as citizens, and build strong evidence for the effectiveness of alternative ways to protect our health. We cannot leave it to companies and governments. And we need to open the black boxes. The data they contain is feeding algorithms that will decide on rights and obligations—when populations will return to work and school, for instance. This data is too important to be left in the hands of companies that refuse to allow citizens to hold them to account.

Saša: Yes, the right to move is another one that will be decided upon based on data. In February, the founder of Forensic Architecture was denied entry to the United States ahead of the opening of his exhibition on the "arbitrary logic of the border" in Miami, because the security algorithm triggered an alert.[3] And this reminded me of a performance in Vienna by the Belgian artist Thomas Bellinck, who was researching European "migration management" and reading a lot of Frontex documents. He found that the term "data subjects" is used to designate people who are trying to enter the European Union, and that it is permitted to use force to get the necessary

---

3   https://www.nytimes.com/2020/02/19/arts/design/forensic-architecture-founder-says-us-denied-him-visa.html.

data from these subjects. What I found interesting is that the GDPR uses the same terminology of "data subjects." On the one hand, we have governments that we don't really trust with our data, and on the other, we have private companies that use our data not in the public interest but for profit. How is it possible to achieve the third option: the civic ownership of the infrastructure or data?

Renata: First, I want to refer to this idea of data subjects and the double standards at work. The connection between the Covid-19 crisis and digital colonialism is very interesting. Through this crisis, there is a risk that people will be forced into a new technocratic regime—there is no "opt-out" because public health is at stake, we are in an emergency, and mandatory new rules apply to everybody. It is now the "infected subjects" who have to provide data, are forced to give data away, on things that they cannot control: body temperature, daily habits, consumption. Companies can be forced to share data on what purchases you make, where you go—and not only you but your wider network. This chase for high-quality data worries me. Privacy International has been documenting the exceptional measures being applied in Europe and around the world, and one of the things that I found interesting was that many of these measures allow people to opt out, to freely choose whether or not to be involved. We need to be very aware of the limits on this so-called freedom once Covid-19 recedes, and in the transition to a post-Covid society. In some countries, precarious workers are not likely to have much choice in terms of, for instance, returning to work. The gig companies will likely demand that workers enroll in a "voluntary" system of testing and of geolocation tracking, like the one in China, and, based on your test results, movements, habits, and those of your families, will decide whether you are allowed to return to work and earn a living. Some freelancers and workers on zero-hours contracts are receiving subsidies from their governments, but others are not. There is a layer of non-legality and informality of work that is the most precarious. Those who are not formally in the system are the most vulnerable to these control measures. What worries me most about the transition to a post-Covid society is that those people who governments couldn't previously track or identify, who were moving around "our" beautiful European countries and free-riding on "our" social systems, as the right wing claims, will be forced to install an app to return to work and, therefore, become traceable. Governments will be able to then monitor, geolocate, and deport people. This use of surveillance is not new, of course. And three companies profit the most from it here in Europe: Microsoft, Amazon, and Palantir (though of course, Google is also involved). Palantir in particular sees this as an opportunity and is already pushing to provide surveillance systems to Europe. The dangerous thing is that Peter Thiel, cofounder of Palantir, is a good buddy of Donald Trump's, and Palantir already provides many of the technologies used to brutalize and to deport people in the United States. ICE, the authority overseeing the massive deportations of Central American families, uses Palantir software. It is a very unethical company and, if allowed, will become a key means of enforcing a new infrastructure of control and repression of the most vulnerable, not only during the Covid-19 crisis but afterward.

Saša: Covid-19 has shown the failures of the privatization of healthcare systems, and the logical response would be to reverse this privatization. However, we are seeing exactly the opposite. The same companies that you mentioned—Palantir, Amazon, and Microsoft—have already started working with the National Health Service in the UK on, curiously, developing a system to secure the reliable allocation of resources, very scarce resources. Not only has public health infrastructure been destroyed, but now these very murky companies are being engaged to provide logistics systems for the public sector. We are seeing another level of privatization, wherein even logistics are being privatized. I'm afraid that it is not the undoing but instead the intensification of neoliberalism that we are seeing.

Renata: I agree, and I think that's why building new infrastructures is very important. DiEM25 volunteers co-wrote a tech pillar with solutions to prevent exactly the kinds of trends that you are describing.[4] And DiEM25's tech solutions are not tech solutionism; they are integrated with pillars on

4   https://diem25.org/wp-content/uploads/2019/03/Technological-Sovereignty-Green-Paper-No-3.pdf.

economy, a European Green New Deal, and a migration policy. This Covid-19 crisis has shown us that when a society really cares about the well-being of all its people, all of these things go hand in hand. The Portuguese government did the right thing by legalizing, at least temporarily, all the migrants and refugees in the country in response to the pandemic.[5] It knew that you cannot have two classes of citizens if you want to address a pandemic. Similarly, we need an integrated approach. We need to realize, and Covid-19 is helping us do so, that data is a key infrastructure. Countries need to have control over the sensitive data of their citizens and use it to the benefit of citizens, not international companies. This is an opportunity to really push back on data sovereignty, which needs to be made a political matter fought at the local, national, and pan-European levels. We need to push for a data model that increases the privacy and agency of citizens, is open-source, and is rights-preserving. I think Europe has a tremendous responsibility in this, because it possesses the resources, knowledge, and institutions to do things differently.

Saša: We have also seen, recently, planning for the introduction of 5G networks, together with this whole "smart cities" and "internet of things" perspective, which is, again, being pursued by the giant tech companies. How might this translate into the surveillance of our lives and impact on our freedom?

Renata: In terms of 5G technology, I think that we, at the European level, need to look at our priorities. Millions of people have been working from home due to Covid-19, many of us in cities and others in rural areas, and what we are finding, across Europe, is that the internet is really crap in isolated areas. Many places don't even have broadband access that is resilient enough to deal with the present crisis. This belief that highly skilled Europeans can swiftly implement a fast-tracked, massive transition to doing everything online is a myth. Reliable internet access is not cheap, and many are being excluded. The European Commission should reprioritize and freeze, for a while, the implementation of 5G. It's very

---

5 https://www.euronews.com/2020/03/29/coronavirus-portugal-grants-temporary-citizenship-rights-to-migrants.

expensive and very exclusive, not to mention the privacy concerns. Can Europe really afford to make a massive investment in this technology that will exclusively serve urban areas? It doesn't improve the communication between people, but only between things, and it will bring yet another set of regulatory problems that perhaps are not immediate priorities for the European Union. With Covid-19, we have seen deficient health infrastructure, precarious services, dependence on Amazon to deliver basic goods, and a complete lack of investment in green transport. We have a long list of priorities to address before 5G. This is really a moment of reflection for Europe in which to rethink the basics, including taking back control of sensitive data and establishing a real democratic governance model for Europe. If governments expect people to adopt these magic apps in order to solve the health crisis, the security crisis, and the many other crises, we must be able to audit the algorithm and make sure our rights are respected. Investment is another basic. The ability of citizens to come together and, in a matter of days, create ventilators to provide a solution to the urgent shortage shows the potential of a little investment in digital social innovation. Imagine if, instead of funding a Chinese or US company to implement 5G boxes everywhere, which are useless to the average citizen, that money was allocated to volunteer communities to build crucial items? I recently read an article in the *Financial Times* in which a former Amazon manger claimed that "Amazon is the new Red Cross."[6] The Red Cross is an institution that I have the highest regard for. It is an institution of almost a hundred million volunteers, founded to protect human rights and alleviate human suffering. How can we compare a predatory company that extracts our data, destroys local businesses, treats their workers not even as data subjects but as disposable objects, and destroys the planet in order to deliver things in record time, to the Red Cross? Local resilience needs investment. And to build trust in the technology that we use requires democratic processes, citizen involvement, and transparency and accountability. If we had these things, Europe would have been much more resilient to Covid-19. We lost a big opportunity to build social digital innovation when we gave up our sovereignty to free trade agreements that

6 https://www.ft.com/content/220bf850-726c-11ea-ad98-044200cb277f.

only benefited China and Silicon Valley. And we lost an opportunity with the Snowden revelations to restore trust and to clamp down on the back doors (and even front doors) through which the US extracts the sensitive data of our citizens in the name of "national security." We need to rethink the model and I think that Europe has an opportunity to do so now.

Saša: You mentioned the digital divide and the rural areas being left behind not only by 5G but by basic internet services. On this, I want to know how DiEM25, or any kind of progressive movement, can reach people in rural areas? They are left behind even in the simple sense that they don't have the infrastructure to participate. There were these proposals, for instance, from the UK Labour Party last year, to ensure free broadband for all. What are some other communal technological solutions that we should be implementing?

Renata: I think municipalities or local governments are key. There is an emerging coalition of cities for digital rights happening at the moment.[7] With Covid-19, there have been huge subsidies to workers and companies, and I am wondering if we could leverage the situation to demand subsidies for basic pieces of infrastructure such as broadband. We need a massive investment to bring broadband to rural areas. However, it is not only connectivity that is needed, but the ability to engage locally. Together with connectivity there has to be an infrastructure of participation that engages people actively. I think that rural areas have a lot of potential for remote work, high-quality lives, and many of the things we want to see in a green Europe. Green transport is very important, but rural areas won't appeal to young people as places to live unless they have good connectivity. We need to really start pushing the narrative that data is a basic infrastructure and that good custodianship of such data is crucial. How did we lose control of such a basic asset that is so important in making public decisions? Citizens' data, especially concerning health, is a key infrastructure of the good democratic governance of tomorrow. This should be among the first of our priorities, not 5G.

7 https://citiesfordigitalrights.org/.

Saša: How can we build resistance against digital colonialism? Recently, a friend told me that in China everyone uses a VPN as part of their normal digital hygiene. Is this something that we should be doing in Europe as well, for instance?

Renata: First of all, it is important to understand how technology works and, second, to understand the economy behind the technology and data extractivism. If anyone is happy about the Covid-19 crisis, it is big tech companies. We are training their algorithms day and night as we work from home and are glued to our screens for news, entertainment, and social media. We need to realize how much of our lives is dedicated to the screen, and who benefits from this, and analyze our choices. The response should not be to simply change our habits and limit our use of technology, but to understand its politics. We need to push for political changes that will enable us to mobilize the necessary funding and political will across multiple sectors to build new technology based on an alternative economic model. And we need new means of funding that don't rely on data feeding the algorithms of for-profit companies that are not our own. Algorithms are fantastic, and a good model with good data can improve people's lives, but first we need to generate the ecosystem to bring a new model to life that is non-extractive, open-source, public-funded, rights-preserving, and secure.

Saša: In terms of basic digital colonialism, big tech companies are extracting the value of very local economies, from things like taxi rides and food deliveries. Silicon Valley companies are reaping the value from these daily street-level exchanges, and I want to know how we can make these economies local again? Does the solution align with what you've mentioned: funding different competitive solutions that are community based, cooperatively owned, and publicly funded? Companies such as Amazon are already established, convenient, and popular, but we are also increasingly aware of the insecurity and exploitation of their workers and their impact on the environment.

Renata: I was in Chile last year when the government imposed a curfew in response to growing social unrest about education, transport, and austerity.[8] We were under military rule and you couldn't go to work or leave the house after 6 p.m. It was horrible. However, what was interesting was that, with everyone confined to their buildings and neighborhoods, with limited outdoor hours, a sense of local solidarity was reborn. We made collective decisions, for instance, to boycott shops and companies that backed the government in this brutalization of society. I think that Covid-19 is an opportunity for rebuilding local solidarity in this way. First, we need to support the unions, and this is an excellent opportunity to organize the tech workers and invite them to expose the abuses in the industry. Second, we need to engage with our neighbors, friends, and family and understand how this crisis has impacted them. We need to think carefully about where we shop and what kinds of businesses we want to support. The economic effects of Covid-19 will create a lot of empty pockets and empty stomachs all over the world. Right now, we have a moment to think, and to build forms of collaboration and mutual support. When we engage with the services of Silicon Valley companies, we pay a heavy price: on top of the upfront costs, we pay with our behavioral data and with the time and attention we devote to advertising. They, on the other hand, do not even pay taxes. Do we really want things to return to "normal" after Covid-19? And do we want to allow these companies to masquerade as the saviors of our normality?

Saša: Many are wondering, also, about the potential for the far right to capitalize on this crisis, with borders closing across the globe. Is it possible to impede or stop this return to the nation-state, and to motivate a different sort of mobilization?

Renata: We have an excellent opportunity right now to demonstrate that crises can only be addressed as an international block. It is possible and it is precisely what we are doing, for instance, at DiEM25, with the pillars we have developed. We are using the space and time that many people around Europe now have with the lockdown to share our ideas, so that our agenda becomes the common agenda of Europe. And when people suffer losses,

---

8   https://www.latimes.com/world-nation/story/2019-10-26/chile-lifts-curfew-a-day-af-ter-massive-protests.

such as the loss of a loved one, a job, or the freedom to walk in the street, they are especially receptive and sensitive to others who can, with compassion and solidarity, propose a way for things to be different. We are living precisely in such a time. And if we do not seize each and every minute of it to make a difference and increase our numbers, then the far right will.

Conversation held on April 1, 2020

The Fall of Public Man 2020

Richard Sennett and Srećko Horvat

Srećko: This is an unprecedented time in human history, with more than two billion people, in one way or another, confined at home. Hundreds of millions of people are working from home. Theaters, sports stadiums, concerts, and cafes are closed indefinitely. Most of your work, Richard, from *The Fall of Public Man* in 1977 to, more recently, *The New Culture of Capitalism* and *Together,* has dealt with various topics directly relevant to the current global pandemic. Topics such as public space, public life, work, cities, urban environments, economy, society, and more, all of which are rapidly changing today. To take just one of these, how do you think the city is changing due to the Covid-19 pandemic?

Richard: When I retired from teaching five years ago, I immediately unretired and went to work for the United Nations on a project about how cities will adapt to and deal with climate change. The advent of the Covid-19 pandemic has changed a lot of the thinking that my group had about cities. This health crisis reinforces issues that we were dealing with before it, like the burning of plastic waste, which is horrible for people's health and a terrible cause of pollution in the atmosphere. But there are other ways in which a healthy city is not necessarily a green city. That set of issues focuses around density. For a green city, for instance, you want to cram as many people as you can onto public transport. For a healthy city not just today, but in the aftermath of Covid-19, that might not be the best way to get people around. We should never go back to the car economy of gasoline engines, but there are lots of other things we need to rethink, too, about how to be green, which are difficult. One of these is housing. In New York City, the seventeen-story housing towers are a very efficient way to deal with energy use and the environment, but, during the present pandemic, to have seventy or eighty people using one or two elevators crowded together is not such a good idea. The question becomes: How do we get forms of density that don't put people at risk of exposure to viruses? At this point, I don't have the answers. A lot of the work that we've been doing for the 2021 United Nations Climate Change Conference has been delayed because of the pandemic, and this has given us a pause to think about how the recommendations we want to make by developing cities can be squared with crises such as this, which is not the last pandemic any of us will see. We need to work out how to build something that's sustainable along these two frameworks.

Srećko: As the chairman of the UN-Habitat urban initiatives program, you are dealing with quite a contradictory situation. We need a healthy city, but, as you said, it's not necessarily green. Many scientists are saying that future pandemics may be worse than Covid-19 because of the way neoliberalism is ruining habitats and the climate crisis is leading to the extinction of species, which makes it easier for viruses to jump from animals to humans. My question is how do you imagine the future city? What kind of transport will we have? I spoke to Saskia Sassen recently and she was advocating for more localism, less densely populated cities. Is that perhaps a solution? Or, if we retain cities as they are, how do you imagine them coping with a future global pandemic?

Richard: One of the reasons cities exist is that when you put a lot of different activities and people together you get what economists call an "agglomeration effect." In a suburb with one shopping center and many houses, there isn't much of an economic engine. If you have, as Microsoft does, an office in the suburbs of Seattle, workers don't get the kind of stimulus that they get in the city from being surrounded by lots of start-ups competing and colluding with one another. Economically, the notion of getting rid of cities, of de-densifying them, is not such a good idea. And socially, it's a disaster. People should be exposed to differences—different ethnicities, religions, classes, and so on. To me, the issue is not whether to have less dense environments, but how to deal with them. One proposal by the mayor of Paris, Anne Hidalgo, is to create what she calls "walking density."[1] That is, to try and remodel cities so that there are these nodes that are dense, with grocery stores, cafes, sports facilities, health centers, schools, and workplaces all accessible within fifteen minutes of walking. The nodes would be self-sufficient so that people don't have to take public transport, and would then relate to each other electronically. That's a good idea, but it would mean a scale of investment that very few capitalists are prepared to make. Imagine

---

1   https://www.theguardian.com/world/2020/feb/07/paris-mayor-unveils-15-minute-city-plan-in-re-election-campaign.

a Paris that was an entirely walking city. The whole infrastructure of the city would have to be reimagined, not to say anything about its politics. It is a possibility, though, and one of the ways to do it is simply to do away with the idea of one center regulated by mass transit. There is a slight problem with that, however, which is that it is a solution of privilege. If you live in a poor part of Mexico City, which is one of the cities my team is working in, your work is at least three hours away, which by foot would be ridiculous. In that case, it would be necessary to reconfigure the whole structure of the economy so that capitalists would invest in building factories in the midst of localities that workers could access. I have thought a lot about pedestrian solutions and I think that they are great, but in the developing world it is a solution of privilege. The question is really a much more fundamental one of economic reorganization so that poor people can actually access their workplaces. In slums like Dharavi in Mumbai, many of the people live and work on the same street, so the idea of a pedestrian city is evident there. But Dharavi has one of the highest rates of diseases in Mumbai because it is so concentrated. The Covid-19 pandemic is really a crisis of neoliberalism. Anglo-Saxon neoliberal regimes like the United States, primarily, as well as Australia and Britain, are proving themselves absolutely incapable of mobilizing resources against these kinds of problems. And that is because they waged war against the idea of the welfare state. What we are seeing with the current pandemic is, in many ways, a natural experiment. Having destroyed basic systems of support, neoliberal countries will be really menaced by Covid-19. The US will have the hardest time of all major developed societies in dealing with the pandemic because it has been the most brutal in its attack on the welfare state. In terms of cities, we need to figure out how to create urban economies that give us the benefits of agglomeration but overcome the problems that density brings. And density is both a technical subject—how you orchestrate a crowd, how it moves, whether it's static, how much space people have in it—and an aesthetic problem: What kind of theater is a healthy theater now? I certainly don't believe that online broadcasting will replace clubs or cafes, but we may have to reconfigure their size, for instance. There are many knock-on effects of the pandemic that are focused on this particular problem of how to design density.

Srećko: Before we consider in more detail the topic of this new online life and whether it can compensate for the public life we had before Covid-19, I would like to talk more about this idea of the "walking city" such as that proposed for Paris. On the one hand, it sounds like it would be a utopia for those living there. But, on the other, what the Covid-19 crisis has shown, besides the necessity of public infrastructure, is the emergence of a kind of dystopian version of the "walkable" city. In Paris, for instance, due to the restrictions on movement, you cannot currently go outside a zone of several square kilometers. And what is being implemented in most European countries now (and already in China to a much higher degree) is a kind of intensification of already existing forms of surveillance capitalism, with the pandemic being an excuse for imposing surveillance measures such as geo-location tracking. How do you see this trend developing? Will we emerge from isolation in a few months, for instance, to find a dystopian city that is completely surveilled?

Richard: This is a general social problem: that crises are opportunities for power to expand its scope, even after the immediate crisis ends, and it goes back to the Greeks during the Peloponnesian War. It is a kind of sociological constant that power tries to normalize the measures that it uses for control during a crisis. It is a political issue that we absolutely need to understand. The politics of post-pandemic will concern how to fight back against the kinds of surveillance implemented. I always thought that surveillance cameras were George Orwell come to life. In fact, the resistance to this in China, which is the home of facial recognition technology, is the strongest political resistance seen in years. People are not just passive victims of high tech and the world of these cameras will be a point of political struggle. There are many problems with the way the Chinese use these technologies, but in "smart cities," which try to use a lot of camera tech— like Masdar in the United Arab Emirates, or even London, which has a zillion cameras—the main problem is information overload. These cities pass a point at which the information is really un-computable in any kind of practical sense. The Chinese haven't passed that point and, because they haven't, there is a huge struggle emerging about it. In London, there is a different kind of issue: surveillance without intelligence. There is just more and more raw data than anybody knows how to compute. We are on the other side of the curve. Either way, whether this situation is Orwellian or pre-Orwellian, the politics of high tech at this point concerns, primarily, how to turn off the cameras. And we could do it, it's very simple to turn off a camera: just take huge industrial scissors and destroy them! More than people being tracked on the internet, I think it is camera surveillance that is producing new kinds of politics; this is the flash point.

Srećko: Let's talk about public space and the internet, since you're the author of *The Fall of Public Man*, a book that was very important for my generation and was originally published more than forty years ago, in 1977. In it, you describe eighteenth- and nineteenth-century cities such as Paris and London and their cultures of public space, including in theaters and cafes. With the Covid-19 pandemic, all of these public spaces are shut down, empty, not functioning. Many people are, instead, having an almost purely online life. What do you think about the relationship between public space and online life?

Richard: I don't think it has to be one or the other. It might surprise you, but I welcome the advent of technologies like Zoom because there is a real limit to face-to-face communication, which is that you have to be where the other person is. That we can now have visual and audio communication across distances of ten thousand miles is great. The question is, of course, how this technology is used and how it might be used in cooperative ways. Technology is an instrument. And it doesn't have to be one or the other. There is something about face-to-face communication that embodies relations between people that can never be replaced, but having tools like Zoom in addition is very positive. Did you know that I started off life as a musician?

Srećko: Yes, you are a cello player, right?

Richard: Yes, I still am. I started recording in the age of the tape, and tape cassettes and then CDs and DVDs were kind of wonderful. You'd feel that, while you were not physically there, you had a proximity to the musicians on stage, hearing and seeing what they were doing. Some musicians don't play as well in performance as they do when they play for themselves. There are ways in which using technology expressively is fabulous. I think that as a result of the kinds developments occurring with the Covid-19 pandemic, we will learn which mediums are appropriate for which purposes. I would much rather see an opera online than pay hundreds of pounds to go and sit in a little seat in the upper level, where you can barely see anything. Zoom is a new tool of expression as well as of communication. *The Fall of Public Man* refers to, as an image, the notion of withdrawal from other people, an inward turn. It's the notion that you are alone with yourself even when you're in the midst of other people. This phenomenon, whereby sociability has been replaced by subjectivities, happened in a crisis in the nineteenth century and came to fruition in the twentieth. Tools like Zoom are a liberation from that, in my view.

Srećko: Recently there have been many concerns, for instance, that Zoom is not as "public" as we thought, that our data goes straight to the desks of the National Security Agency in the United States. I am concerned about what Renata Ávila calls "digital colonialism" and the prospects of a kind of new technological barbarianism. Neoliberalism is spreading platform capitalism and exploiting the current crisis to monopolize all spheres of human activity, to privatize the spaces we perceive as being public, but which are not public in the same way as, for instance, a state-owned, publicly financed theater.

Richard: That is a real threat, but the answer is not that we shouldn't use the tech, but to find ways where the corporations can't get at our data. We have the technical means we need to shield ourselves from that kind of surveillance. This is not a problem of the machine, but a political problem. One of the things that it might spawn is the kind of hidden level of communication that my friend James Scott has studied among slaves, who had no protection against being surveilled but developed a kind of language that was very difficult for the masters to understand.[2] Maybe we'll develop something like that? It is of course a problem of corporate capitalism. When you have five or six huge tech companies dominating the market, every other tech company

2 James C. Scott, *Domination and the Arts of Resistance: Hidden Transcripts* (New Haven, CT: Yale University Press, 1992).

aspires to become similar. What if Zoom, for instance, were de-privatized? Or an alternative to Zoom that was run like Mozilla Firefox or DuckDuckGo? We need to reinvent tech in resistant ways that don't feed into the monopoly tech stream. I feel similarly about the media reporting of the Covid-19 crisis, which is very exploitative. It's as though the media gets more of a reach by exciting panic and fear. This is a very serious crisis and the worst way to deal with it is to say, "My god, another five hundred people died yesterday!," or, "This is the future, we're all done for!" That is a good way to keep journalists in work, but there needs to be a sobriety about this issue. The same thing is true of tech. Instead of saying tech is the devil's instrument (or Bill Gates's), we should consider it as a serious problem that needs to be solved, and can be quite easily. Perhaps it is because I'm so old, but I'm resistant to the notion of crisis as a moment from which truth emerges. That is almost infantile to me. A crisis is just that: a difficulty that you have to face calmly. A lot of the left sustains itself on demonizing tech, but an apocalyptic view is not productive.

Srećko: Besides *The Fall of Public Man*, your books *Craftsmen* and *Together* are particularly useful in this moment of a global pandemic. I love the passages in *Craftsmen* where you talk about the skills that were created under the NHS and how a public sector was created as a common good that reinforced social cooperation. As is now evident in the UK, once a country privatizes and quantifies the public sector it is not able, any longer, to resist pandemics. Considering the huge number of people who are now at home using online spaces, do you think new sorts of social cooperation will emerge from the Covid-19 crisis (notwithstanding the surveillance and privatization that we anticipate)?

Richard: Yes. Using communication tools such as Zoom enables people who are very far from each other to cooperate. I know a PhD student at LSE, Shani Orgad, who studied the way in which some women with breast cancer set up an international network to share information, including things they weren't getting from their doctors.[3] They developed incredible com-

---

3   Shani Orgad, "The Use of the Internet in the Lives of Women with Breast Cancer: Narrating and Storytelling Online and Offline" (London: London School of Economics, 2003, PhD Thesis) https://core.ac.uk/download/pdf/4187465.pdf.

munication skills to share stories, experiences, and knowledges, and that was before video calling was possible. The thing about cooperation is that it is informal and context-dependent. We are in a situation now where that informality and context-dependence does not require people to be together in one place, and that is an incredible possibility to exploit. I am also interested in the notion that high tech be used as a kind of workshop for the left. I feel that the British left, for instance, has always pushed tech to the background. It's obsessed with the notion of class and there is very little thinking about how to build solidarity. It is assumed that solidarity comes out of anger at injustice. But that is not true; solidarity is a craft. One of the things that I hope comes out of this moment is that the left thinks less about Piketty and more about the internet.

Srećko: Do you think the Covid-19 crisis will be used to justify fascism in Hungary and other Western European member states?

Richard: The answer is yes. Of course they will! It's a golden opportunity.

Srećko: In that case, let me mention a very interesting detail from your biography, which is that your father and uncle fought in the Spanish Civil War as part of the International Brigades. If fascism is our future, what are the possibilities for creating some kind of new "International Brigades" using the internet?

Richard: As a background note, most of the people who joined the International Brigades went into it as Communist Party members and left Spain as anarcho-syndicalists or anarchists. That was certainly true for my father and uncle. They were good Party members who believed in the revolutionary vanguards, but the war changed their minds—particularly after the Hitler–Stalin pact. The reason I say this is that I think we need to have a lot more inquiry into "how" rather than focusing on having "a movement." I'm very resistant, and have always been, to manifestos. I don't think, "the Left" should have "a position." That is what the dominant powers have; that is called "hegemony." I think we need a different kind of politics now. Your generation needs to find a way to have many different workshops rather than a single Church. That is why I am optimistic about all these internet groups coexisting, but not fitting neatly together. This debate among the left about how to mesh identity politics with a critique of capitalism to me seems ridiculous. Why mesh them? They don't have to fit together. The lesson is that anarchism is the aftermath of communism, rather than the precursor.

Srećko: Is your view closer to Michel Foucault's concept of heterotopia?

Richard: Well, we did write together for a decade. And heterotopia was a very prescient idea. I think that if Michel had lived longer, he would have gone back to it after he'd finished the books on sexuality and power. Heterotopia was also, I must say, the idea of Jacques Derrida, Foucault's great enemy. The idea of heterotopia goes back to the 1930s, but it got pushed aside by the notion of that there is "a Left." I probably won't live to see this, but the left shouldn't have a program; it should have a procedure.

Srećko: How, do you think, will the so-branded "open" neoliberal city be maintained despite surveillance intensification?

Richard: Neoliberalism has an ideology of individualism but the control mechanisms are very enclosed. In the West, the impulse in everyday civil society to live in an open way is pretty strong, and this is a privilege that we shouldn't scorn. But it doesn't come out of neoliberalism, it comes out of a kind of localized sociability. That's certainly true in London, which doesn't have a dominant culture. Sociability is something that is particular to a relationship between two people, and we've been privileged to have a form of sociability in which those two people can be strangers to each other, but this has not been true for our Chinese friends. Their sociability has been rigidly controlled so that that doesn't happen. For us in the West, this kind of sociability has an anarchic element, communitarian without being claustrophobic. That's why my project has been to figure out how to put the "social" back in socialism.

Srećko: Could you explain further what it would mean to put the social back in socialism, and whether you think this current crisis might evoke and reinforce that process?

Richard: I'll tell you what it would mean in terms of the NHS. The cleaners and the nurses in the NHS were subject to a regime where they were asked to constantly move from ward to ward, task to task. These are people whose skills were thought to be so primitive that they weren't really credited as having anything to do with the care of patients. However, now what people are discovering in the NHS as a result of Covid-19 is that the workers who really know what's happening to patients in horrible distress are those who are cleaning up, the night nurses. They're not the doctors. There has been, in the last couple of weeks, a huge reevaluation of the role of these workers, who, because most of them are foreigners, were previously menaced by this immigration discourse wherein Britain only wants "highly skilled" workers. Suddenly, that's no longer an operative claim. Their social skills are much more important, for instance, than the social skills of the Secretary of State for Health and Social Care. What we are seeing is that the right has dropped its anti-foreigner rhetoric and is now desperately wondering how to retain and expand this workforce. Once you start asking what the actual social skills needed in a crisis like this are, a different kind of picture of social relations forms and that has a knock-on effect on things that seem to have no relation to the disease, like immigration policy. That is what the Brits, who are very slow learners, are learning; in two weeks, they have had an accelerated course in the perils of nationalism. A similar thing might happen in Hungary, although of course Orbán will try to prevent that. My point here is that when you start with the social, you then work out to the political. The social is not a consequence of the political. In my view, it is the other way around. That is what Michel Foucault's notion of heterotopia was about. You start with the social relationship, not with the scopic regime. The regime gets challenged by the social relationship. It's also close to the idea of James Scott, who is probably the world's greatest anarchist philosopher at this moment, which is that if you work out socialism from the social, you will arrive at the political.

Srećko: Earlier you claimed that the left shouldn't have one common program and you proposed, instead, a "common procedure." What do you mean by this?

Richard: What I mean is a set of ideas about how to develop social skills. I'll give you one example—when I go to political meetings, and I hear one person arguing with another, they always use the declarative voice: "I believe," "I think," and so on. There's never a space open for a different kind of speech, which is a subjunctive speech, one allowing for ambiguity: "I would have thought," or "perhaps." If I were running those meetings (which I sometimes do at the UN), I would say, "Okay, your position is very clear, what is wrong with your position to you?" That is to introduce more self-doubt, subject questioning, and ambiguity into the process. And that is political; it is not a weakening of politics. It is a creation of a social bond because the other has an opportunity to reflect on and address any uncertainties in their position. It is for a similar reason that I don't like voting. What does it matter if a majority of people think one thing or another? Why is the majority, the 51 percent, more right than 49 percent? Also, it leads to a false notion that something is resolved by taking a vote. Life is too complex for that. We have to be different kinds of animals on the left. We have to be much more interactive and communicative, rather than having a clear, defensible, robust position. Leave that to the right; that belongs to them.

Srećko: You mentioned this question of "how to be together," which reminded me of our last physical meeting in Zagreb, two or three years ago, when we were talking about another dear friend of yours, and a huge inspiration for myself, and that is Roland Barthes. In one of his last lectures at College de France, he was talking precisely about "how to live together" and he used the term *idiorrhythms*, coming from *idios*, in the sense of "one's own," and *rhuthmos*, or rhythm, the rhythm of a community in which one lives with others.[4] I think this resonates with what you are saying; namely, this idea that we have to reinvent the ways not just of how we cooperate, but how we live together and how different rhythms of living together can actually come together in order to create a community, in the sense Roland Barthes was talking about.

---

4 Roland Barthes, *How to Live Together: Novelistic Simulations of Some Everyday Spaces*, trans. Kate Briggs (New York, NY: Columbia University Press, 2013).

Richard: Yes, I was also very inspired by him. He was a terrible pianist but an inspiring writer. That notion of Barthes's is the same as that of Foucault, which is that "being together" doesn't mean being on the same page. And how to manage that relationship is, to me, radical.

Conversation held on April 2, 2020

Internationalism in a Pandemic

Astra Taylor and David Adler

David: It's day twenty-six of the lockdown in Rome and I feel like I'm adjusting to a new normal. We have moved through several different phases: first, there was panic and adjustment, followed by the honeymoon, where we dreamed of the reading and yoga we would achieve, then came the boredom and restlessness, and, now, in a surreal and dangerous way, we are all adjusting to the possibility that we might be inside for a long time. The general point that keeps returning to me is that this is not one thing. Even though we call it "the coronavirus crisis," it is not one thing over time, and it is not one thing across different places in the world. It is also not one *thing*: it's not just a health crisis, but an economic crisis, social crisis, and, above all, a political crisis. We often talk about plagues as the "great equalizers," but we can clearly see the ways in which the present pandemic is fragmenting along very familiar fault lines in terms of class and social position. I'm hoping you can give us an update about the situation in America, Astra?

Astra: I think you are exactly right in that this is a multifaceted crisis. The word *crisis* is interesting in itself; its original meaning refers to illness, and in particular the turning point of an illness where the person either recovers or perishes. Covid-19 is a novel form of the coronavirus, one which we have no immunity to and is rapidly spreading. However, many people will perish not solely because of the virus, but because countries don't have the resources or public health infrastructure to handle it. This isn't a natural disaster, in that sense, but a social disaster. There is a second sense, too, in which this is not a natural disaster or an act of God. Covid-19 emerged out of what is often described as the human–wildlife interface. As human beings engage in environmentally destructive forms of agriculture and land use, we encroach upon wildness and that increases the likelihood that these viruses will jump from animal species to domestic lifestyles or to humans. Almost every terrifying illness in recent years—HIV, Ebola, and now Covid-19—jumped species. Covid-19 evolved in the natural world, but that it jumped to human beings and is now spreading so rapidly is very much a product of our political and social reality, our exploitation of nature, and the impact of this on biodiversity.

David: The pandemic is not simply mixing in with existing crises, but is in many ways a product of them, and a fundamentally global one. On the one hand, there is something almost universal about this moment in a way that feels novel, and we can talk about the potential emancipatory possibilities of this. On the other hand, this pandemic feels incredibly personal and many people are asking themselves some variation of "Why me?" and "Why now?" We are toggling between the global and the personal. At the same time, our discussions of the pandemic and how it has been handled are still mostly framed in national terms. We still haven't figured out how to make sense of the scale of this thing, as we toggle between our personal experiences, how it is affecting our lives and those of our families and friends; the virus as a national crisis, interacting first and foremost with national institutions; and then as an international crisis. How are you making sense of this? Is there a sense that this is something more than American?

Astra: Feminists have long said that the personal is political and it's quite true. The political is also very personal, as we are seeing. Massive phenomena like land management and industrial food supply chains are now coming home to roost. I'd also like to go back to the question of whether Covid-19 is an equalizer and point out two things. Firstly, if you read the right-wing media in the US, you notice a particular frame being used that is old and tired and somehow extremely resilient, which is that disease is spread by the poor. You will often see comments positioning homeless camps and cities as epicenters of the virus, as well as a strong anti-immigrant motif, evident, for instance, in Trump's attempt to frame this as "the Chinese virus."[1] This is ancient news in the US, where there has always been a mix of racism and fearmongering around disease and contagion. These tropes linger on and reassert themselves and are a kind of virus in themselves. Secondly, I'd like to point out that a pandemic does not spread at such a rapid pace unless people are traveling by plane, and only 20 percent of human beings on this earth have ever flown in an airplane. In other words, at least in its initial spread, a major vector of this disease was wealth. This is evident in both the United States, where those with second homes are fleeing New York City because it has become a hot spot, and Europe, where it is being spread via ski resorts. It is evident

---

1   https://www.aljazeera.com/news/2020/03/outrage-trump-calls-coronavirus-00chinese-virus-200317130157057.html.

that people of means are bringing the disease to world communities that don't have the care infrastructure to battle it; there's a class politics already to its distribution. People are told to shelter in place, but this assumes that they have a home. Many people don't, or they are staying in confined spaces. And many are forced into workplaces that are crowded and unsanitary. As Keeanga-Yamahtta Taylor recently wrote, this is a virus that thrives on the intimacy of poverty.[2] I think the left absolutely needs to push back on the idea that there's a national solution to this. A pandemic by definition is international, and borders don't make sense when you are battling a pathogen. As it stands, there's no vaccine for Covid-19, so we are using fourteenth-century methods of quarantining and isolation. Shutting everything down does make sense, but there is no reason to assume that the boundaries by which we shut things down at all correspond to national borders. It is true that we need less human movement to slow transmission, but that doesn't mean we need to shut down movement along the arbitrary line that runs between the United States and Mexico, for instance. Borders concern geopolitics; they are human-made structures irrelevant to a disease.

David: I want to dwell a bit here on what it really means to take this seriously as a pandemic. So far, the Covid-19 crisis has by and large been an experience of middle- and high-income countries. We are just seeing the beginnings of what it means for it to go South, to countries with far less infrastructure and resources at the household and individual level for quarantining. Certainly, we should understand this pandemic as a test—of our institutions, our ability to unify and make sure everyone has the appropriate provisions. Because it is a pandemic that makes true the basic premise of solidarity, which is that we are only as healthy as our sickest. In Europe, we are failing that test in ways that will seem remarkable to future historians. This is a European Union that is thoroughly integrated, its leaders hang out in Brussels and their kids go to the same colleges, and yet they seem incapable of acting in solidarity, delivering on the promise of universal provision, and creating the necessary fiscal resources. At the same time, we have Trump literally behaving like a

---

2 https://www.newyorker.com/news/our-columnists/reality-has-endorsed-bernie-sanders.

pirate, seizing masks from a shipment destined for Berlin.[3] There are forms of warfare taking place between high-income countries. Turning to the South, in the past two and a half months, more money has flown out of the Global South than in history. Ninety billion dollars have flown out of emerging markets—more than three times the outflow of capital in the 2008 financial crisis.[4] What this means is that just as Covid-19 arrives in the Global South, just as the health crisis begins to intertwine with political and economic crises, these countries are likely to face a balance of payments crisis such that they can no longer afford to import basic goods like food, let alone ventilators. This international crisis will bear down on domestic crises. What do you think we should expect to see in terms of America's role in the world, as well as the pandemic "going South"?

Astra: "Going South" here has a double meaning—both that the virus is heading toward the Global South and that things will be getting worse. Attention needs to be paid to both the spread of the disease and to the movements and distribution of money as it flees certain areas and takes shelter in the dollar. The outlook is really fucking bleak; there is no silver lining. The United States and Europe are concerned with sourcing ventilators, with Governor Cuomo of New York, for instance, requesting an additional thirty thousand ventilators.[5] The country of Liberia, with a population of five million people, has three ventilators.[6] None of them are in the public healthcare system. Mali has fifty-six ventilators for nineteen million people.[7] We, in the affluent West, need to lift our heads above the parapet and realize what is happening in countries that are not just less affluent but have been robbed by our countries for centuries. The US also has the privilege of the imperial

---

3 https://www.bbc.co.uk/news/world-52161995.

4 https://www.cnbc.com/2020/04/03/coronavirus-way-worse-than-the-global-financial-crisis-imf-says.html.

5 https://www.cnbc.com/2020/03/24/gov-cuomo-says-new-york-needs-ventilators-now-help-from-gm-ford-does-us-no-good.html.

6 https://www.theatlantic.com/ideas/archive/2020/04/why-covid-might-hit-african-nations-hardest/609760/.

7 https://graphics.reuters.com/HEALTH-CORONAVIRUS/AFRICA/yzdpxoqbdvx/.

dollar, which enables it to do things with money that other countries cannot do. And what have we done with it? We have decided to give away 450 billion dollars in corporate handouts, which can be leveraged into 5 or 6 trillion dollars, as a reward to companies that have spent the twelve years since the 2008 financial crisis enriching themselves, not paying their taxes, banking offshore, laying off workers, attacking unions and pushing money out the doors to their shareholders.[8] This instead of leveraging our privilege to create, for instance, a Green New Deal that addresses the public health crisis, or sending desperately needed assistance to regions that lack resources. As activists, we need to change people's political understanding with the goal of building power. This has gotten a lot harder in the present circumstances, but you are exactly right to lay out the economics. On the cover of the *New York Times* the last few days have been different articles about how great Germany is for having so many ventilators, but why is Germany so wealthy? To answer that question, we need to look at Germany's economic relationship to poorer countries in the EU and the rest of the world. The left wants a world in which there is public affluence, but not affluence based on exploitation, colonialism, and a murderous disregard for human life.

David: This brings us to the question of "Where to for globalization?" It seems so wild to me that we have these glorious depictions of the great Germans who have managed this crisis without speaking about the invention of a new kind of international political economy that we can call "sicken thy neighbor." This builds upon the now familiar "beggar thy neighbor" policies that make one country rich at the expense of another, which is the core of the German economic model within the context of the eurozone. What concerns me is that we like to pretend that globalization is an on/off switch. Trump preaches "deglobalization" on the basis that the US shouldn't depend so heavily on global supply chains. However, we know that globalization involves the movement not just of humans but also goods and capital. We also know that a crisis like this, the volatility it entails, offers tremendous opportunity for deeper, accelerated forms of financialization which,

---

8 https://www.politico.com/news/2020/04/09/coronavirus-recovery-bill-fed-records-176371.

as you pointed out, could serve as an excuse to harden the borders. The left hasn't yet gotten to the point where we are really grappling with borders, but there is a feeling that, perhaps, there has been *too much* movement. I'm hoping you can speak a bit more about this.

Astra: From what I've read from public health advocates, there is no scientific rationale for closing the borders. In terms of disease management, it only makes aid more difficult. And the claim that we are only as well as the sickest among us is not only a moral assertion, but a self-interested, rational one, for, as long as this pathogen exists, we are all at risk. The left needs to be very critical of the delusional push to close borders. It is the default because of centuries of ideology and anti-immigrant politics and is a very cheap way for states to act like they're doing something proactive. The United States doesn't even have solidarity across the fifty states, let alone across international borders. Whatever this "test" is that you mentioned, we are failing. On the other hand, many human beings are really rising to the occasion and this crisis is really driving home the extent to which altruism and solidarity are taken advantage of in the current system. Regular people are stepping up and doing the care work the state should be assisting with.

David: To me, it boils down to a fundamental difference between two basic ways of organizing at both local and international levels—one is competitive and the other is cooperative. The present failure to deliver necessary public goods even within a particular country is a failure of market competition in the crudest, most Hobbesian form. The competitive federalist model that many thought would work in the United States has failed disastrously and the need for stronger, more institutional forms of solidarity, driven, as you said, not by altruism but by a sense of mutual benefit, is very clear. Recently, a group of nine countries in the eurozone, including Italy, France, Portugal, and Spain, came together behind a proposal for a so-called coronabond: a eurobond that would be jointly issued by all the members of the currency union in order to create fiscal resources for investing in public health and economic recovery.[9] It was based on the logical, obvious idea that these countries

9 https://www.cnbc.com/2020/03/25/nine-eu-countries-say-its-time-for-corona-bonds-as-virus-deaths-rise.html.

share a currency and if one tanks, they all will. But the Dutch balked at it because they didn't want to be on the hook for the "profligate spenders" in the South. We at DiEM25 have also made the case that, without building unity, the eurozone will sink and fall apart, and released our own 3-point plan to this end. I worry that, in the aftermath of the pandemic, globalization trends will double down on a framework of charity, where some wealth is redistributed from the North to the South but no institutional frameworks are built. After World War II, countries came together around the world to design the so-called Bretton Woods institutions to help coordinate cooperation and regulate international economy in ways mutually beneficial to countries of the North and South. We should be thinking on that level of ambition.

Astra: Advocates of neoliberal globalization used to work under the pretense that the world was flat, that globalization will lift all boats. However, that veneer seems to have given way to an "every country for themselves" approach. This is not simply a matter of rhetoric, because it sets the stage for particular kinds of mercenary economic policies. What we are seeing with the collapse of the "coronabond" idea is a variation on what happened to Greece in the economic crisis, emblematizing a kind of fiscal cruelty within the EU. I think we have to ask what solidarity is. Solidarity is not charity and it is not being an ally. Solidarity had its first appearance in ancient Roman law and comes from the phrase "in solidum," the state of debtors holding a debt in common such that if one person failed to pay, everyone else had to come and bail them out or risk collective default. Solidarity always has an economic component. It's not a sentiment, an ethos, or a Tweet, but economic bonds. And it's imagining a world where banking, bonds, and mutual funds would actually tie us together in positive ways that create commonly shared prosperity. The word solidarity was revived in the 1700s and became a key part of thinking about socialism and the welfare state. We need a similar awareness now of the need to create institutions of economic cooperation. Globalization is a fact, but it seems we have all of the bad international structures and none of the good. We need an international environmental protection agency that has the ability to enforce and police rules and regulations. We need international institutions that can enforce labor standards and taxation.

David: In past months, DiEM25 has worked to bring together a group of people, groups, and institutions to form a new Progressive International, a central task of which will be to reimagine international institutions and to connect domestic struggles to international ones. I can only hope that we are able to match the scale of the global finance with the scale of the activism itself.

Astra: On a strategic level, though, I think many people take that idea too literally and believe, for instance, that if we are facing a global company such as Amazon then our movement has to be global and massive. I think that, as organizers, we need to build power where we are. I don't mean organizing should always remain in your own backyard, but at this moment the left is not able to operate at the macro international scale. We need to organize our municipalities, states, and federal government in order to affect global issues. The right only got so powerful in the United States through decades of the most banal forms of organizing: taking over school boards, writing legislation at the local level, and so on. Yes, their campaigns are funded by billionaires and the left has to come up with a different, radical model of sustaining its organization, but my point is the right doesn't only operate on a macro level but on a local level, too. I'm always interested in the paradoxes of organizing, and one is that if we want to change things at the global scale, that involves being very strategic in the grounded, bounded communities we inhabit.

David: Again, we are toggling between the personal, local, and global levels. Now, there is a lot of—I think premature—excitement about rewilding at the moment, and this idea circulating that "we are the virus." Would you be able to speak a bit about how the ecological crisis is tied into the Covid-19 crisis?

Astra: The science is pretty clear on this. Covid-19 emerged because of human beings encroaching on wildlife. Pundits like to blame the Chinese wet markets and engage in a racist exoticizing of the animals being sold, as though eating pigs and cows is any more normal or natural than eating bats and snakes. However, what seems to be the case is that part of what drives people into these other markets is industrial agriculture and smallholders' inability to compete with the scale of "big agriculture." We see this with the climate emergency, too. The ecological crisis and climate change cannot be separated from industrial agriculture, which produces a very substantial part of the emissions and pollutes our air and water. There are many ways that environmental determinants shape people's abilities to survive crises. Yet, we have leaders such as Trump denying these interconnections and, in fact, using the present health crisis as justification for ignoring pesky environmental regulations.[10] The right wing is again practicing the art of science denial, which they have cultivated for decades regarding climate change and are now turning against Covid-19. Just as with climate change, countries are refusing to have a scientific or rational conversation about the origins of the present pandemic. Many of the solutions to the climate crisis overlap with the kinds of measures that would be necessary to prevent more virus outbreaks, including rewilding. These are interlocking crises.

David: I want to go to another form of crisis that you've worked a lot on, and that's debt. I mentioned the evacuation of capital from emerging markets and their retreat to [the] dollar, this imperial currency that gives tremendous power to the Fed to essentially determine who lives and who dies in the Covid-19 crisis. It is likely that countries in the Global South will be stacked with unsustainable debts and forced, again, to reach out to international institutions that, historically, are unreliable managers of this challenge. The debt crisis plays out and will play out on multiple levels. In the last fifteen to twenty years, there has been an explosion of credit card and household debt in general in countries such as the US, which will be compounded by the coronavirus. We can also expect to see huge amounts of sovereign debt and potentially crises at the national level. How do we link these together? Where can organizing around the question of debt go from here?

Astra: They *are* linked—we just have to recognize the linkages and figure out strategically how to respond. The personal is definitely political in terms of our personal financial realities. We are currently facing mass unemployment in the United States and around the world, and this is neither the

10 https://www.theguardian.com/environment/2020/mar/27/trump-pollution-laws-epa-allows-companies-pollute-without-penalty-during-coronavirus.

fault of workers nor, even, the virus. It is the result of a capitalist economy that refuses to prioritize saving lives over securing profits and that is determined not merely to stabilize the financial sector, but to further enrich and empower it. I'm part of the Debt Collective, a union for debtors that is based on the idea that debt is a form of leverage. Over the last four to five decades, easy access to credit has masked the fact that wages have stagnated. We use words like "financialization" and "neoliberalism," but how are these experienced? For most people, the experience is one of debt. Americans owe an average of $36,000 just for going to college.[11] The majority of people owe debt for medical bills because they don't have health insurance, and every person who loses their job as a result of the pandemic will lose their health insurance, too. People are in debt for their housing because there is no social housing, and they amass credit card debts and payday loans because they are not paid enough. The idea of the Debt Collective is that our individual debts are someone else's asset and, therefore, as a complementary move to traditional labor unions, people should be organized into debtors' unions to give them another form of economic leverage. Our claim is that debts entered into for the necessities of life are "odious" or illegitimate. In a sense, this is a scaled-down version of the "Jubilee South" campaigns that, in the early 2000s, campaigned for the elimination of sovereign debt for developing countries. Right now, we need to decide how to talk about personal debt, public financing, and international financial flows in concise terms that drive home the fact that the enrichment of a few through financial mechanisms is the reason why so many of us are broke and, in turn, desperate when crises hit. The simplistic demand I suggest is, "Can't pay, shouldn't pay, won't pay." These debts are illegitimate and based on domination and extraction. People like Jared Kushner and Donald Trump have bankrupted companies and simply walked away from their debts countless times. It's only the little people who are subjected to the discipline of debt and must pay up. We see this double standard playing out in the present crisis, where corporations, who have amassed huge amounts of debt over the past twelve years, are being bailed out, while

11 https://www.investopedia.com/student-loan-debt-2019-statistics-and-outlook-4772007.

individuals and households, already in debt, are losing their homes to pay for Covid-19 treatment. Debtors around the world must unite.

David: Yes, this is the essence of internationalism. We have discussed how internationalism is not charity, or symbolic forms of solidarity, but is fundamentally about taking the links between multiple different crises that bind us all together and using them to arrive at mutual benefit. I hope that the calls for a debt jubilee for the Global South are revived. Before we end, I would like to discuss the question of the unreliable institutional managers that are in place to deal with international debts. I think that a multilateral institution would be better than the unilateral decision-making of an administration, especially an imperial one. In the context of the present global crisis, the UN has been missing in action, for all intents and purposes. Where do we turn? And how do we build energy behind a vision that can seem so utopian?

Astra: It's interesting to have this conversation while the Sanders campaign in the US comes to terms with the fact that Biden is the Democratic frontrunner. The left in the US, UK, and countries such as Greece before us, have banked heavily on electoral strategies and on the idea that if we could take power at the national level, it would be a huge stepping stone to building a new kind of internationalism. I think the strategy, again, is related to this question of power. I can analyze debt all day long, highlighting the reparations the North should pay on top of erasing sovereign debts in the Global South, or the carbon debts we've accumulated and which must now be urgently paid to those countries and communities least responsible for climate change. However, analysis is not enough; what we lack and need is power, which can only be built through association and organizing. Labor unions are first and foremost, but we also need debtors' unions to respond to the present financialized reality, and tenants' unions to respond to rental and housing crises. And we need to democratize and restructure political parties. We cannot immediately campaign on the international level; as Jane McAlevey says, there are no shortcuts when you want to build power for working people. The present situation is one we couldn't have imagined a month ago, but we already knew that we need to get organized, and this hasn't changed, it's just become harder and more urgent.

David: In terms of moving out from social isolation to an explosion of associational activity and organization, we need to think about how we can prepare ourselves to slingshot from the present moment of isolation and anxiety and fear.

Astra: This is the moment to start thinking through the question of what good democratic international institutions would look like and to figure out how to articulate this in an exciting way, perhaps through the question of how would our lives be different right now if X, Y, or Z were in place? For instance, what if we had a truly universal health framework that was concerned not just with human health but that of the environment as a whole? Would the pandemic be as devastating, or even have developed, under such conditions? What would this moment be like if we had robust public financing mechanisms that could fund a global Green New Deal, or fund the development of pharmaceuticals including vaccines that would be kept in the public domain, or fund the development of a privacy-respecting digital communications infrastructure? We have to keep these alternative possibilities in mind, especially when things seem bleak.

David: Let's take hope from the idea that crisis originally refers to a turning point.

Conversation held on April 4, 2020

Reflecting on Our Post-Virus World

Brian Eno and Yanis Varoufakis

Yanis: The Covid-19 crisis seems to have had three effects on our political reality. Firstly, it has magnified magnificently the never-ending crisis that began in 2008, and which has morphed into all sorts of different sub-crises. Secondly, it has proved that the government can act and must act massively in the common interest against everything that Thatcher, Reagan, and their followers have been saying since the late 1970s. Thirdly, this crisis, caused by a mindless piece of RNA, has temporarily revealed the true nature of politics: who has the power to do what to whom. The question for this conversation is very simple: How will Covid-19 change society? And is there a realistic utopian vision of a post-virus society that can help avert nastier potential scenarios? In grappling with this question, I cannot imagine a better conversation partner than an artist whom I worshipped as a teenager, and whom I have been honored to get to know in the last five years, Brian Eno, a co-member of DiEM25. So, Brian, where is the hole in which you are hiding from Covid-19?

Brian: I'm in Norfolk, in the east of England, the part of England closest to the continent, and near where you used to teach in Norwich.

Yanis: Yes, I used to ride my motorcycle from Norwich to Ipswich.

Brian: You probably passed through this village on the way!

Yanis: So, share your thoughts with us: What would a vision of the post-virus world, one that is worth fighting for, look like?

Brian: Well, I think we can see the beginnings of it already. One thing that I've noticed in the last few weeks is that there has been a sense of relief among people that they could suddenly be nice to each other again. Anyone familiar with English politics over the last year five years will realize it's been very bitter and divisive, with an anger stoked by the media, and particularly the media outlets that support our present government. For five years, people have pretty much been at each other's throats. It seems to me that this upsurge of solidarity that's happened in the last few weeks is not only a sense that "we're all in this together," but also that we can actually be nice to each other as well; we can help one another. While people are frightened of the virus, at the same time, they are delighted to be able to like one another again. That is the beginning of something, I think, and it's something that I hope we won't forget. It's as if we are rediscovering certain things that had been forgotten for quite a long time—not only that we like each other's company, but that we can do creative things together, that we don't have to be wholly dependent on having our entertainment supplied to us. And we are rediscovering that certain parts of the community are extremely important. When, a few weeks ago, the government classified certain workers as "essential," who are those allowed to continue living as normal, it was interesting to see that nearly all "essential workers" are the lowest paid people in our society. Essential workers: the people we don't pay very much, essentially. On Thursday nights, there is this wonderful sight of people coming out to applaud the National Health Service, which is tied into a broader recognition that carers in general are the people who keep society running. It wouldn't matter a fig if all the bankers disappeared for a year, nobody would notice the difference. If the nurses disappeared, we would notice it the very next day. There is a societal reevaluation occurring in terms of who we are and what we are worth. And one of the positive upshots of this is that the NHS should be safe for a few more years, it will be harder for the government to sell it off to American corporations as planned. Right now, we occupy an interesting moment in which we are designing the future of civilization. The decisions we make in the next few months will persist for a very long time. If you travel through any airport, you can see that the residual emergency powers from 9/11 are still in place. I don't think they will ever be removed. We have to be very careful that we don't end up in a society that is dominated by a sense of fear, emergency, and threat. I will talk about what we might aim for soon, but what we risk now is a voluntary surrender of power and control to the state. The most efficient way to concentrate power is to encourage a situation in which people are willing to surrender it. The present moment is a perfect example of that. There is always a dialogue occurring between security and freedom, and we must now be very careful not to sacrifice freedoms in the name of security that we will later be unable to get back. Historically, it has been very difficult for societies to say, "Actually, we are prepared to live a slightly riskier life now, for the sake of having some liberty." Generally, civilization tends toward increasing security, not lessening it. After 9/11, a huge industry called "Homeland Security" was suddenly built up, with hundreds of billions of dollars invested and nobody really knowing what for. It gave rise to this wonderful phrase of the twenty-first century: "For security reasons." This is now an ultimate, unquestionable justification given for why people cannot do all sorts of things. It doesn't even need to be explained, we are simply told that "for security reasons" we cannot do this or that. It is simply a way that the powerful justify and protect their actions. Now, those who would like to control power understand the value of an emergency situation like the present Covid-19 pandemic. Governments are establishing a kind of war footing. For one way for so-called democratic governments to achieve consensus is to create a threat big enough to make all people want to agree, so as to not complicate the business of government. We can see how war has been used historically as a resort for rulers who feel that their power is under threat: they imagine, or generate, or promise a war and suddenly it becomes possible to enforce unity among the population. But to have a war, you need an enemy. In the past, the enemy has been other tribes, races, nations, or ideologies. Most recently in Britain, immigrants have been the enemy. But this is perhaps the first time in history that we've declared war on another organism—and not even a very impressive one, as you say, just a piece of RNA. Nevertheless, it works. It gives countries all the benefits of being at war, such as being able to constrain social freedoms. I understand fully the need for those constraints right now, but I think we have to be very careful to make sure that they don't fossilize in place and become the new normal. Let's now turn to the question of what kind of future we could imagine, other than the rather dark one I have just suggested. I am hoping that the skills that people are learning in these few months (or longer), of sociability and being together, of working with each other to overcome the huge gaps left by the sudden stoppage of conventional industries, will become part of the way that we build the future. I agree with Richard Sennett, who said on DiEM TV that solidarity is a craft. It does not happen automatically but is something we have to practice and refine together. He also said that he didn't believe that solidarity is the product of rage. Anger has a role in inciting people to build solidarity, but we also need reflection, care, and thought. We have to ask, "What can we do together now that we could never do before?" Because, remember, we have many new tools for the craft of solidarity, one of them being the technologies that enable us to converse when we are thousands of miles apart.

Yanis: I was touched by your mention of the recognition of essential workers. As Slavoj Žižek pointed out on DiEM TV recently, those millionaires who isolate themselves on their yachts in the middle of the Atlantic cannot do so unless there is an army of poor Italians working for them. When DiEM25 put together our European Green New Deal, we made a point of extending solidarity to those who are those now recognized as "essential workers," the maintainers who ensure the operation of national services, social care, and technologies like sewers, for instance.[1] In terms of the craft of solidarity, Covid-19 has given us an opportunity and a prompt to support the maintainers. However, my great worry is that the fascists are pretty good at looking the maintainers in the eye and saying, "We're going to look after you; we are going to make you proud again." We progressives have our work cut out for us. The fascists are surpassing us in doing solidarity work on the ground, giving workers what is, in my view, a false sense of importance on the basis of hating others, of demonizing the foreigner, the Black, the Jew, the Palestinian, the other. How do we navigate this terrain where, in the midst of Covid-19, the hearts and souls of the maintainers are being contested by the nationalist internationalists: the Trumps, Johnsons, Bolsonaros, and Mitsotakises?

Brian: In England, at least, the situation has become much clearer recently. Everyone knows that the NHS has been under attack for some time now and, suddenly, health workers are the heroes of the day, even to those responsible for undermining them. There is not much ambiguity about this right here and now in England. It is suddenly very clear who the essential workers are, and who supported them and who didn't prior to Covid-19. The difficulty, of course, is that the fascists are always prepared to lie, and we aren't. And they can rely on the media to help them make people forget that they ever said what they did. The performance of Trump has been astonishing. Recently, he claimed, "I always knew this was a pandemic," and a lot of people seem to believe him, even though it doesn't take much research to

---

1   https://diem25.org/wp-content/uploads/2017/03/European-New-Deal-Complete-Policy-Paper.pdf.

find him denying the existence of a pandemic just a few weeks earlier. Like so many of the battles we face, this is a media problem. Despite the alternatives in media and communications, mainstream news outlets continue to set the atmosphere around things. In the 2019 Jeremy Corbyn campaign, we witnessed what was likely the most naked exercise in propaganda to occur in British history. It was really quite astonishing to see (as I did on the doorstep) how carefully cultivated people's opinions were about Corbyn. No matter how much we chipped away at all the propaganda, debunking all the untruths, we couldn't get rid of the smell. The mass media is very good at instilling vague feelings in people, which don't have any real underpinnings but nevertheless have strong effects on, for instance, voting.

Yanis: Do you think things will return to some kind of "normality" after Covid-19, or are we facing the end of normal?

Brian: I think we're facing the end of normal for a while, yes. I find it very difficult to imagine what the future will be like. I know what I hope for and what I fear, but the reality will likely be a mixture of the two, and more. I think the end of normal has already happened, actually. I don't think we can simply get the industries up and running again, or slip easily back into nine-to-five jobs. There are going to be so many things changed. How many business meetings, for example, are not going to happen as a result of Covid-19? How many flights? Many of these disruptions will have knock-on effects.

Yanis: Are you not worried, though, that people fall back into old habits very quickly? It's like being pulled over on the motorway for exceeding the speed limit—once you get stopped, you might drive carefully for the next twenty miles or so, but soon enough you are speeding again. In terms of Covid-19, central banks have pumped millions into the financial sector and the recovery of capitalism will be widely celebrated, but real level investment to alleviate inequalities will have plummeted, and things will return to "normal." For many of us, the 2008 financial crisis felt like a turning point in history. And it was, because capitalism in its financialized, globalized form has not since recovered. Nevertheless, most of society was lulled (in the same way they internalized a hatred of Corbyn) into accepting that the crisis has been overcome, the system is resilient. Don't you feel that, in two or three years' time, Covid-19 will be remembered in more or less the same way as 2008?

Brian: Yes, I think that is very possible, and our mission is to make sure it doesn't happen. That really is the mission, and particularly of artists. Because, among other things, artists provide material for imagining different futures. Art is a way of trying to experience what it would be like to live in a different world. And that world might be represented by something as elaborate as the works of Charles Dickens or Tolstoy, or as simple as a pop record. To make art is often to create something that gives you the chance to experience another set of values and relationships. And we've really got to be working on this now. We have a little window in which people will still remember this period, and possibly fondly. British people still remember the Blitz as though it was the most wonderful time of their lives. Why? because, for the only time in their lives, probably, they felt unified, like they really belonged to something. I think that what matters to humans more than anything else, including money, is a sense of belonging. People love that feeling and, when they don't have it, they miss it and try to satisfy it with various false sorts of belonging, buying a red sports car as a surrogate for actually being part of something real and meaningful. The Covid-19 crisis is a spectacular difference in our lives and I think that for a little while, maybe the next three to five years, people will remember this time. Artists need to find ways to express the story of this time, and what was unique, positive, and wonderful about it. We know the awful side of the story: people are dying and living in terrible situations. But we must try to remember that we can learn something from this.

Yanis: I feel what you are saying in my bones, because I grew up in a military dictatorship. I was constantly in fear of the state police breaking down the door and taking away my parents. It was not an irrational fear. It actually happened to people. The beauty of that awful military, ironclad oppression was that you could recognize the bloody enemy: they wore a uniform. Similarly, in the Blitz, which you mentioned, you could see the Stukas in the middle of the night, you knew the enemy and could see the bombs coming. The problem with neoliberal capitalism is that, unlike these examples, no one is as fault. As Marx explained, so vividly and poetically, in *Capital* volume one, you can't blame the capitalist, because the capitalist lives in fear. If he does not exploit his workers, he will go bankrupt; if he goes bankrupt, he becomes like his workers; if he becomes like his workers, his life is finished. I experienced a similar reality in the Eurogroup, where I could see that if any of those ministers who were trying to destroy the Greek people were to outwardly state that they were convinced by what I said, they would lose their jobs, immediately. I was talking to people whose salaries depended on not being convinced. Do you agree that one of neoliberalism's most intense and irreversible powers is that nobody is, in the end, at fault?

Brian: I just read an interesting essay by Douglas Rushkoff called "Survival of the Richest," in which he describes being hired to deliver a speech to a group investment bankers on the subject of "the future of technology."[2] He was paid a huge sum of money, the equivalent of half his annual salary as a university professor. Just five men, hedge fund managers and CEOs, attended the talk, and they were not interested in the future of technology. All they really wanted to know was, "How do we escape?" They felt that humans were on an inevitable trajectory toward doom and there was no future (and this was before Covid-19, by the way). They wanted to know how to escape from and protect themselves from the future. These are the same people who own ranches in Nevada and elsewhere, surrounded by huge numbers of proletarian guards. They are the wealthiest people in society, and they really don't see a future. They have given up trying to guide the course of events in any way, all they want is to protect their world, their power, and their privilege. The rest of us are going to burn in hell, for all they care. But it's kind of encouraging to me that they've given up. That means that we can take over, if we're lucky and if we're smart. We can't, after Covid-19, go through a repeat of the 2008 scenario where everything goes back to some kind of normal. We have to say, "Look, we've realized now that social services matter, that caring is what a society does for its inhabitants, and that it needs to be paid for." Now is a very good

2 https://onezero.medium.com/survival-of-the-richest-9ef6cddd0ccl.

time to start saying, "Tax havens, let's get rid of them"; it would have a lot of popular support.

Yanis: To return to the subject of art, could you elaborate, perhaps, on the possibilities for new cultural and artistic forms in a post-virus world?

Brian: Art in and for other worlds is something I think about a lot. One of the problems we encounter in talking about art is that nobody knows why it is important. We all understand why food and exercise are important, but not art, and that's partly because the people who traditionally talk and write about art are such bad thinkers. They are so unclear in the way that they think and articulate. Now, we all know that play is what children do, and it is how they learn to understand the world. They touch things, squeeze them, pretend they're other things—and nobody would say to a child, "You're wasting your time doing that." Play activities are clearly an essential set of tools for learning social and physical skills and understanding the world. At a certain point, we send children to school and say, "Now you are properly learning," as if they weren't before. Quite soon, to tell someone they're playing becomes a criticism that implies they should be working. My theory is that art is really a way of continuing to play throughout the rest of your life. It is continuing to engage in those ideas of pretending, thinking about materials in different ways, seeing how things fit together, seeing what you're excited by, and wondering why you're excited by those things. People can either play directly, which is to say by making art themselves—including through cooking, sewing, building, and many other activities—or indirectly, by experiencing other people's art, listening to music, for instance. The first thing people do once they've addressed the basic problems of staying alive is to make art: to dance, to sing, to write. Now, what is the point of all of that human activity? Why do we do this? I think we do it because the most essential thing that humans have, the only thing that makes us really different from anything else in the universe (as far as we know), is our ability to imagine: to think about and examine something that doesn't exist outside of our minds. All of us are constantly creating other worlds in our minds, and that is what makes us distinct and enables us to survive. And we need to rehearse it all the time. I think that if—in the same way that we understand the importance of food, exercise, and communication—we can start to understand the importance of this deliberate and continuous act of imagining that we call art, then we can start to take it seriously, as something essential to the ecology of our lives. This will enable us to move away from this horrible idea that the only things that are important to learn are the STEM subjects.

Yanis: My training is in mathematics, and some of the happiest moments of my life were those in which I would lose myself in mathematical play. The happiest and most productive moments, too, in the end, were when I was playing around with mathematical equations that I made up completely out of my own head. I would say, "Okay, this proposition is impossible, assume that it is not impossible: What would happen?" I would spend hours, in the middle of the night, lying on the floor with pieces of paper, and I would come up with stuff that was just nonsensical, about a world that doesn't exist. It was immensely gratifying. And it led to some ideas that later on percolated into my work, which got me jobs and made me an academic. Although these ideas were not, then, completely useless in the end, they would never have been generated if I did those play exercises *in order* to achieve something else, as a means to an end. Descartes came up with a nonsensical question which was, "What if there was a number that, when multiplied with itself, equaled minus one." Now, that number can never exist. He came up with an imaginary. Descartes himself dismissed it as a stupid idea, but then Leibniz and Euler took it and turned it into complex number theory, without which the technological revolution of the past one hundred years would not have been possible. Descartes did that for the hell of it, for play, not in order to gain something. That is a kind of art. Art and science are totally similar in the sense that they only produce great things if they are done for nothing—which is exactly the opposite of neoliberalism, which only does things in order to realize money. In a sense, therefore, doing proper art and proper science is the very definition of opposing neoliberalism.

Brian: Good!

Yanis: Now, so far, we have touched a bit on the effects of Covid-19 in the global North, for instance, in the United Kingdom, but perhaps we could turn our attention to the global South for a moment?

Brian: It's hard to make a single prediction, because different things will happen in different places, but it seems to me that as long as we still have a neoliberal structure to our economics, the third world will always suffer. Because the great triumph of neoliberalism is not so much the creation of wealth, but the concentration of it, and that process carries on unstopped and continues to accelerate. This might seem trivial in economic terms, but one thing that I think might make a difference is a shift in societal attitudes toward wealth. I think that displays of wealth will soon seem very coarse, gross, and crude, and that this shift will impact people's actions. For example, when minimalism began as an art movement about fifty years ago, it seemed quite radical in its questioning of this idea that "more is better," and that more detail and luxurious materials were better. Minimalism has now, however, translated into a broader cultural movement from its beginnings as a stylistic notion. While it takes a long time, these aesthetic shifts do eventually have societal effects. I think it does make a difference if austerity, for instance, becomes a kind of cultural value, expressed in stoicism, reduction, and parsimony.

Yanis: In the last week, there has been an exodus of money from the global South to the North in response to Covid-19. In recent decades, so-called smart money rushed into developing countries based on speculators' expectations that their economies would take off. This smart money then creates bubbles, empowers the local oligarchy, accelerates the exploitation of resources, shifts resources to the North—and then, the moment the "first world" has a crisis, all of that smart money is withdrawn, because speculators fear the devaluation of the local currencies. This withdrawal then enhances and accelerates the devaluation of the local currency, leaving nothing but smithereens behind. In the last week, an unprecedented amount of capital, unmatched since the 1970s, has left the developing world. And, of course, we don't live in a world that has any kind of international solidarity amongst those powerful enough to prevent this. As a movement, as a progressive international, we need to address this, because personal parsimony amongst us in the North is not going to provide a solution to the collapse of industries around the developing world.

Brian: No, no, of course it isn't. It won't work like that. But humans do evolve in their feelings about what constitutes appropriate kinds of behavior, and this is necessary to wider change. Our understanding of climate change is, of course, one of those evolutions. We are now aware that we are woven into the ecology of this planet, and that our previous attitude toward the climate is unsustainable and impossible: namely, that it was an infinite reservoir of resources that we could draw upon freely. These changes in our thinking do happen, and they normally start as almost aesthetic changes. In the beginning, they are hardly scientific, but grounded in a feeling that "this doesn't feel like the right way to be any longer." Now, art is what deals in feelings like that. Art is the exchanging of those feelings with other people, the communication of their universality, that actually consolidates them into ideas and actions. And that, actually, is the important part of the revolution. Alexei Yurchak wrote a book called *Everything Was Forever, Until It Was No More*, which is about the end of the Soviet Union. He wrote that up until the night before the Soviet Union collapsed, it was there and solid and eternal. The next day, suddenly, it was gone. And life went on. Things can change very quickly. The other point we can take from Yurchak is, as I recall, that there are two stages in a revolution. The first stage is when everyone realizes something is wrong. The second and important stage is when everyone realizes that everyone else realizes it as well.

Yanis: It is similar with the stock exchange, which collapses when somebody thinks that somebody else thinks that somebody else has realized that things are bad.

Brian: Yes. So, I'm kind of optimistic. If only all the billionaires would piss off to Pluto and live in their bubbles there . . .

Yanis: They keep promising, but they are failing to deliver. Instead, they will remain here and suck the blood out of every last human being. I hope that they don't colonize the rest of the galaxy, though, because I'm a *Star Trek* fan, and I want Captain Picard and Captain Kirk to be the first representatives of humanity, using the good old high-tech communist principles of star flight. Imagine if Elon Musk is the first representative of humanity in space? I prefer to die than to even think of that. So, once you are out of isolation, what will your next artwork be?

Brian: I am participating in a project at the Serpentine Gallery called "Back to Earth," which has been delayed due to Covid-19. It is an attempt to bring together people who are interested in the future design of our relationship with the planet. For my part, I attempt to make this point that many important human changes start out quite vaguely, as either aesthetic senses, or spiritual feelings. They don't usually arise from facts and figures, though, of course, those are incredibly important. What usually gets these movements going are rather vague feelings of "this doesn't feel right"—or, on the other hand, "this feels great," "this is what we'd rather be." I would like to make a place where those feelings can come together with the evidence, the science. The most important thing we have to nurture, now, is hope: hope that we can make something great and beautiful in the future. And we know what will stand in the way of that, it is obvious. What we are not so clear about is where the seeds of hope already exist. I think we should use this period of lockdown to ask, "What is beginning here?" I see little signs of it here and there. I see people starting to communicate and collaborate again, and those are green shoots. I want us to all grasp those shoots and assert, "This is the future starting here."

Conversation held on April 4, 2020

Capitalism, Covid-19, and the US Election

Jeremy Scahill and Srećko Horvat

Srećko: Hello, Jeremy, could you describe the present situation in New York?

Jeremy: I live in one of the largest immigrant communities in the city, Sunset Park, and it is being hit very hard by the virus. One of the most striking aspects of the Covid-19 crisis is the banality of the terror that it is reaping on so many particularly vulnerable communities. The death toll has skyrocketed in New York City and has already surpassed that of 9/11. Nonetheless, I live by a bus stop that is used by a lot of workers to travel to and from their places of employment, and it continues to be packed with largely nonwhite workers. In contrast, those with means are able to shelter in place. Local and family-owned grocery stores often provide masks and gloves to their workers, but the large chains, including Amazon, owned by the richest human being in the world, have some atrocious practices. In fact, in Staten Island, a young warehouse worker named Chris Smalls, an African American father of three, started organizing because he was concerned that the company was not taking the outbreak of Covid-19 at his workplace seriously. They forced him into quarantine, but did not quarantine other workers on the same grounds. Then, he successfully organized a walk-out of the workers and was fired by Amazon in response. In recent days, notes were leaked from a meeting attended by Jeff Bezos himself and high-powered lawyers, including a major fundraiser for Joe Biden, where they discussed how to smear this young African American worker and make an example of him in order to destroy organized union activity among Amazon workers.[1] To me, this encapsulates what has happened in this country in the midst of this pandemic; namely, that we have immediately reverted to an all-out feudalist system where the richest and most powerful will be taken care of and the poorest and most vulnerable are lucky to get a few crumbs off their tables. Let's be clear: they want you to die. They want you to work, and if you can't, they want you to die. At a time of crisis with ten million people applying for unemployment in the last two weeks, and more than three million people losing their healthcare

---

1 https://www.vice.com/en_us/article/5dm8bx/leaked-amazon-memo-details-plan-to-smear-fired-warehouse-organizer-hes-not-smart-or-articulate.

because it is tied to their employment, we have a sociopath as president and a spineless opposition that refuses to fight for free healthcare for all.

Srećko: In Europe, by contrast, most countries introduced measures swiftly and have universal healthcare. I come from Croatia, formerly part of socialist Yugoslavia, which still has a more or less functioning healthcare system that is free to all. I am currently in Vienna where I have been in isolation for twenty days already, and public events were banned two weeks ago. From a European perspective what is happening in the United States is really horrifying. A month ago, an Iranian minister said that Covid-19 is a "democratic virus," in the sense that it doesn't discriminate between rich and poor. I think this is ideology at its purest because, as you described, the virus is hitting those who don't have a choice but to work the hardest. Shop assistants, delivery drivers, mail workers, and waste collectors are highly vulnerable. How do you see the situation in the United States developing further with this sociopath in power who won't even wear a mask?

Jeremy: It's important to remember that Donald Trump lost the popular vote in the United States by three million to Hillary Clinton. Trump ran on a fascistic platform and mobilized a large sector of society that generally do not vote comprised of racist, bigoted individuals. This was akin to how Ronald Reagan mobilized evangelical Christians to vote in the 1980s, who, again, were traditionally nonvoting. Trump thrives on the notion that people want leaders who are dumber than they are, these cartoonish characters. Obama, arguably one of the most intelligent individuals to ever hold office, was absolutely despised by large sectors of Trump's base and not because he was a Kenyan Muslim socialist, but because he was smart and he happened to be Black. In terms of the supposed "democracy" of Covid-19, I grew up in a in a city called Milwaukee, where African Americans comprise 26 percent of the population, yet they account for 80 percent of Covid-19 deaths. The virus doesn't discriminate in terms of who is infected, but our system does. Capitalism is a death sentence that is being meted out against the poorest and most vulnerable populations in the United States, especially those who are not white.

Srećko: I'm hoping you can help me to understand the fact that recent polls show that Trump is actually rising in popularity.[2] Do you think that those who voted for Trump will vote for him again in the upcoming elections, given his handling of the Covid-19 outbreak?

Jeremy: First of all, I want to clarify that I don't think everyone who voted for Donald Trump is an ignorant, backward asshole. Obama voters and people supportive of Democratic candidates voted for Trump and he appealed particularly to suburban white women, such that 53 percent of white women in the US voted for him. He also appealed to people who were hurt by Democratic Party policies on trade like NAFTA or World Trade Organization dictates. As for the current uptick in Trump's support in response to his handling of Covid-19, America is a peculiar country in many ways and one particular form of American exceptionalism dictates that you have to rally around the commander in chief at a time of crisis, even if that means checking your conscience at the door. In terms of the upcoming election, Joe Biden, the likely Democratic nominee for president, has a forty-year track record of terrible policies; has been accused of inappropriate conduct by eight women; is often unaware of what room he's in; cannot speak clearly unless he has notes in front of him; has repeatedly lied about his role in the civil rights movement; and there are questions about nepotistic exploitation that led to his son, Hunter Biden, working for a Ukrainian oil interest, Burisma. Donald Trump is going to fillet Joe Biden if they actually have a debate. It is as though the Democratic Party wants Donald Trump to rule for another four years. The ridicule the Democrats reserve for supporters of Bernie Sanders is much more passionate than the war on Donald Trump in some quarters. This may seem confusing for people in Europe, but the US is the only country that I know of to have had large demonstrations against healthcare!

Srećko: There are similarities in Europe and particularly in the UK elections in December 2019, where it was very evident that the establishment hates the social democrats and the left more than it hates populists and autocrats.

---

2 https://news.gallup.com/poll/298313/president-trump-job-approval-rating.aspx.

Members of Corbyn's own party hated him and tried to thwart him.[3] Yet, compared to what is needed today, Corbyn's program was moderate. In terms of Bernie Sanders, what do you think his chances are now? Will Donald Trump postpone the elections if the crisis continues? Will the Democratic Party realize that Medicare for all is the only solution to saving lives?

Jeremy: I don't think it is impossible, yet, for Bernie Sanders to become the Democratic nominee. I think it is important to analyze the mistakes Sanders made in his campaign, as the media is doing, but this shouldn't take place at the expense of analyzing the wider consequences of *not* running someone like Bernie Sanders as the Democratic candidate. To attempt to close the debate by pointing out that Biden beat Sanders in South Carolina and on Super Tuesday, ignores, first of all, the fact that Sanders won the state of California, where one in ten Americans live, and, second, the role of the institutional elites within the Democratic Party, the behind-the-scenes role of Obama in trying to force other corporate candidates to drop out, and the role of corporate media outlets. Even the so-called liberal television network in the United States, NBC, streamed one-note propaganda trying to destroy Bernie Sanders. Michael Bloomberg, one of the wealthiest people in the world, spent hundreds and hundreds of millions of dollars mostly on ads aimed at undermining Sanders. Yes, Biden won a number of primaries and has a sizable lead at the moment, but about 50 percent of Americans haven't yet had a chance to vote in the primaries. Why is it that the most powerful Republicans and Biden, as the presumptive nominee of the Democratic Party, are both currently advocating the continuation of in-person voting during the Covid-19 pandemic, effectively pursuing a reckless disenfranchisement of voters that could kill people?

Srećko: Yes, the choice between Donald Trump and Joe Biden seems like a choice between Ebola and SARS.

---

3 https://www.independent.co.uk/news/uk/politics/labour-leak-report-corbyn-election-whatsapp-antisemitism-tories-yougov-poll-a9462456.html.

Jeremy: I think that there is validity to that mentality, given that we have a corporate-controlled duopoly in this country and the Democratic and Republican parties do everything in their power to prevent third parties from entering debates or getting on the ballot. When it boils down to a choice between Donald Trump and candidates like Hillary Clinton or Joe Biden, you can make a reasonable case for making a harm reduction vote, choosing the least damaging option to try and stop Trump from further consolidating his fascism. We are in a code red emergency and it will be women, immigrants, and people of color who will suffer the results of another four years of Trump. By way of illustration, Joe Biden's top health adviser, Ron Klain, is a long-time Democratic Party lawyer and legitimate expert on public policy at a time of pandemic who led the Obama–Biden response to the Ebola crisis. When you compare him to Jared Kushner or Mike Pence, who literally believes that Adam and Eve were alive at the time of the dinosaurs, there is no comparison. Voting for harm reduction is a legitimate approach, but it shouldn't come at the expense of demanding that we fundamentally dismantle the system that creates the reality where our choice is restricted to Joe Biden or Donald Trump.

Srećko: What worries me are not just the immediate effects of the Covid-19 crisis but the roll-on effects. The pandemic will continue for many months, if not years, and beyond the hundreds of thousands of people who will die now, many more will die because of the forecasted recession. After 9/11, Bush used the "war on terror" to sweep away many civil liberties and implemented a total surveillance later revealed by Edward Snowden and others. We are now in the beginnings of a "war on virus," with a lot of the rhetoric used by politicians being similar to that of 9/11. The measures implemented in these "states of exception" typically remain in place long after the perceived danger has receded. In Austria, a democratic country, the technology sector and the state are cooperating to implement geolocation tracking of people and I fear the potentially repressive results of this becoming permanent. How do you see this developing further if Donald Trump uses Covid-19 as his 9/11?

Jeremy: I've been starting to call it "Covid-1984" because of the domination by corporations of social and political life. We are living a corporate feudalism of the kind Martin Luther King talked about: socialism for the rich and rugged individualism for everyone else. This was evident a few days ago in the US, when not a single member of either party or either house of our Congress voted against the most consequential corporate bailout in the history of this country.[4] Not a single one—not Bernie Sanders, not Elizabeth Warren. Why did this happen? It happened because Donald Trump controls the White House; our Supreme Court is stacked with right-wing judges; and the US Senate, a white supremacist relic of a previous era, is controlled by one of the vilest human beings to ever serve as a lawmaker in the US, Mitch McConnell. Essentially, the Republican Party and some corporate Democrats used poor, sick, and working people in this country as hostages in an effort to free billions upon billions of dollars to give to corporations in return for very minimal aid in the form of one-off $1,200 checks for the millions of people who can't pay their rents. One Republican, Thomas Massie, demanded a recorded vote, in order to hear all 450-odd members of the House of Representatives vote on this hugely consequential bailout bill, and the Republican and Democratic leaderships conspired to make sure it did not happen. After 9/11, there was just one member of Congress, an African American lawmaker named Barbara Lee, who voted against the "forever war" authorization.[5] She received death threats and had to have security because of it. She was right. We had one US senator, Russ Feingold of Wisconsin, who voted against the Patriot Act, and he too got death threats. He was right. This time, we have nobody.

Srećko: Europe is not much better. We don't have transparency when it comes to voting, there is nothing on record. DiEM25 recently released the so-called Euroleaks showing what the Eurogroup was doing during the Greek crisis and the ways decisions were made by bodies which are not

---

4   https://theintercept.com/2020/04/09/coronavirus-stimulus-package-congress-vote/.

5   https://theintercept.com/2016/09/11/barbara-lees-lone-vote-on-sept-14-2001-was-as-prescient-as-it-was-brave-and-heroic/.

even constitutional.[6] How probable is it, do you think, that the Covid-19 pandemic will incentivize the US to make systemic changes?

Jeremy: In the US, one thing that corporations and the right wing have PhDs in is exploiting crises to alter society for the worse. The corporate bailout just authorized in the United States will be one of the greatest transfers of wealth from the federal budget (ultimately, from taxpayers) to the private sector. And Trump issued a signed statement that almost completely nullifies the ability of Congress to oversee how that money is used and what restrictions will be placed on it. Yet ordinary workers are subject to means-tested aid, where their earnings and tax returns are scrutinized before they can receive a mere $1,200 check.[7] The elite is way ahead of us and is already restructuring society. When we are told that our demands for universal healthcare are unrealistic, we must remember that, as Frederick Douglass said, power concedes nothing without a demand. What the Democrats ask us to believe is that power concedes nothing unless the people concede everything beforehand! This society will be radically transformed for the worse unless people unify and force those in power out or, at least, to make concessions. Trump occasionally comes out with surprising statements that we should seize upon. For instance, when he realized that 30 percent of people may not have health insurance as a result of Covid-19, his response was to suggest expanding Medicare.[8] We should demand he follows through.

Srećko: What do you think of Yanis Varoufakis's recent idea of supporting Amazon striking workers by organizing a one-day international consumer boycott of the Amazon website?

Jeremy: I love the idea of a one-day boycott. However, if we were to pursue a longer term boycott or a dismantling of Amazon, we would need to be aware that many people, including many poor families and elderly people, rely on

6 https://euroleaks.diem25.org/.

7 https://www.cnbc.com/2020/03/25/coronavirus-stimulus-bill-updates-whats-in-the-2-trillion-relief-plan.html.

8 https://www.businessinsider.com/coronavirus-trump-says-he-might-help-millions-of-uninsured-americans-2020-4?r=US&IR=T.

Amazon for basic goods, especially during crises, and would suffer if it was abruptly taken away. It has become a monopoly so we would need to tread carefully and offer alternatives for the vulnerable. We should be careful not to shame those we claim to support or represent. I think Amazon should be determined as a public utility and be nationalized. I would also like to see, coming out of this crisis, the building of networks of small shops, farmers, and producers that can present viable alternatives to the monopoly.

Srećko: After a crisis, or at the moment of crisis, we can also see "resilience," although I don't really like that term. In the financial crisis of 2008, people in Greece set about establishing alternative markets, in part in response to the potato crisis, where the producers avoided supermarkets and middle-men and sold their products directly to consumers. As well as being more ethical and fairer to both consumers and producers, it creates a much more sustainable model. My question is, in the face of monopoly capitalism, how do we scale such efforts up?

Jeremy: Part of it requires understanding how this functions on a global scale. Cuba, an island of eleven million people, has been under a ferocious US economic blockade for almost its entire postrevolutionary history from 1959 [to] 1960. And one of Cuba's chief crimes at the beginning of the revolutionary period was aiming to try to achieve self-sufficiency through the exporting of sugar cane. Any time you see governments rising up and trying to shift from a cash-crop economy to sustainable agriculture, the United States tries to break it up. It's not, therefore, sufficient for us to organize locally in our communities. We need to think about what it means to break the constraints of borders in our minds and view our lives as linked to that of a rural farmer in France, or a factory worker in China. History has been written by people who dare to think outside of the parameters defined by those in power and the rich, but with the ascent of the internet-era corporate power has become more effective in limiting debate to particular parameters than we have been in breaking them. I believe in the cliché adage to think globally and act locally, but we also need to act globally, and the internet is a two-edged sword in this regard.

Srećko: You mentioned the Cuban Revolution. About eight years ago, I met Aleida Guevara, Ernesto (Che) Guevara's eldest daughter, in Zagreb. She is a doctor and she was asking us whether we could help her to find some medicine to bring back to Cuba. Why? Because of the US sanctions. In the present crisis, the Cuban doctors have been exemplary in acting in solidarity with other countries and volunteering abroad to fight the virus. But, instead of the US helping these doctors to help the world, they continue to impose sanctions on Cuba.

Jeremy: Similarly, in the United States there is the most vicious propaganda spouted against Iran by both Democrats and Republicans. But, like Cuba, the "evil" Iranian regime is doing the right thing when it comes to fighting Covid-19. Iran has released more than 100,000 prisoners since the outbreak of the virus, while in New York City there are now more than two hundred cases of Covid-19 at Rikers Island alone.[9] There are dozens of prison guards who are infected. At the same time, the state of New York just passed one of the most racist budget bills in recent history that will cut certain people's healthcare and make it easier to put people in prison.[10]

Srećko: Thank you, Jeremy, for raising the situation of prisoners in the present crisis. Today, the UK government said it would release 4,000 prisoners due to their vulnerability to Covid-19, which is already spreading throughout the prisons.[11] However, it is refusing to release Julian Assange into house arrest, a person who committed no crime and, since 2002, has had a chronic lung condition.[12] The UK and US governments are leaving him to die in a cage. Assange of course not only revealed the crimes of the United States,

9 https://uk.reuters.com/article/uk-health-coronavirus-iran-toll/iran-extends-prison-furloughs-as-coronavirus-death-toll-rises-idUKKBN21G0CC and https://www.theguardian.com/us-news/2020/apr/01/rikers-island-jail-coronavirus-public-health-disaster.

10 https://theintercept.com/2020/04/03/andrew-cuomo-coronavirus-bail-criminal-justice/.

11 https://www.theguardian.com/society/2020/apr/04/up-to-4000-inmates-to-be-temporarily-released-in-england-and-wales.

12 https://uk.reuters.com/article/uk-health-coronavirus-britain-assange/wikileaks-founder-julian-assange-denied-bail-by-london-court-idUKKBN21C26G.

but also released valuable information on Ebola, SARS, and the avian flu on WikiLeaks. We need an Assange today.

Jeremy: Assange should have never been placed in prison and the charges against him in the United States are some of the most far-reaching and dangerous legal assertions ever made on the question of press freedom. Assange provided a public service to the citizens of the United States and the world in helping to create WikiLeaks and by publishing documents that demonstrated in clear, raw form the crimes that the United States government commits around the world. The only reason that Assange is in prison right now is because the United States wants him dead. None of the criticisms people can level at Julian Assange justify the horrid human rights–abusing treatment that he continues to receive. If he dies, his blood is on the hands of the United States government.

Conversation held on April 4, 2020

Tech in the Time of a Pandemic

Evgeny Morozov and Renata Ávila

Renata: We are now one hundred days into the Covid-19 crisis, which has tremendously shifted the discourse on technology and its possibilities. I have the pleasure to exchange ideas with a much-needed voice at this time, tech critic Evgeny Morozov.

Evgeny: I have been in Rome, close to the epicenter of the virus, for the past five weeks now. I've had some time to reflect upon some of the structural changes occurring in global capitalism, and on the behavior of technology firms, which has been instructive, though not particularly surprising. First off, let me warn you that I'm less sanguine about this crisis signifying the end of capitalism, or the onset of a new era driven by solidarity, than many other thinkers on the left, who I think have taken a rather optimistic, at times naïve, reading of the predicaments. Though I am an optimist, I want to urge a more cautious approach and bring some more complexity to the ongoing discussions about what the present situation means for democracy and for progressive movements that are trying to chart their own paths on it. On the other hand, I equally don't subscribe to this quite cliché framing that is popular at the moment that posits the Covid-19 pandemic as marking the onset of a new techno-totalitarianism, where we are entering the future Orwell predicted and our privacy will be destroyed. This way of thinking about democracy inherently falls into these clichés and ways of thinking that we inherited from the Cold War. There are different and more complex ways to think about what this privatization of politics by means of technology means for democracy. The reason why I'm more sanguine than some others about this heralding the end of capitalism is quite simple. While I agree that neoliberalism as an ideology is now morally and intellectually bankrupt, capitalism as such does not survive and advance solely on neoliberalism. In an article I've just written for the *Guardian*, I argue that neoliberalism is essentially the "bad cop" of contemporary capitalism, but there is also a "good cop" and that is the ideology of solutionism.[1] Neoliberalism and its attempts to spread entrepreneurship and innovation around the globe causes a lot of havoc, and solutionism

---

1 https://www.theguardian.com/commentisfree/2020/apr/15/tech-coronavirus-surveilance-state-digital-disrupt.

presents a universal Band-Aid to this. It offers seemingly cosmopolitan and humanitarian solutions to clean up the mess left by neoliberalism—and implements them cleanly and at a happy profit. The existence and activities of this better, well-intentioned cop will only be amplified significantly with and beyond the present crisis. Regardless of how privacy-secure and privacy-aware many of the new technologies that will be rolled out might be, the increased mediation and privatization of public life and political activities by a set of private firms is quite dangerous, and this is because neoliberalism has a quite particular blueprint that it seeks to implement. This blueprint is to essentially prevent spontaneous social coordination among people from taking place, because the function of coordination in society belongs to the market. The blueprint of neoliberalism is quite clear, and we know what to expect, but the goal of solutionism, the sibling of the neoliberal project, is quite distinct. The goal of solutionism is not to promote a particular blueprint, but to disable the blueprints of others. Importantly, where neoliberalism privatizes our infrastructures and technologies, solutionism privatizes politics; where neoliberalism controls and shrinks our budgets, solutionism shrinks our imaginations and the space available for alternative action plans. My fear is that, when we look back on this crisis five, ten, or fifteen years from now, we will see the present crisis as a defining moment when the public surrendered its capacity to engage in acts of collective world-making and gave in to the neoliberal project, aided by its solutionist friends in Silicon Valley. This is not a typical reading of the situation. I think that much of the debate at the moment remains dominated by frameworks that we have inherited from the past, where we like to imagine a Big Brother watching us, that there is manipulation of our minds by fake news fed to us by governments. These are real problems, but we also need to reflect on the longer-term effects of this kind of thinking—what it means for collective action and for the social imaginary that allows us to imagine alternative worlds. The services of Amazon, Palantir, Google, and Apple have become almost inalienable parts and the default background condition of public life as such. We saw this recently in the United Kingdom where, as the pandemic began to rapidly worsen, Boris Johnson called upon the tech industry to step up and play the savior role. If it is true that these industry giants have managed to establish themselves as the gatekeepers of public life, and of fundamental aspects of it like healthcare and education, this suggests that they are not only "too big to fail," in the sense that Wall Street is, but that it's impossible to imagine a world without them. That's, I think, the point we are at.

Renata: In the last hundred days, states around the world have failed totally to gain control of the pandemic and we have seen companies stepping in to assist them. On the one hand, many are saying that everybody is now realizing the importance of the state and state intervention in crises, but, on the other, most of the key infrastructure necessary to sustaining human life is mediated by tech companies that are concentrated mainly in two countries. If the state is so dependent on big technology companies concentrated in such few jurisdictions, how can we even think of a different future?

Evgeny: I tend to take a historical reading of this incapacity of the state that is currently being highlighted. It's not an essential feature of public bureaucracies that they are inefficient, malfunctioning, or corrupt, but a consequence of numerous historical factors. In the last few decades, these factors were connected to the neoliberal agenda and the reconfiguration of the state to function in ways akin to a company or firm, where bureaucrats were reimagined as entrepreneurs and engaged in ransacking corporations. In much of the Global South—again, for historical reasons tied to colonialism and imperialism—the neoliberal agenda was to attempt to bypass the emergence of autonomous and sovereign state entities and replace them with a kind of quasi-algorithmic entity that would just respond to external incentives provided by the World Bank and IMF. In such conditions, where there was very little opportunity for the state to become a well-functioning entity geared to work in the public interest, it's not particularly surprising that states are now not functioning and are unable to deal with the challenge of the pandemic. This is where the "good cop" of solutionism and the "bad cop" of neoliberalism split and pretend that they're not part of the same story. The solutionists say, "If you just run your infrastructure from Amazon Web Services, put AI into every public agency, or hire the services of Palantir, you can turn your country into Denmark." Their message is that you can have a very well-functioning bureaucratic system, you just need to buy it as a service. We are confronted with a very interesting dialectic at the moment. On the one hand, many on the left have fears about an omnipotent state that is capable of monitoring communication, surveying everything, and taking full advantage of modern communications in order to constrain the liberties of people. However, there are also fears about a completely incompetent state that is not able to even manage the infrastructures necessary to implement contact tracing, for example, in order to tackle Covid-19. In that case, the solutionist temptation is even greater: Surely you would rather have Apple or Google run these systems than a malfunctioning, decrepit state that has been paralyzed by decades of neoliberalism? It's not a very easy position to argue against, because to do so is to ask people to accept the need to resist the pressure of the efficient giants of Silicon Valley and, at the same time, to expect them to hope that, somehow, states which have failed to reform themselves for decades will rise to the challenge. It is complicated, and this is why we have to resist an ahistorical framing of the situation that presents states only as bandits interested in ransacking and not as prisoners and hostages of global neoliberal capitalism.

Renata: You also have a third way of approaching the situation, which is squeezed between monopoly tech companies and the neoliberal state, and that is social innovation. We can see this, for instance, in the ventilator parts being made by 3D-printer enthusiasts from their homes. There are communities of active citizens who are trying to create meaningful change through technology, innovation, and collaboration. However, this particular effort was squashed by the system, with the "makers" receiving legal threats and the tech companies jumping in with patent infringement claims.[2] I am interested to hear your view on these obstacles to the abilities of citizens to organize.

Evgeny: It relates, to some extent, to my earlier point that solutionism exists to disable alternative blueprints of organizing society. The initial neoliberal agenda of spreading markets and commodification, as well

2   https://www.theverge.com/2020/3/17/21184308/coronavirus-italy-medical-
    3dprint-valves-treatments.

as preventing nonmarket modes and methods of social coordination, became much easier with the fall of the Soviet Union because there was no longer a viable communist enemy. From the early '90s onward, it was clear that we would have a liberalism on steroids and this is why, for instance, Francis Fukuyama wrote about the "end of history" and there is a lot of commentary from that time about globalization and digitalization working together to spread markets and democracy around the world. What has happened, though, is that digital technologies, while they do not *naturally* favor social coordination or collaboration, can at least make it easier for us to imagine an alternative future where production is completely automated and decentralized, where digital technologies support universal education and healthcare systems. This, of course, is a much more appealing picture than the current dystopia of mass death. However, this is precisely where the ideology of solutionism kicks in to try and disable the deployment of the radical potential of technological infrastructures for the sake of a social transformation that might distance or remove us from the market economy as the central and essential coordinating mechanism of social relations. The whole point of solutionism is to convince us that the disruption of everything on the periphery is worthwhile so that we can keep the central institution of modern society, the market, completely intact and unchanging. Solutionism is an ideology of common sense that buys legitimacy through the neoliberal project. We have to contend with this and understand how our pragmatic, practical decisions intersect with it. In crisis situations like the one we are currently experiencing, everybody wants solutions and fast, and this is highly conducive to the emergence, intensification, and solidification of paradigms that, in retrospect, we would have never accepted.

Renata: It is also a matter of rights. There is often a rapid erosion of people's rights for the sake of a solution that is needed, especially when combined with widespread fear, state incompetence, and general chaos. Here I am thinking of contact tracing and all the surveillance technologies that have been deployed with very little questioning and broad acceptance as ways to manage Covid-19. Would you be able to speak on this?

Evgeny: Abstracting from the ways in which it is technologically implemented, I do not have much of a problem with contact tracing. Done right and done correctly, the idea makes sense. Of course, we have already seen that contract tracing can be implemented in a punitive way. East Asian countries, especially, for various political reasons, have chosen a highly punitive version of it that is not entirely optional and is very intrusive. From this, it is possible to speculate on less permissive implementations of the technology where, for instance, contract tracing is joined with predictive analytics that will then determine whether a person can enter a particular part of the city, or receive certain services, based on probabilistic evaluations of how likely they are to be sick. That has all sorts of implications and we have seen some of them realized in China. Looking at it more abstractly, however, what interests me more is how we have arrived at a situation where Google and Apple have quite explicitly co-opted the work of European privacy researchers, and our inability to encourage other institutions in society to act upon those ideas. As long as the infrastructure with which we can act remains in the control of just a handful of corporate players, they will likely be able to act upon it quicker than others, simply by virtue of having all the resources and expertise. The key lesson to learn from this is not that we should fear Google or Apple, but rather to think about why we have not managed, in democratic societies in Europe, to encourage others to do something with these insights that have been present for quite some time. Where are those encouragements? Where are the methods of social coordination that could enable us to build truly bottom-up implementations with the funding, scale, and robust public policy that are needed? We no longer expect anything innovative to come out of actors other than technology companies. We need to reflect upon the noncorporate actors and the kinds of schemes we'd like to have in our broader ecosystem so that alternative forms of social coordination between hackers, activists, citizen groups, neighbors, hospitals, and universities can come to the surface faster, with much more effort and support, and not just die off as prototypes.

Renata: The support has to come from somewhere, but the areas of the world with resources and opportunities, such as Europe, are also highly colonized by technology. There is increasing mediation of the political activities of

European citizens by Silicon Valley. What would be a compelling argument that we can make for politicians to seize the present moment as an opportunity to reposition Europe and take back control of key infrastructures?

Evgeny: The task is clearly a political task and there are concrete steps of realizing it, but before we get to them, it's very important to understand what it is that we'd like to argue. A lot of movements on the left have not entirely recovered from the knockdown they received when communism fell apart. We have not yet found the right ways to articulate the argument for a different technological universe and have instead learned to speak the language of rights. We can easily find faults with digital infrastructures and say that they're not compliant with the GDPR right to be forgotten, or socioeconomic rights in general. That may achieve something, but it does not answer the pragmatic question that anyone who has money to invest would ask you, which is, "But do these technologies pay off?" We have to show, document, and argue that pulling people together, equipped with powerful digital technologies, and enabling ways of collaboration across them are good not just because people will feel less alienated in contemporary society, but because it will result in immense social innovation and discovery of new ideas, practices, and techniques of production. If we can make that argument at the abstract, theoretical level, we can address the great theoretical challenge that neoliberal thinkers like Friedrich Hayek, for example, have traditionally put to leftist, socialist governments. Their own arguments, shaped by the binaries of the Cold War, conceived of only two paradigms: centrally planned economies of the Soviet Union kind, where everything is planned by central planners and there is very little discovery of new knowledge, or the fully neoliberal economies of the Global North, where the more deregulation there is, the more entrepreneurship is unleashed, and entrepreneurs and consumers, in a strange dance with each other, discover new things, new tastes and ways to satisfy them, and new ways to produce more cheaply than competitors. We need to more coherently articulate a paradigm that will transcend this binary and show that solidarity can be good for collaboration as well as production and innovation. We need to start building infrastructures that can harness that value, package and integrate it, and make it available to the wider public. In the absence of concrete projects that can show us how social coordination unleashed from commercial incentives of competition can produce tangible value that can make us buy things and produce things at a very trivial level, it will be very hard to convince anybody that we need a different way of doing things. We need to radically change the paradigm and demonstrate that if we let Google, Amazon, Apple, and Microsoft continue to dominate technology, not only do we potentially lose the opportunities of harnessing all of the genius knowledge that people are producing, but we are also entailing huge costs. And unless we manage to calculate what those costs are—the kinds of futures being disabled and the kinds of resources that cannot materialize because tech giants control the infrastructure—we will not be able to make a cogent argument.

Renata: You wrote a piece calling to "Socialize the Data Centers" for *New Left Review* in 2015.[3] We are currently in a dangerous position where pharmaceutical companies want data on our health and social interactions, and tech companies want that data as well. Is this the moment for pushing the idea of socializing at least the health data?

Evgeny: On a very specific, tangible level, of course we have to be making political claims about the immense value residing in the data and companies leveraging that data for their own good. We should not pretend that data is some kind of a gift that these companies take from nature. They grab it from us as a result of very specific, extractive, and artificial practices and hijacking our attention. Beyond this, we have to understand the danger of grabbing all the data for an alternative political project and then realizing that the other parts of the stack that we need to use and make sense of that data just do not exist. The idea of "socializing the data centers" made for a good slogan that I and others have flirted with, but it downplays the degree of the struggles to come. Unless we manage to build infrastructures of artificial intelligence, cloud computing, predictive analytics, and machine learning that can actually process that data, it will be largely useless. Socializing the data centers needs to be part of a more holistic project

3 https://newleftreview.org/II/91/evgeny-morozov-socialize-the-data-centres.

of digital socialism that looks more broadly at feedback infrastructure, as I wrote in a follow-up article for *New Left Review* in 2019.[4]

Renata: In terms of the algorithms that shape our priorities and perceptions of situations unfolding, Google recently made a very generous donation of $100 million toward the Covid-19 effort, but the majority went to ad placements. These tech companies collaborate with governments and other organizations to place particular information at the center of our attention and have huge influence on public perception. At the moment, of course, access to accurate information can be the difference between life and death. Could you speak on this and explain what you are doing with the Syllabus project to address this?

Evgeny: First of all, individual companies largely behave quite rationally and follow the imperatives of the system, and to blame them for doing so can be counterproductive. We need to shift to a higher, more abstract level of critique and try to understand how those imperatives are constructed. Platforms like Google, Facebook, Twitter, and YouTube have very particular economics of knowledge discovery and knowledge distribution built into them. Institutions around the globe—art galleries, think tanks, universities, libraries—produce a lot of videos related to the events that they hold, and they upload these to YouTube. There is a vast repository of information on YouTube and a little bit of this is high-quality information. None of those videos tend to make it into the most highly recommended and suggested videos by the YouTube algorithm, and most of them never get discovered. This is not because high-quality content doesn't exist but because our public sphere, tied to online advertising as its driving imperative, does not create new incentives for the discovery of such content. About a year ago, I founded an initiative called the Syllabus, which tries to break the economics of how high-quality information gets discovered and distributed online. We go after sixty relatively high-brow and important topics, from human rights, neoliberalism, and work, to artificial intelligence and climate change, and try to systematically find the most

4 https://newleftreview.org/issues/II116/articles/evgeny-morozov-digital-socialism.

relevant, recent, and interesting content to package and distribute to our subscribers. The idea is that, while we cannot compete with YouTube—which milks users for data and trades on it to sell advertising—we can show that a very different arrangement of information is possible. You don't need to end up in in a black hole of trivial content every time you start your browser—that's not a gravity force of the digital economy, but only of the form of digital economy that is tied to advertising. It's a scandal that there is no library or university model, and no tax-funded model, for people who would like to build a different digital economy to get access to those resources and infrastructures. The idea that we are living in the most innovative economy imaginable is simply a lie; rather than the peak of innovation, this might actually be the bottom.

Renata: For this, we need politics. Unfortunately, our political system is behaving like Google's algorithm, giving us the most sensationalistic politicians who are terrible but attract a lot of attention and distraction. There needs to be a break with the current forms of privatized politics. What plan of action would you recommend?

Evgeny: What I find missing, not in specific movements, but in the general left, progressive forces, is a raison d'être—what are they here to do? They focus on reducing inequality, tackling climate change, ridding us of surveillance, or restoring privacy, which are all reactionary moves against problems caused by decades of neoliberalism. I don't believe that this reactive program suffices for the left to win; we need a proactive program. I would argue that this proactive program has to involve the empowerment of the citizen and (reasonably) of institutions, and of citizens vis-à-vis each other. This can only happen if we put digital technologists at the heart of the transformation. Digital technologies allow us—and maybe the quarantines enforced for Covid-19 will prove this—to relate to each other in ways that are very different to those present when, for instance, people worked largely in factories. We have to reexamine our political life with the centrality of mediation by digital technologies, but *not* by digital platforms, but right at its center. If we start from the assumption that everything is digital and there is metadata about everything, then what kind of institutions of solidarity would we build? For me, the goal is not to invent a hundred ways through which we can defend the public health-care system or the public education system. Such efforts have my respect, but they cannot define the horizon of possibility for the progressive pro-ject. It also has to invent new institutions of solidarity and collaboration.

Conversation held on April 11, 2020

Capitalism Depresses the Soul, Not Just the Economy

Johann Hari and Yanis Varoufakis

Yanis: Covid-19 has turned our lives inside out and upside down. It has put capitalism in suspended animation, destroyed lives, caused a new tsunami of poverty, and demonstrated huge class and race divides, with some of us privileged enough to be in splendid isolation, while an army of garbage collectors, hospital workers, farmers, and others labor for a pittance and at risk of infection to cater to our needs. As always, there are silver linings. The planet is breathing more easily now that we humans emit fewer poisonous gases, and everyone has recognized, after decades of neoliberal sermons, that government is, and ought to be, instrumental in safeguarding our lives and our capacity to reproduce our lives. Politics has become more real and more interesting, liberated from the media's portrayal of politics as some kind of sport in which parties score points against each other in search of winning the electoral championship. Now, under lockdown, with governments flexing gigantic muscles that had atrophied for so long, the truth about politics emerges. Do you know what politics is all about, in the end? It is not about who wins elections but about who does what to whom. That is what politics always was, and now we can see this clearly courtesy of a mindless piece of RNA, a virus. Of course, these silver linings will mean precisely nothing unless progressives do this time what bankers and racists did after the last capitalist implosion back in 2008—that is, cooperate transnationally. Will we allow them, the masters of finance and the nationalist international, to emerge yet again triumphant once the pandemic recedes? Or will we succeed this time, against the odds, to change the world instead of keeping on interpreting it? Before we can even begin to coordinate, so as not to let this terrible crisis go to waste, we need a vision of how we would like the world to be. The oligarchs, the beneficiaries of our current irrational system, don't need a vision. All they want to do is to freeze things as they are, to ensure that nothing changes, and that the status quo is preserved for their benefit, even if this means the end of the world. What is our vision? What realistic utopia should we work toward, so as to avoid the dystopia awaiting if we fail? This question has been on my mind for some time, well before the pandemic. Ever since we met, my partner has been encouraging me to write my vision for a postcapitalist, rational, humanist world. The truth is, I had no clue where to begin, so I made excellent excuses. I told

her that no human brain has sufficient processing power, or the information necessary, to imagine an alternative world. I would say to her—going
back to Marx—that it is history which creates new modes of production,
distribution, and exchange; it's not the imagination of some feeble human
mind. But I must admit that, deep down, I knew those to be near excuses.
The real reason I did not attempt to put on paper a realistic vision of another
society, another now, was that it was too hard. Then something changed. A
couple of years ago, my book *Talking to My Daughter About the Economy* was
published. With it, I tried to convey to folks young and old how I understood life under contemporary capitalism. The book did very well and got
many reviews—one of which hit a nerve. It was written by Ireland's finance
minister, a gentleman with whom I have huge ideological, analytical, and
political differences. His review, I have to say, was incredibly generous in
that he endorsed my description of how money and banking works. His
criticism was, however, even more useful to me. In effect what he said was,
"Okay, Mr. Varoufakis, let's agree that capitalism is problematic—what is
the alternative? And, if there is an alternative, are we not running a huge
risk that, like in the past, the attempt to build a postcapitalist utopia will
lead to something far worse?" The Irish finance minister's question was the
jolt I needed to realize that my partner was right all along. Analyzing our
capitalist now, and agitating against it, is just not enough. Without a vision
of a realistic other now, we risk creating a new social order that is worse
than what we have. So, when my publisher asked what my next book was
going to be, I answered that I wanted to have a crack at penning a vision of a
realistic utopia. And I chose to approach it through the medium of political
science fiction. The result was a novel-like narrative with three characters in
which I placed many people that I have met and who have influenced me in
the past. These three characters accidentally discover another now. The idea
was that time's arrow bifurcated in 2008 due to the severity of the capitalist implosion, the crash of Wall Street, the City of London, and the banking
system generally. There was one trajectory, which is the one we experienced
and live in now, in which financialized capitalism reinforced itself courtesy
of the 2009 bailouts, but, to their astonishment, my characters discover in
2025 that there is another trajectory, another now, a second vector which

began with the crash of 2008 and evolved very differently. In effect, by 2013 in the other now, capitalism died and was replaced by a very different economic and political system, a system that my characters find out about by conversing with their counterparts in that other now. Why am I telling you all this? Because Covid-19 hit just as I was finishing the first draft of this damn book. With seven out of nine chapters completed, my partner and I found ourselves in our house, isolated in something that feels very much like, yes, another now—not a postcapitalist other now, but a strange other now in which capitalism is suspended. The difference between this and the other now in the book is that, while we're in lockdown, capitalism is not finished, it is merely suspended, and yet, we don't have an alternative vision. We haven't had such a capacity at least since 1991, especially those of us from a left-wing tradition. With this serving as something of an introduction for our discussion, greetings, Johann, from the island of Aegina off the coast of Attica. I believe you are in London, working as hard as ever in your flat.

Johann: There are so many things in your introduction that are really important for us to think about. Although this is a terrible tragedy for all the people who are going to die, and its especially terrible for particular parts of the world—for instance, the virus has now arrived in the Gaza Strip—I also think that, as you said, we can't let this crisis go to waste. There's a lot we can learn from the current responses to the crisis, and one of things I really care about is how we might think differently about questions like addiction, depression, and anxiety. This is a real opportunity for us to understand those problems better, in line with the ways that leading scientists like the World Health Organization have been urging us to do for a long time. The reason I wrote *Lost Connections* is because there were two mysteries that were really haunting me. The first was the question of why depression and anxiety had been rising throughout my lifetime. To understand why this is, you have to understand two concepts. One is neoliberalism, and the other is the biomedical model of understanding what are called mental health problems. The biomedical model essentially says that depression or anxiety are primarily problems located in your brain, genes, and biology. There is some truth to this—biological factors do contribute to mental health issues. However, the idea that these issues are *solely* biological problems doesn't work, because obviously human biology hasn't radically changed over the course of the forty-one years I have been alive. I thought that there must be something else going on, and I wanted to understand what it was for a quite personal reason. When I was a teenager, I went to my doctor and explained that I felt like pain was leaking out of me, I didn't understand it. My doctor gave me the biomedical model in its purest form and said, "Some people naturally get a chemical imbalance in their brains and you're clearly one of them, all we need to do is give you some drugs." I was prescribed an anti-depressant and it gave me some relief, but it wore off quite quickly and I was given higher and higher doses until, for thirteen years, I was taking the maximum possible dose you are allowed to take, at the end of which I was still quite depressed. And I thought, *What's going on here?* For the book, I spent three years traveling all over the world interviewing leading experts about depression and anxiety. I interviewed people with very different perspectives—from an Amish village in Indiana, because the Amish have very low levels of depression; to a lab in Baltimore, where they were giving people psychedelics to see if that reduced depression; to a city in Brazil, where they banned advertising to see if that would improve how people felt. I learned a huge amount. But what was hugely striking to me was that the World Health Organization has been saying for years that depression and anxiety are primarily social problems that require primarily social solutions. It has said that the biomedical model is diverting people from the most important solutions and is helping to excuse some of those responsible for these problems. In the United Nations' official statement for World Health Day in 2017, a leading doctor said that we need to talk less about chemical imbalances and more about power imbalances.[1] There is scientific evidence for nine different causes of depression and anxiety, and I want to talk about two in particular that I think really illustrate the power of the different way of thinking that we need to develop. There is a huge amount of evidence that financial insecurity causes depression and anxiety. For example, people who have an independent income from property are ten times less likely to develop severe anxiety than people who have no income from

---

1   https://www.ohchr.org/EN/NewsEvents/Pages/DisplayNews.aspx?NewsID=21484&LangID=E.

property. This, of course, is not surprising. And one of the things that has been happening prior to the present health crisis—and for the whole era in which neoliberalism has been regnant—is a massive increase of financial insecurity for a majority of the population. Unsurprisingly, that has caused a lot of depression and anxiety. And this is one example where we begin to see the relationship between neoliberalism and the biomedical model. When neoliberalism wins, electorally, and wealth is transferred to the rich, there is a big increase in both risk and financial insecurity for everyone else. So, we have a huge increase in anxiety and depression which has largely political causes. People feel profoundly distressed for entirely understandable reasons, but they go to their doctor and what happens? They are given, in many cases, an entirely biological explanation for their distress: that there is just something wrong with their brains. According to this model, it is an extraordinary coincidence that the people of West Virginia seem to have much more wrong with their brains than the faculty of Harvard. If you interpret this in a purely biological way, it makes no sense. Once you understand the environmental causes, however, it makes perfect sense. The biomedical model has helped to depoliticize a lot of the distress caused by neoliberalism. It has encouraged people to transfer their anger downward and to transfer their sense of what causes their problems inward. Drugs can give some relief to some people, but we have to understand mental health issues in a wider context. We know this is true because of what happens when you break with neoliberalism. I'll give you one example. In the 1970s, the Canadian government chose a town, seemingly at random, called Dauphin, about four hours out of Winnipeg, Manitoba, and as an experiment, they gave a guaranteed basic income to lower-income households in the town. It was the equivalent of US$11,000 in today's terms. The recipients did not have to do anything in return for this, and there was nothing they could do which would result in it being taken away, unless they were sent to prison. The results were studied by a brilliant social scientist named Dr. Evelyn Forget.[2] To me, the most important finding was that there was a huge fall in mental health problems of all kinds. This tells us something that should

2 Evelyn L. Forget, *Basic Income for Canadians: The Key to a Healthier, Happier, More Secure Life for All* (Toronto, ON: James Lorimer & Company, 2018).

be obvious: giving people a baseline of financial security reduces depression and anxiety. The problem is that this seems counterintuitive in our present culture because we've been taught that depression and anxiety are biological, individual problems. The current pandemic can further help us to see the limits of the biomedical understanding. For obvious reasons, there has been a big increase in depression and anxiety in the last three weeks. Human beings have needs. And, to return to your question of what we might build an alternative future around, I think one possible model is to think about what people need. Everyone knows that they have natural, physical needs like food, water, shelter, and clean air. However, there is equally strong evidence that all human beings have psychological needs. You need to feel you belong, that your life has meaning and purpose, that people see you and value you, and that you've got a future that makes sense. The culture we've built has made many improvements from the past, but we are getting progressively less good at meeting people's deep psychological needs. We need to build our alternative society around, first, what the planet needs to maintain a stable ecosystem and biosphere and, second, what human beings need, as individuals and as communities, to have decent lives and not be distressed. To achieve this, we need to change the notion that depression and anxiety are effectively malfunctions. We need to explain to people that, although there are some real biological contributions, depression and anxiety are largely signals that our needs as human beings are not being met.

Yanis: There's not a single word that I would be unwilling to endorse. You've also reminded me of something that influenced me when I was a very young lad, which is Michel Foucault's work on the shift from feudalism to capitalism, and the corresponding triumph of exchange value over experiential value. Once upon a time, experiential value was God. If you read Homer, for instance, it's all about human relation, glory, and righteousness. When Achilles died and his arms were looking for new owners, they never thought of holding an auction in order to distribute them, but convened a sort of jury to decide who deserved them more. The other crucial point from Foucault is that to understand modernity, you have to understand three buildings: the factory, the prison, and the madhouse. His book, *Madness and Civilization*, talks about how madness was systematized, which links both to your point that it's all about power imbalances and to my earlier point about power concerning who does what to whom. Foucault shows that power gets to decide who is mad and who, therefore, should be interned in the madhouse. The pseudoscience that accompanied this power grid went hand in hand with the creation of the factory—where the factory owner could make twelve-year-old kids work fifteen hours a day in the pursuit of surplus value—and also the idea of the correctional system. Those three buildings together are part and parcel of capitalist modernity (neoliberalism, for me, means nothing; it's simply the ideology by which the financial sector regained huge power after the end of Bretton Woods). If you put all this together, it sheds light on what you experienced when you first consulted the so-called experts and were told, "This is a hardware problem, here is a commodity, take it and you're done." That is, if you want, the archetypal paradigm of the triumph of exchange value. Remember Oscar Wilde's wise definition: "The cynic is he who knows everything about prices and nothing about values." According to this, the drugs cost a certain price that reflects the utility you will get from them—they will sort out the hardware problem that you have and, if you're not interested, off you go to the madhouse because you're not rational enough to know what's good for you.

Johann: I've thought a lot about Foucault and the ways in which these ideas are constructed, and I'll give one example that really connects with what you're saying. In the 1970s, the American Psychiatric Association (APA) decided that they would standardize, for the first time, the definition of depression. Up to that point, psychiatrists had been using their own working definitions that were kind of mixed up. The APA drew up a list of ten symptoms (obvious things like crying a lot or feeling hopeless) and they told psychiatrists that if their patients showed at least six of these symptoms for more than two weeks, they should be diagnosed as mentally ill and helped to recover. Quite quickly, a psychiatrist came back and said, "Hang on a minute, if we use these criteria as they are laid out, we will have to diagnose every grieving person in the United States as mentally ill." The APA acknowledged the mistake and added what became known as the "grief loophole," which added an exception for patients who had experienced the loss of someone they love in the last year. As the years went on, employers became annoyed that people were allowed to grieve for so long and the grieving period in the APA criteria was cut back—first to six months, then to two months, then to two weeks, and now it's been abolished entirely. If your child dies in the morning and you are really distressed, you can be diagnosed that same day with mental illness. Dr. Joanne Cacciatore has done really important work on this, and she explains that it shows us something about the nature of capitalism and its relationship to the biomedical model. The biomedical model permits a person a certain amount of distress in certain limited situations before they are diagnosed as outside of the norm—exactly in the way that Foucault talks about in *Madness and Civilization*—and those constraints are entirely arbitrary. As Cacciatore points out, why are you allowed to feel terrible without being mentally ill if your mother dies, but not if you lose your job, are made homeless, or are stuck in a job you hate for forty years? Under the guise of being a dispassionate medical science, these are highly political judgments built very deeply around the valences of capitalism. On the idea of the shift in value that occurs with the transition to capitalism, which you mentioned, Yanis, in relation to Foucault, there has been a very deep internalization of capitalist values, and the fact that this makes us depressed should tell us something about the inhumanity of that system. I think about how, when I was a child, Margaret Thatcher famously said, "There is no such thing as society," and about all those years I was depressed, and I wonder why it took me so long to even consider whether my depression might have social causes. I take that as a sign of how deeply Margaret Thatcher won: that even someone like me, when it came to something as profound as my own depression, had internalized those neoliberal values to the extent that I thought my depression was a flaw in me; I didn't think about possible social and cultural causes. Everyone knows that junk food has taken over our diets and made us physically sick, but there is also strong evidence that a kind of "junk values" have taken over our minds and made us mentally sick. For thousands of years, philosophers have said that if you think life is about money, status, and showing off then you're going to feel like shit (that's not an exact quote from Schopenhauer but it's basically what he said). Professor Tim Kasser actually investigated this question and discovered, firstly, that the more you think life is about money, status, and showing off, the more likely you are to become depressed and anxious.[3] One very persuasive reason for this is that it trains you to look for happiness in all the wrong places. People don't lie on their death beds and think about all the shoes they bought and all the likes they got on Instagram, they think about moments of love, meaning, and connection. As Kasser puts it, we live in a machine that is designed to get us to neglect what is important about life, and if there was a mass realization of this, capitalism would be in crisis. He also proved, secondly, that these "junk values" have become increasingly dominant, to the point where they are now regnant. One of the opportunities the present crisis gives us is to see how badly awry our values have gone. Who are the people we really need in a crisis? Turns out it's not billionaires and Instagram influencers, but those who have been mocked and derided by this system of values for a very long time: people like cleaners, bus drivers, and shelf-stackers.

Yanis: Your focus on psychiatry and the biomedical complex has thankfully shielded you from the tragedy that befell me, at the age of about seventeen, when I became familiar with the world of economics. I was a young lad from Greece, just arrived in Britain, when I opened my textbook of microeconomics and suddenly saw the whole five thousand years of human wisdom dismissed in one line. The first chapter of the microeconomics textbook says that the rational person is he who maximizes a given degree of satisfaction from pre-existing exogeneous and objective preferences, subject to constraints. This model of the rational man—which is at the heart of every economic model from the Bank of England and the Treasury to the Royal Bank of Scotland and any idiot using economic tools—is one where you are defined as a bundle of preferences that human reason has no right to pass judgement on, and you are rational to the extent that you can weigh up the amount of satisfaction you will get from meeting those preferences. Suddenly you have no capacity, for instance, to love. The whole point about *falling* in love is that the only way of being truly happy in love is, of course, to lose control. Why would you ever love if you are just a machine weighing up different options on the basis of

---

3   Tim Kasser, *The High Price of Materialism* (Cambridge, MA: MIT Press, 2002).

expected utility? Think about the millions of poor students who have been schooled by economists, like myself. You are reading microeconomics and suddenly everything you thought you knew about human nature is dismissed as subservient to a model where you are just a pair of scales weighing up different expected options. Your depression would be much worse, Johann, and you really would be in deep shit, if you studied microeconomics.

Johann: I've tried to think about the profoundly erroneous conception of human nature that is embodied in economics, and someone who helped me in this is Dr. Brett Ford, whom I interviewed in Berkeley. She was part of a research team that wanted to figure out what people would do when asked to consciously try and make themselves happier, studying groups in the United States, Russia, Taiwan, and Japan.[4] They found that if you try to make yourself happier as a person in the United States, in the main, you don't become happier, whereas in the other countries, you do. The reason for this was that people in the United States generally tried to make themselves happier by doing something for themselves, such as purchasing something or working to get a promotion, in line with the neoliberal model that microeconomics teaches. They instinctively had an individualistic, almost Randian, conception of happiness. In the other countries, people largely did something for others, their friends, families, or communities. They had an instinctively collectivist conception of happiness. I don't think these findings can be separated out from economics. The profound individualism that economics teaches has been so deeply propagandized and culturally ingrained that it effects how we express even deeply personal concepts like happiness. The failure of classical economic models to account for human behavior and the fact that they make us feel like shit is also a damning indictment of those systems—they literally don't work, even in delivering the utility that they promise! They fail because the grammar of the thinking is wrong: we're not individualists. In the present crisis, we continually hear this message that we are a social species, we stand or fall together. It has illuminated how socially connected and interdependent we are. Prevailing theories about economics and mental health don't describe reality, but

4 https://pubmed.ncbi.nlm.nih.gov/26347945/.

they can distort our perception of reality in ways that lead to dysfunctional economies and distorted individual lives, where we pursue money and status and are then puzzled when get depressed, in turn feeding into the biomedical model that locates the problem in the individual's biology.

Yanis: It reminds me of John Kenneth Galbraith's idea of the mouse on the spinning wheel, where the faster you go, the more exhausted and less satisfied you are. Perhaps we can learn from the ancient Athenian philosophers who talked about persons, not individuals. For them, if you are individual it means you are isolated, and if you are isolated you are stupid by definition— you don't even have language, you're not a rational person, you are nothing, you are a beast. The difference between the Anglo-Celtic tradition and the Ancient Greek tradition is that Aristotle, Plato, and others knew that the person becomes a person through interacting with others in a social context. In the Anglo-Celtic tradition, there is a tendency to think of individualism and collectivism as mutually opposed, but the Ancient Greeks understood that this is not the point, it's about personhood, and personhood can only be achieved in a social context, in the *polis*, therefore within politics. Further, they had a word that is not exactly happiness, which is *eudaimonia*, and Aristotle, Socrates, and the rest of the Ancient Greek philosophers believed that you only discover how eudemonic your life was just before you die, when you look back and ask yourself a pertinent question: "Was that a successful life?" This is of course different to the question, "Did I maximize my utility at every moment in time?" I wonder whether you will permit me to ask a personal question: From what I understand, you have experienced depression; how do you deal with it personally?

Johann: People often say (and I used to, too) that "I have depression," or "I've got anxiety," as though these are permanent and fixed conditions. I come at this with all sorts of privilege, but I now realize that my depression, which I experienced intermittently over nearly twenty years, was a signal that something had gone wrong in my life. The primary thing is that I experienced some very extreme abuse as a child, and I hadn't ever been able to release the shame, or challenge the destructive thinking, that it caused. When I did, I found that my depression largely went away. When I learned to interpret my depression not as a malfunction in my biology but as a signal that something wasn't right, that opened up a set of solutions I could not have seen had I remained in the biomedical paradigm of thinking. I think we should listen to the World Health Organization, which says that the vast majority of what are diagnosed as mental health problems are social problems, and that solutions should be primarily psychological and social, although there is some place for drugs. I'll tell you a story that really helped me to think through this. Derek Summerfield, a South African psychiatrist, was in Cambodia in 2001 when chemical antidepressants were first introduced there. The local people had never heard of these drugs, and when Summerfield explained what they were they said, "Oh we don't need those, we've already got antidepressants." Summerfield didn't understand and he thought the people must be referring to an herbal remedy, but instead they told him a story. One day, one of the rice farmers in their community stood on a land mine leftover from the American attack on South East Asia, and he got his leg blown off. He was given an artificial leg and went back to work in the rice fields. It was extremely painful to work in the water and, presumably, very traumatic to work in the fields where he was blown up. The man started to cry all day and refused to get out of bed. This is when the Cambodian doctors gave him an "antidepressant." They went and sat with him, listened to him, and realized that his pain had causes that were perfectly understandable. One of the doctors figured that if they bought the man a cow, he could become a dairy farmer and wouldn't be in the position that was causing him so much pain. They bought him a cow and within a month his depression was gone. They said to Derek Summerfield, "So you see, Doctor? That cow was an antidepressant, that's what you mean, right?" Those Cambodian doctors knew, intuitively, what the leading medical body in the world, the World Health Organization, has been trying to tell us for years. In my opinion, anything that reduces depression should be regarded as an antidepressant. For some people that will include drugs, but we need to radically expand our concept of antidepressants—a higher minimum wage: really good antidepressant! Universal basic income: really good antidepressant! Transforming corporations into democratic cooperatives where the workers are in control: really good antidepressant! To return to the initial question of "another now," when we think about the alternative societies we want to build, one of the things we should do is heed the signals of what's not working now and assert that, for instance, we want this to be an antidepressant society—a society that meets the full range of people's needs. And there are all sorts of things that we already know to be massively beneficial in achieving this.

Conversation held on April 13, 2020

Debt, Bullshit Jobs, and Political Self-Organization

David Graeber and Maja Kantar

Maja: I, like many people, have been closely following the news for updates on Covid-19. And one thing I have picked up on is this discourse urging people to be "reasonable" in their expectations of potential economic routes out of this crisis. The European Union recently looked at ways to help countries most affected by this crisis, such as Italy or Spain, and the idea of "coronabonds" was proposed to help them recover their economic losses.[1] However, Germany and the Netherlands (in particular) declined the idea because they did not want to risk sharing in the debt. This should not surprise us, of course, especially in light of the EU's response to the 2008 crisis. Then, as now, we were told again and again to be "reasonable," and that rich countries should not bear the burden of less organized, poorer countries. How is it possible that the ritual of rich countries declining to act in solidarity or cooperation is being received, this time, with a certain outrage and surprise?

David: I think that 2008 blew the cover, to a certain degree, on the line we had all been given about debt and finance in general. We were told about the financialization of the economy, but as though this occurred in a kind of casino that is completely detached from the real economy, where financiers are just rolling the dice and making bets among each other. Before 2008, there was a general consensus that we, the public, don't really understand how finance works, that it's some kind of arcane science beyond our understanding. At the same time, debt was redefined in basic moral terms. This discourse of being "reasonable" is very surprising in this context, because normally "reasonable" means compromising, and debt is one of the few things that can make completely unreasonable things seem reasonable. It is used to justify things that people would never approve of in any other context. So there is this moral element, on the one hand, but there is also the idea that financiers are exceptionally clever people who have understood the science of economics in a way that most people cannot. No one was quite sure how finance was supposed to be driving the world economy toward greater happiness and prosperity, but we kept being reassured that it was and to trust in the experts. After 2008, both the moral and intellectual justifications completely

---

1   https://www.cnbc.com/2020/03/25/nine-eu-countries-say-its-time-for-corona-bonds-as-virus-deaths-rise.html.

collapsed. It turned out that not only was the world of finance built on scams, but on really stupid scams. The supposed "experts" were completely corrupt as well as very clumsy. There was a brief moment in which many people then reconsidered everything they knew about money, capital, finance, and debt. Even the *Economist* was running headlines like "Capitalism: Is it Really a Good Idea?" Of course, their answer was yes, but nonetheless there was a moment when it seemed like everything was thrown into question. Even when things returned to a form of normality, there was an enduring sense that we were sitting on a time bomb and that "next time" those in power would not be able to cover things over again. People realized that the entire economy was based on a series of completely dishonest delusions, and the idea that there is anything moral about debt was shown to be completely absurd. The EU attempted to portray the Greek people as improvident for having made irresponsible loans and, therefore, as breaching the basic morality of economics and deserving any resulting hardship. However, the reason the economy was able to turn into a gigantic bubble in the first place was precisely because those who were making irresponsible, stupid loans never had to take a hit.

Maja: Your own book on debt and that of Maurizio Lazzarato finally presented the problem in a clear way that enabled us to do away with the notion that economy is a science completely detached from any other aspects of life.[2] You point out that three centuries ago, "the economy" did not exist as a discrete sphere as it does today, but was always connected to other aspects of life such as the family and religion. Today, we have this narrative of morality surrounding debt, which almost always turns into moralism, especially, as Lazzarato discusses, in connection with guilt.

David: Yes, it's all theology. We have to remember that even three or four hundred years ago, economics was a branch of moral science which fell under theology. Economic questions were handled largely by clerics in the Middle Ages. Even Adam Smith was a professor of moral philosophy.

---

2 David Graeber, *Debt: The First 5000 Years* (Brooklyn, NY: Melville House, 2011); Maurizio Lazzarato, *The Making of the Indebted Man* (Los Angeles, CA: Semiotexte, 2012).

Maja: In terms of the situation unfolding now, we have IMF officials reiterating that debts have to be repaid, structural adjustment programs have to be implemented, and so on.

David: They won't even cancel the African debt, which, of course, has been repaid five times over and it is now just interest payments that are owing. They will drag the payments out no matter how many have to die. Noam Chomsky often makes the point that when Stalin arranges an intentional famine in Ukraine, knowing that this will lead to the deaths of thousands of people, we count that as mass murder, but we don't apply the same charges to the actions of the IMF. If the IMF insists on policies that it knows will kill people, how is this not mass murder? I am not sure that it will last because so many bubbles have been punctured this time around. The traditional justifications for capitalism have almost all withered away, they are indefensible. For instance, almost nobody still believes the claim that "the rising tide will lift all boats." It's very clear, especially in rich countries, that the next generation—leaving aside the climate disaster—will be economically worse off than their parents. The second major justification was the idea that technology would save us, which, again, nobody sincerely believes anymore. The third appealed to the democracy and political stability that capitalist countries supposedly inevitably create in creating a larger middle class. Now, this argument has given way to a weaker one which seeks to justify capitalism by holding up North Korea or Venezuela as the alternative. In place of these traditional justifications, proponents of capitalism resort to moral arguments of the sort that "if you don't pay your debts, you're a bad person." This morality of debt is also connected to a morality of work. People have internalized the so-called Protestant work ethic, according to which if you are not working hard, you are a bad person undeserving of public support. I wrote a book on each of these moral justifications (*Debt* and *Bullshit Jobs*, respectively) because both have really stuck.

Maja: The morality aspect of debt always comes to mind when this discourse of being "responsible" and "reasonable" emerges, in a constant reiteration of the confinement of the "possible." Suddenly, when a crisis like the Covid-19 pandemic happens, we can see that everything that was deemed impossible somehow becomes possible, whether that is writing off the National Health Service's debt in the UK, the nationalization of private hospitals, or squatting a McDonald's in Marseilles and turning it into a food bank.

David: There has been a thirty- to forty-year war against human political imagination. In the 1930s through to the 1960s, it was just assumed that we were living in a somewhat terrifying, but nonetheless exhilarating, new age where almost anything was possible. Creations such as the United Nations or the space program were epical feats of statesmanship. This is inconceivable now. We are given this line that there are economic machines beyond our control that are propelling us toward a better future and we just have to trust in them; we certainly can't intervene in history. It's a strange version of historical determinism, in a way, which I think is one reason why many old apparatchiks in Eastern Europe were able to quite easily switch from a Marxist-Leninist philosophy to neoliberalism without too much conceptual dissonance. It is this idea that history moves in a determined direction and if we just listen to the experts we will arrive at a better world. It entails giving up on the idea that human beings can have an impact on history and, today, it has gotten to the point where even those in power can no longer control the mechanisms they have created—they seem at a total loss in the face of urgent calls for them to mobilize on a global scale.

Maja: To merely have someone in power who actually behaves like a leader is an impossibility now.

David: I've always thought Obama represented the ultimate death of visionary politics. He managed to get elected by portraying himself as the kind of person who would have a vision—but it never occurred to anybody to ask what the vision actually was. I have said, for some time now, that capitalism is obviously on its last legs and what I fear is not a capitalist future but something even worse. If there was ever a stupid time to give up on trying to imagine a better future, this is it.

Maja: Keeping our political imagination alive is more important now than ever. Some will dismiss our efforts to reimagine the future as theoretical musings, but the real fictions of today are those of finance. Ours is a much more material project. My favorite political group at the moment is a UK-based group called Nihilists for Labour that appeared during the Covid-19 lockdown. Two or three weeks ago, they did a shout out to everybody who just realized how pointless their job is. *Bullshit Jobs* has perhaps never been so pertinent.

David: That book sort of inflicted itself on me. I kept meeting these people who, when I asked them what they did, would reply, "Oh, nothing really." At first I figured they were just being modest, but when I pinned them down, they would admit, "No, actually, I meant that literally. I do nothing all day, I just pretend to work. Maybe I do fifteen minutes' work a day, but, basically, I'm just on Facebook." I wrote a piece postulating that perhaps bullshit jobs were the reason that we are not working fifteen-hour weeks, as was predicted with increasing automation. We are so dedicated to the idea that if you are not working hard you are undeserving that we invented dummy jobs just to keep people off the streets. Basically, it was kind of a joke, but within two weeks of publication it was translated into a dozen different languages. A survey was then done and it discovered that over a third of people said that if their jobs disappeared it would make no difference at all.[3]

Maja: Your style resonates, at least to my mind, with Bob Black and other old-school anti-work anarchists. The opening sentence of Black's *Abolition of Work* is clear and simple: "Nobody should ever work." Of course, what he meant was work on the basis of the capital–wage relation. He makes the case for play as another form of creative engagement. The problem comes down to the system of production, which needs justification through different kinds of nonsensical activities. And part of our work is developing a new system of production.

David: The idea of production itself needs to be examined because it's one of these theological notions. One of the odd features of Abrahamic religions is the idea that God created the universe out of nothing, *ex nihilo*, and it is very

3   https://yougov.co.uk/topics/lifestyle/articles-reports/2015/08/12/british-jobs-meaningless.

important, because production literally means to "shove out" (from the Latin *produire*). In the Bible, Adam is cursed to work by the sweat of his brow and Eve is cursed by God, who says, "I will multiply your pain in childbirth," which of course we call "labor." This idea of labor as work that is productive, either of grain or of babies, is envisioned in a certain way in political economy. The image of production in Adam Smith, Ricardo, and Marx, carries with it a sort of male fantasy of birth: factories are shoving out objects, fully formed, through a painful process, which, through consumption, are used or eaten up, and we also "produce" workers who are then consumed in the workplace. That whole image assumes that work is "productive," that it makes something. But, of course, it ignores most work. It is an incredibly gendered conception that is rooted in the male fantasy of pregnancy. It ultimately implies that the work of making something is more important than the work of maintaining or caring for it, which is absurd. Most labor isn't making things, or even transforming them, but maintaining and taking care of them. Feminist economists always point out that even productive labor can be thought of as a form of caring labor. We need to expand our notion of care and see meaningful production as a subset of that. Care and freedom, instead of production and consumption, should be the bases of our economy. Obviously, if you endlessly maximize consumption it will ultimately lead to disaster, but freedom can be maximized without killing anyone, necessarily. I would propose that care be considered as any sort of behavior, productive or not, that is aimed toward maintaining or enhancing another person or entity's freedom.

Maja: That's a beautiful idea. There always seems to be this clash between freedom and necessity, even on the left.

David: Play is a key concept here, because, if you think about it, play is the quintessential form of human freedom: freedom for its own sake.

Maja: I would add that we are talking about a play that is not childish or reckless, but is passionate and has high stakes and, similarly, a care that is not reliant on a patriarchal notion of femininity, but is militant, almost, and generates a solidarity that is noncompromising. Do you think it is likely that more useful jobs and forms of global justice will be produced by the Covid-19 pandemic and related economic crisis?

David: That's up to us, isn't it? One of the most telling things for me was this debate about whether to shut down Wall Street for a few weeks when it kept crashing incessantly. I remember reading a fairly long debate about this in a mainstream magazine, and I noticed that at no point in the article did anyone suggest that shutting down Wall Street would itself have negative economic effects. So, why does it exist? The point of Wall Street seems to be itself: the economy is there for it, rather than the other way around, and this is the quintessence of how we got things backward. Now, we have certain politicians saying, "We need to save the economy, and if a lot of pensioners die, that's too bad," but that is just the latest version of this ongoing insanity.[4] In the '90s, we heard people trained by the World Bank, who are now ministers of health, saying, "We need to stop the AIDS crisis because, if we don't, in ten years' time half of the population will be gone and that will have terrible effects on the economy." Economy was supposed to facilitate the provision of necessary material goods; now, the best reason we can think of not to be dead is that it will hurt the economy. Today, we are again in a situation where politicians will tell us that what we just went through was a dream, that it's now time to wake up and return to normal. But, actually, "normality" was a dream; the crisis is reality, for through it we discovered again what is necessary and what is not.

Maja: Do you think this pandemic is marking the beginning of a fascist technocratic new world order?

David: I don't know, actually. Has it ever not been at least a technocratic order? I must admit, I was writing a piece right before the pandemic hit about climate change, and it began by saying that, at this point, when there are large portions of the earth that are literally on fire, and every year is the hottest year on record, even the most stubborn right-wing climate change denier will have to concede to what is happening. If there is anything scarier

---

4 https://www.theguardian.com/politics/2020/mar/22/no-10-denies-claim-dominic-cummings-argued-to-let-old-people-die.

than a fascist who denies climate change, it's one who doesn't, because we know what kind of "solutions" they would implement. We have to assume that the right has been brainstorming plans for when the climate crisis gets to genuine emergency levels. There are plenty of people employed to brainstorm contingencies and agencies tasked with predicting and modeling bad things that may eventuate, some of which are secret and some of which are not. We need to grapple with these possible approaches that are being played around with, because they can give us an idea of what we can expect if we do try to pretend that we can just go back to "normal" after the current pandemic—an apocalyptic climate scenario.

Maja: Yes, the "normal" is what started this whole thing.

David: The normal is standing on the tracks looking at an oncoming train and arguing with each other about how fast it's going. We've now had somebody knock us off the tracks, out of the way, and what are we going to do, get back on? In fact, about ten years ago, a scientist showed that a series of sunspots had slowed down global warming and we'd be in a much worse position had that not happened.[5] This is a similar jolt—a completely random event which has given us a moment of breathing space and reminded us that we have the ability to take dramatic action, that, perhaps, we should stop listening to those who tell us what is possible and impossible.

Maja: We all recognize the problems, but the question is how to organize to solve them? This is, of course, an eternal question, and I like the answers we gave in terms of rebuilding economics around play, freedom, and care, but what about political organization? In the United Kingdom, many people have recently been surprised to see that people within the Labour Party have worked to sabotage its chances of success in the December 2019 election.[6] Why do we still count on forms of liberal representation, and why are we still surprised to see that politicians from the left and right remain

---

5 https://www.scientificamerican.com/article/sun-spots-and-climate-change/.

6 https://www.independent.co.uk/news/uk/politics/labour-leak-report-corbyn-election-whatsapp-antisemitism-tories-yougov-poll-a9462456.html.

opportunists playing power games? Are there other ways to be politically present besides representation as we know it?

David: When you ask "Why are we surprised?" my question is, who is "we"? There is an attempt to have politics polarize around an opposition, between what is called the left, the neoliberal center built around the perspectives of the professional managerial classes, and what is called the radical right, crypto-fascists, or "populists." This opposition is based on a disaffected working class being divided between the two poles. In fact, the professional managerial classes that now represent centrism are the only people who really believe in the rules. For them, life is built around rules, regulations, and institutional structures and they claim that all people want is for the integrity of these to be upheld. I noticed this in America in the Bush–Gore election. The spokespeople of this centrism that campaigns on form over content are the same people who questioned why, if Hillary Clinton didn't break any laws, people accused her of corruption. These people, who truly believe in rules and regulations, are those who are continually shocked and surprised. In contrast, right-wing figures like Trump manipulate the cynicism to trick people into thinking that they are the tricksters and aren't being tricked. That's the real secret of so-called right-wing populism. After Trump won, he embarked on a series of rallies. At one point, he mentioned Hillary Clinton and everybody started chanting, "Lock her up, lock her up." He said, "No, no, you don't have to use that line anymore—it was good during the campaign, but now that we've won, we don't need it." He manages to convince everybody in the audience that they are all part of the scam, and they are so cynical that they are not surprised by anything. Against this, the centrists remain defiant and insist on "the rules." While the one is manipulating intentional cynicism as a weapon, the other is manipulating intentional naivety.

Maja: As Jarvis Cocker would say, "Cunts are still running the world." There's nothing new about that. But there are of course places where different sets of rules and ideas have been enacted throughout history. For instance, I know that you are familiar with the Kurdish struggle. Could you specify some elements of difference in terms of the political organization in Rojava?

David: One of the key differences is taking seriously the issue of gender rather than simply paying it lip service. Second, the dissemination of knowledge and the awareness that a lot of power is really based on the illusion of expertise. Part of their idea of a revolution is to disseminate practical knowledge as widely as possible, so they have academies with six-week courses where people can learn anything useful that they can think to disseminate. They say that their dream is to give everyone in the country police training and then abolish the police, and that all forms of knowledge should be made available to everyone as quickly as possible. Finally, bottom-up direct democracy. What the Kurdish project has discovered is that all the things we were experimenting with in Occupy and the global justice movement in terms of consensus-based, decentralized decision-making can actually work to run an entire society, if you have the will and patience. And not everyone in Kurdish society was or is a revolutionary, of course, but it only took 20 percent of the population, mainly young people, to commit to a certain idea and completely transform the society. Kurdish society was one of the most traditional and patriarchal societies in the Middle East, and what they have managed to do in seven years is just dazzling. The Spanish anarchists would have been one of the greatest inspirations for the left of the twentieth century. Their experiment lasted about two years. The Kurdish people have managed to hold their project together, in one of the least friendly places in the world to have a feminist–anarchist revolution, for almost a decade now. It's one of the most remarkable things I've ever seen and, if nothing else, it shows that those who claim that such ambitions are impractical or impossible are simply wrong—you try fighting ISIS!

Maja: You told me earlier that there is no Covid-19 in Rojava yet?

David: Yes, that's right. As of yesterday, there have been no cases. They immediately mobilized a bottom-up approach implementing mass hygiene, shutting down institutions, and preventing large gatherings of people—but they haven't implemented a lockdown and the measures have still been completely effective. It is very interesting to think about what different countries are doing to stop the spread of Covid-19, and what is effective and what isn't. It has nothing to do with authoritarianism versus democracy, as some are claiming. In East Asia, countries like South Korea, which is known as the most individualistic and rebelliously democratic in the region, did the best in terms of handling the outbreak. China and Japan did about equally well, and all of them did better than Europe. The major difference that researchers have been able to find is trust in institutions. The countries with the greatest infection rates are those in which nobody believes what they read in the papers or hear from the authorities. This might sound like an argument for authority, but it's not. The reason that people in the United States, for instance, don't believe what they read and hear is that the papers and politicians usually lie to them. We are now dealing with the wake of a wave of aggressive cynicism, which is literally killing us.

Maja: That's why it is so important to look at outlets of real struggle where things have been done differently and with success. The rate of success is irrelevant in the end; the attempt itself testifies a lot.

Conversation held on April 15, 2020

Covid-1984 and Surveillance Capitalism

Shoshana Zuboff and Renata Ávila

Renata: Professor Shoshana Zuboff is best known for her book *The Age of Surveillance Capitalism: The Fight for a Human Future at the New Frontier of Power*. And that is precisely what we want to discuss together in connection with the Covid-19 crisis: a human future. I have been reading the numbers of preventable deaths in the United States, where you, Shoshana, are based, and it's frightening. At the time that you wrote the book, the future, perhaps, looked a little bit green. Now it is more confusing, accelerated, and conflicting than ever. I don't know if you feel the same, but I feel like we are part, right now, of a global experiment, with so many of us depending very heavily on what you describe as surveillance capitalism. I would like to ask you to start the conversation with a reflection on your personal experience. How are you seeing things unfold from where you are at the moment, given your closeness to these topics?

Shoshana: To a certain extent, I see the daily events unfold in the news and sometimes I feel like I am reading the pages that I spent so many years composing. There is an obvious way in which it looks like, "Here we are again, a state of exception; here we are again, shock doctrine; here we are again, surveillance capitalists exploiting our fear and the global uncertainty in order to aggressively expand their empire." But I want to talk about a different kind of story tonight and it starts with Orwell, who is on everybody's minds. When he wrote 1984, it wasn't because he expected the nightmare of 1984 to constitute itself. He spent his last years, when he was working on 1984, in a little cottage in the Hebrides. There was no heat. He had tuberculosis, which steadily worsened. He had a strict publishing deadline, and even the typist his publisher had promised him never materialized. In the end he chose to keep working at any price, tucked up in bed typing the final draft. The book was declared a masterpiece upon publication, and six months later Orwell died of TB. He literally sacrificed his life in order to complete that work. Why? 1984 was Orwell's warning, a flare into the darkness of complacency with the message, "This is what can happen if we stop paying attention, if we fail to mobilize our mental and moral faculties." It was, in a sense, the negative of the photo of the future that he hoped for. Orwell was a prolific essayist, and my favorite of all is his 1946 review of *The Managerial Revolution* by James Burnham, originally published in 1940. This is Orwell at his best, excoriating Burnham. He shows nothing but contempt for the author and his despicable conclusions. Burnham looked at the Third Reich and he was impressed with its administrative, managerial capabilities—after all, it was administrating mass murder within its own borders, and eventually across Europe. He predicted that the Germans would win the war because they were the superior managers. Then, a couple of years later, when the war turned in favor of the Allies, Burnham came out with another edition of the book in which he changed his entire interpretation and predicted that the Allies would win. Orwell considered this kind of behavior to be the definition of cowardice. It bows to whatever force is dominant at that moment. Burnham can only draw a straight line from the present to the future. He assumes that the future is always determined by whoever is, or appears to be, on top. I want to suggest that we are reading essays, op-eds, and newspaper coverage every single day that is cowardly, because it looks at the might of the tech companies and of the empire of surveillance capitalism—which is increasingly allied not only with authoritarian governments but with the underlying authoritarian yearnings of democratically elected governments—and it bends down to this and declares, "This will be the future after Covid-19: everyone will have given themselves up to complete bio-surveillance and pervasive tracking." I say that is cowardly for the same reason that Orwell said it: because the future is unknowable. However, there is one overriding factor that determines the future, and that is us, the people, and all the conversations we are having, the articles and blogs we are writing. The indignation and anger, the sense of rights that are still unnamed but nevertheless ruthlessly violated. What *we* do, whether or not we can mobilize at this moment–– that is what will determine the future. Until we know that part of the story, no one knows the future.

Renata: What an exciting start. We do, however, face a problem, because we often communicate and mobilize our network through platforms like Zoom, YouTube, and Facebook. It feels like we are engaging in completely incongruent behavior where, on the one hand, we know that we are feeding these systems actively, and with each interaction we make them more powerful and ourselves weaker but, on the other hand, we need to use these tools in the meantime as we build an alternative future. We are often obsessed with small details like encryption, which is very important, but we are not attacking the monster as a whole. Your book is, in a sense, the *1984* for our generation; it is that signal. You make the point that asking Silicon Valley to protect our privacy is like asking a giraffe to shorten its neck. And it often does feel like we are just modifying small details. So what would you say to activists who want to create a new future, about where to start?

Shoshana: Your description of our predicament is, to me, itself an illustration of the huge leap forward that we have already taken. The last time a state of exception allowed the massive expansion of the surveillance state and surveillance capitalism was 9/11. Before 9/11, there were active discussions in the United States about comprehensive privacy legislation. And twenty-four hours after the planes hit the Twin Towers, the conversation had changed dramatically to one focused on total information awareness. These fledgling Internet companies were already acting improperly with secret cookies and web bugs to monitor and track users. Most of the folks at the Federal Trade Commission had concluded that the Internet companies were never going to be able to self-regulate. That's where the impetus for comprehensive legislation was coming from. After 9/11 the American intelligence community and their colleagues around the world looked at these emergent surveillance capabilities in the private sector and said, "Forget about legislation." They decided to draw a wide berth around those companies and to encourage those capabilities, because they knew that they were going to need them. They understood that the Internet companies would be able to do things outside the rule of law, such as bulk surveillance, while the agencies of the Five Eyes would be constrained by the constitutions of their own democracies. That was the starting bell for surveillance capitalism and what allowed it to grow into the mighty power that it is today in just two short decades. This, the absence of law, is key. The lack of law was complemented by our ignorance. All these systems were engineered with significant skills and capital to keep us ignorant and bypass our awareness. Hold that thought for a minute, and let's go back to what you said, Renata, about how we continue to make platforms stronger every time we click into a Zoom call. The very fact that you are saying that is immense, because twenty years ago we did not know it. Millions of people now have a very deep sense that our lives, our private experiences, are being harvested without our knowledge or consent, and that data produced from our private experience has been used to fund the business operations of what have now become trillion-dollar market capitalization empires. And we have started to understand more about their use of our data for methods of social control that serve the optimization of their revenue flows. Public awareness is on the move, and that in itself is huge. For example, there's been a critique of Zoom for quite a while, but it's been sequestered in specialist communities. In the last three weeks or so, as lockdowns have begun, this information about Zoom and its anti-privacy practices has erupted out of those specialist domains right into the bloodstream of the public conversation. Even Google, ironically, is telling its employees that they can no longer use Zoom for company business. Here we have, in a very short time, public mobilization and awareness driving a new standard. Granted, some of us continue to use Zoom, but the point is that we know, we are thinking critically, and we believe that its extraction practices are illegitimate. That's just one way in which we are already showing signs of exactly the kinds of strengths that are going to shape our future, despite the mightiness of the tech companies. A second thought concerns your question, Renata, about whether we are overly concerned about encryption and particular techniques at the expense of taking on the broader issues. The point I want to make is that this is not a story about technology, but about institutions. We have just embarked on the third decade of the twenty-first century, the digital century, and we remain naked in the encounter with the digital. This is like living through the twentieth century without child labor legislation, without the rights to join trade unions and bargain collectively, to safe and healthy working conditions, to fair pay, to not be discriminated against in the workplace because of race, sex, religion, or anything else. If we tried to make our way through the twentieth century without those rights, and the laws and democratic institutions that legitimated and governed them, we would simply be societies of oligarchs and serfs. Yet, right now, our lives unfold in the digital century without the laws, regulatory paradigms, institutional forms, and democratic governance that would make the digital safe for people and for democracy. Without a new era of institutional creativity,

the possibility of a "market democracy" is lost. Digital technology is not surveillance. Only institutions can do that. Digital technology is what democracy wants it to be. This institutional challenge is our work now.

Renata: I have two quick challenges for you. One is a push-back against
legislation, because we are currently in a situation where Brussels and
Washington, DC, the main centers of legislation that can influence surveillance capitalism, are completely captured by corporate lobbyists. When
Edward Snowden's revelations came out in 2013, many of the bad practices
that were documented and explained by journalists were rapidly legalized
and normalized. The intelligence agencies responsible for the wrongdoings
wanted to seize the opportunity of regulatory change using the excuse of
terrorism and passed legislation to make it legal and even acceptable by
the general public. Just like then, normalization of the current situation
is a risk. The present moment is characterized by a lot of stress, fear, and
anxiety, and we are negotiating a "return to normal." I'm seeing two things
here. On the one hand, there is a narrative that the situation demands a
massive deployment of surveillance technology—in liberal democracies it
won't be mandatory to submit to this, but if you don't, you will be seen as
being greedy about your personal data and privacy and as preventing others from returning to work and normal life. Nine/Eleven demonstrated how
exceptional regulations can become enshrined into law and normalized.
Similarly, today, increased surveillance and control relating to Covid-19 is
already mandatory in China and elsewhere. The second thing that worries
me is that, in the twentieth century, we only declared some sort of victory
in the fight for rights, creating institutions like the United Nations (which
are, by the way, collapsing right now), after terrible war, human loss, and
the complete abandonment of human values on a global scale. The technology of the time, the atomic bomb, was geared toward the sophisticated,
systematic elimination of human beings. Now, we are in the third decade of
the digital revolution, and with all of the science and capabilities we have
developed, we are (again) letting people die. The ability to classify people
by their biological characteristics and social status is being automated and
optimized by technology, and this can create worrying situations where
governments divide populations into those who have antibodies and those

who do not, with privileges like returning to work dependent on this classification. Further, those who are poor, elderly, or with existing health conditions are being designated as those whose lives are dispensable and can be sacrificed. In short, the institutions of the past are failing, and the institutions of today are normalizing the life of a few at the expense of the vast majority. So, my follow-up questions to you are: Is regulation really our friend now, or is it captured? And are we heading down a dangerous path where we risk repeating history?

Shoshana: There's nothing that you say that I would deny, but what we don't know is what our response to this will be. Politics, inherently, is the world of the unknown. It is inherently uncertain because it depends upon human action, which is not programmed—at least not yet. To address your earlier remarks, between January 2019 and January 2020, there have been twenty-six significant pieces of legislation introduced into the United States Congress that address privacy in various ways. None of them perfect, none of them comprehensive, but all of them are a great start to addressing surveillance capitalism and its ability to do whatever it wants. We also had, earlier this year, the beginning of a dial back of some of the illegitimate practices that were institutionalized in the Patriot Act. Lawmakers around the world have begun to be mobilized. Much of the analysis I've read finds that this whole wave of new legislative impetus has been driven by public opinion. We cannot underestimate our power. A lot of this began with Cambridge Analytica and whistleblower Christopher Wylie, and then successive revelations and leaks. I hope that my book contributed, at least a little bit, to some of this. The fact is that the consciousness of both the public and lawmakers today is different than it was two years ago. Is this a difference that is irreversible? I believe there are signs that, yes, it is irreversible, but in the end it depends on how much noise we can make on the streets, what we do in our communities, how we use our local political organizations, and how we put pressure on elected officials, companies, and other institutions.

Renata: You talk about mobilizing public opinion, but we must recognize the reality we face, in many countries in the world, of the monopoly of the media. We now have an integration of the monopoly of the media and the monopoly of the platform, and the result is a kind of tyranny of the algorithm pushing certain discourses to be louder than others. Never before have so many people been connected via the same platforms, but, at the same time, never before has it been so easy to hide and silence certain voices. Making noise on the streets will sound very loud if you are in Capitol Hill, but if you are in Myanmar and a genocide is being perpetrated, facilitated by Facebook, it is only if the *New York Times* raises the alarm that anyone will care. There is an inequality of tools and means, and we need to tailor our actions and mobilizations depending on the country we are in. In some countries, some citizens have big influence.

Shoshana: You are absolutely right. These dynamics are unfolding under very different political conditions around the world. In my book I talk about "instrumentarian power," which refers to totalizing data systems, the form of power that they produce, and the asymmetries of knowledge that enforce that power. It is the kind of power that works its will on human behavior through the medium of digital instrumentation. And I draw a distinction between this and the kind of totalitarian power that dominated the middle of the twentieth century, a form of power directly aimed at people's bodies and directly employing the violence of terror and murder in order to maintain control. Instrumentarian power operates differently, through the medium of social media, by nudging, herding, tuning, and coaxing the behavior of individuals, groups, and populations. In countries with authoritarian political systems, we can see what it means to combine these control systems—these data flows that are often developed under the aegis of surveillance capitalism or just straight up surveillance—with the aims and operations of authoritarian governments. That is a kind of societal endgame where there is not only the will to total power, but also the means to total power. That's why comparing the Chinese case and the European or American case requires a very different kind of analysis. We began by saying that we want to understand whether there is hope for our democracies. My premise, to make it explicit, is that we still have democracies on Earth today. They are flawed and under siege, as perhaps they have not been since the 1930s, but they are still functioning as democracies. One illustration of this is that we are having this conversation right now, and there are tens of thousands of others having conversations like this, online and in their homes. People everywhere are talking about the new contact tracing systems and asking themselves, "Am I really going to let my phone do that? I don't think so." My view is that we have an opportunity to finally bring our democracies up to the challenge of what it means to live in a time when 100 percent of information is digitally stored. The story of the rapid digitalization of our social milieu is literally about ten years old. It was not very long ago, in 2007, that we could first see that 97 percent of all information was digitally stored. Two thousand and two was the first year that we had more information in digital than in analog. Technology has gone through this tectonic shift, but our institutions have not. The correct institutional practices, systems of laws, and regulatory paradigms have not yet been invented. This is a huge creative undertaking for democracy that began, in earnest, in the fourth decade of the twentieth century, after economic collapse.

Renata: One of the most important things that I want to discuss is the huge increases in a range of inequalities, which have been one of the huge shames of our generation. You often refer to the concept of epistemic inequality, which I am hoping you can elaborate on. In connection with this, there's a lot of talk about universal basic income at the moment, and one means of addressing multifaceted inequalities might be to have a kind of equivalent of the universal basic income that works to equalize access to information. We need policies that not only equip citizens with economic means, but that help to level up critical thinking. Could this be a way to address the epistemic inequality that you speak of?

Shoshana: Epistemic inequality refers to the gap between what I can know and what can be known about me. Here we are, two decades into the rooting and flourishing of surveillance capitalism, and we've created huge information empires in the form of private companies like Google, Facebook, Microsoft, and Amazon. We went into the digital century saying, "This is going to be our century, the new Gutenberg century, the democratization of knowledge, disintermediation, a golden age of democracy in a digital world!" Instead, we created surveillance capitalism, which moves in the opposite direction, namely, on a collision course with democracy. It does so by virtue of its own economic logic—it must collect everything and it must do so in scale and in scope. It's not content just to have what you're doing online; it wants everything you're doing in your life, in your city, in your bedroom, in your kitchen. As an aside, in terms of Covid-19, one of the key aims of surveillance capitalism has been, for a long time, to get your body. That's been an important aspect of expanding its economies of scope and is, of course, one of the key opportunities that it sees now. Instead of the democratization of knowledge, surveillance capitalism has created massive asymmetries of knowledge. They know everything about us; we know very little about them. They can use that knowledge to shape our behavior in ways that are designed to bypass our awareness. This is a new axis of social inequality that defines the social order at a time when the West already struggles with economic inequalities unknown since the late nineteenth century. Epistemic inequality means exclusion and division, which amplify economic inequality. So, what is our response to this? Our response is that epistemic asymmetries could only constitute themselves in an environment absent of law. That's why Eric Schmidt, former CEO and chair of Google, celebrated the Internet as "the world's largest ungoverned space" in his book, *The New Digital Age*. Being ungoverned is the critical success factor for this asymmetrical knowledge and power. That's why I say that our challenge now is not a technological challenge but an institutional one. We have to create the institutional forms and laws that will interrupt and outlaw the economic logic that produced this inequality. When we say "epistemic inequality," we're talking about inequalities of epistemic rights. Epistemic rights refer to who gets to know, who decides who knows, and who decides who decides who knows. This is the arc of knowledge, authority, and power. Epistemic rights follow the trajectory of all other rights that have been codified in law. Take the right of freedom of expression—every baby can open its mouth and make noise; it doesn't need a juridical right to make noise. Provided our anatomy and physiology is healthy, every single one of us can speak and express ourselves, and that has always been the case. We didn't need a right or a law to make this so. There was a moment in history, however, when our political and social lives became complex enough that our right to voice was challenged and threatened. It was at that point in the development of humanity, society, and, especially, democracy, that we understood we needed to make the elemental right of expression into a juridical right, something fixed in law, under the power of democratic governance. That is the birth cycle of new rights. We are at a similar moment now, where our "rights to know" are elemental. I'm the only one who gets to know about my experience or my feelings, about what I do in my kitchen or bedroom. This is an elemental right that belongs to me. Because of the rise of surveillance capitalism and epistemic inequality, we have now entered that moment in history where my right to know my own experience can no longer be taken for granted and must be translated into law. Those laws will interrupt and outlaw the very systems of power that we're discussing.

Renata: There's a lot of public concern about the question of whether we are heading toward something like the Chinese social credit system. The rule of law operates well in normal times, let's say, but in these exceptional times we have heard crazy stories of drones surveilling people in parks and police entering people's houses to enforce quarantines. The United States is increasingly authoritarian and increasingly using technology to get away with police brutality—for example, the targeting of undocumented workers through the alliance between Palantir and the Immigration and Customs Enforcement Agency (ICE). Would you be able to comment on that?

Shoshana: In terms of the drones and the police brutality—power fills a vacuum. I said earlier that we've entered the third decade of the digital century naked. That nakedness is another metaphor for this vacuum. We have all these technological capabilities that have been given to what has become a tight-knit group of companies and their alliances with the state. The nature of those alliances varies from country to country, but we now see, in this time of crisis, a little bit of the veil lifting. We can see the alliances between these companies and the state, and the degree to which the state has become dependent on these companies for the knowledge that it needs. This, of course, is the fulfilment of the governments' original plan: let these fledgling companies develop their surveillance capabilities because we'll need them. This has been working all along, but now we see it in a very dramatic way. We are now reaping the results of the fact that we've made it through the first two decades of this digital transformation without the law and necessary institutional forms to uphold democracy; to sustain individual sovereignty, dignity, and rights; and to sustain what we think of, however imperfectly, as equality. Power, which has constituted itself faster than our institutional response, fills the vacuum. We all feel the pressure of the present crisis, but we must remind ourselves that creating the institutional forms, laws, and regulatory paradigms that we need does not happen in a month, a year, or a legislative cycle; it is the work of this decade. In the United States, we entered the 1930s with nothing like social security. There was little to protect people who tried to bargain collectively and use the right to strike. It took most of the 1930s to create the institutional forms that we now can't imagine living without. So, how do we mobilize today? The effects of our mobilization will be felt within the Western democracies but also in places like Myanmar or the Philippines where there is much less opportunity to organize and make a difference. We need to establish a democratic digital future that stands as contrast to an authoritarian future. The people of the world will look at these contrasting futures and one will be more appealing than the other. It is up to us to reject the determinism and the inevitablism that we read in the papers and are taught by the gaslighting rhetoric of the tech companies. We must avoid James Burnham cowardice in bowing to the forces of the moment and saying that our future is already doomed. We reject this.

Conversation held on April 18, 2020

Snake Oil or Socialism?

Roger Waters and Yanis Varoufakis

Yanis: In the present moment of a coronavirus pandemic, it is normal to crave a return to normality. But it would be an inexcusable waste not to use the lockdown to envision an altogether different now, a now worth fighting for once we are out there again. Just like the great wars, so too the Black Death, the Spanish flu, and now Covid-19 turn a mirror to our faces and force humanity to rethink its ways. There is no doubt that the powers that be will do their upmost to force us back to "business as usual." Are we going, like sheep, to return to the dystopia passing for normality, with no questions asked? Or are we going to seize the moment, ready to imagine another now and, indeed, to fight for it? I have the overwhelming honor and joy to be joined by Roger Waters—yes, girls and boys, friends and foes, *the* Roger Waters.

Roger: It is extraordinary what a huge change it is—even if you are living in the lap of luxury like I am—for there to be no soccer to watch three times a week, or whatever it might be in your life that is now missing. I was talking to a friend in England today who said, "Isn't it strange, I take the dog out in the morning and then the missus takes it out again in the afternoon, and, apart from that, we don't do anything." He hasn't used the car for six weeks, which really is a bizarre thing. The cricketer Harbhajan Singh tweeted the other day that the Himalayas have become visible from the rooftop of his home in Jalandhar for the first time in forty years. He said he had never imagined it was possible. Just by stopping all the traffic for a few weeks, or however long it's been, suddenly, the Himalayas become visible.

nis: The last time we were together was in London, in the demonstration inst Julian Assange's extradition. Now we are in lockdown to save our 1. We have a duty to remember the man who's been placed in solitary finement *not* to save him, as well as the thousands out there, the hordes borers, who are working so that you and I can isolate in our luxurious undings.

: Trust me, the two names that are in my head every day are Julian Assange and Vanessa Baraitser, who is the appalling magistrate who is keeping him locked up in Belmarsh Prison, even though that in itself might be the death sentence that she and the lackeys of the "grossest machine" are looking for. It is an absolute disgrace, and you and I could rant and rave for an hour, easily, just about that one small microcosm of how malign the powers that be are, and the dangerous way they are running the world. You mentioned at the beginning the question of whether we will be able to draw anything positive from this pandemic, whether our isolation will allow us the opportunity to recognize our predicament more clearly than we did before. My predicament was largely intellectual, but imagine being on the breadline where most people in the world are, living from one grain of rice to the next, constantly on the brink? People often ask me, "How do you explain, in North America, the fact that the poor people, the working classes, the disadvantaged—which is everyone except Bezos and fucking Zuckerberg—don't rise up and say, 'No, we can't live like this'?" And I have come to accept the following view: they are so oppressed and so engaged with the awful situation of having to make five dollars turn into seven just to get to the end of the month that they haven't got the energy to rebel.

Yanis: This has always been the case. One of my favorite quotations comes from a French aristocrat of the eighteenth century, Marquis de Condorcet, who said that the key to understanding successful oppression lies not in the guns of the oppressor, but in the mind of the oppressed. And the beauty of what we are experiencing now with the Covid-19 pandemic, the one thing that I get a modicum of hope from, is that people have actually seen what politics is about. Up until the lockdown, the media portrayed politics as a kind of football league, where it was about which team was scoring points and who was winning the championship for government. Now, however, we can see that politics is all about, as Lenin used to say, who does what to whom. The government decides who can stay and who will go, they can give trillions to their friends, or they can give it to the poor. Suddenly, we can see naked power and the extreme nastiness of it, which the Julian Assange case portrays very well. This is a chance for people to see through those layers of obfuscation and alienation that stop them from realizing who the real oppressors are.

Roger: Wouldn't that be a wonderful thing? The fact of the matter is, though, that the propaganda war, which is the most important war of all, grinds on—the bombardment hasn't stopped for a single second. In consequence, if we are to believe the polls that filter through, we are seeing that people approve of the way Trump is handling the Covid-19 pandemic and his approval ratings haven't gone down but, if anything, have gone up. The fact that he lies through his teeth constantly, that he always makes the wrong decisions, every single day, about everything, including this virus, affects people not at all. The fact that he is a product of reality TV and has this cheap veneer of showmanship about him is enough to persuade the people that he's a leader—notwithstanding the fact that he has no education of any kind, he is dumb as shit and knows nothing about anything.

Yanis: I thought we weren't going to waste our breath on Donald Trump! But I think we should speak about him briefly. My view is that the vast majority of people who support Trump don't do it because they think that he's telling the truth, or that he's competent, or that he is good for them. I think they have given up on politics. Look at the previous administration: Obama was a complete catastrophe. Obama is the reason for Donald Trump. He took the architects of the 2008 collapse, people like Tim Geithner and Larry Summers, and put them back into power to refloat and re-empower Wall Street. The fake news and fake policies were happening long before Trump. In my estimation, most people ask themselves, "Who should I vote for to piss off the establishment?" I don't think that the majority of those who vote for Trump actually believe in Trump.

Roger: You may well be right, maybe they don't. I t about the only day of the year in a small town in W body can get free health treatment of any kind. Peo days before and sleep in their cars to get free dental a woman with no teeth who said she had voted for Tru promised that he was going to save the coal industry and the working classes in America, and she had finally had th saying, "I'm beginning to believe maybe he didn't mean it know this isn't a breakthrough because we know that it's absolutely central to the whole system—not just in the United States of America but in most of the world. Rich white people figured out how they could colonize the rest of the world, and they did, and now they're going to screw everybody in it as hard as they can until we're all dead. That is basically the system. Occasionally there is a blip and, actually, the blips are becoming much bigger, which is great. The blips are Bolivia and Venezuela and Mexico, and these "pink tide" revolutions, where the teachings of Simón Bolívar rise to the surface, or Lenin, Marx, or whoever it might be who says, "Don't you think we should share this shit out a bit more fairly?"

Yanis: It is not looking good for us, though, is it Roger? I was speaking to Rafeal Correa two days ago and the news from Ecuador is just abysmal. That fantastic revolution, that hugely democratic effort by Correa, was totally usurped by what was, effectively, his vice president. Then there is Venezuela and, even though I am completely opposed to the United States' embargo on it, the fact is, it is still a military regime. Venezuela is not like Ecuador, which, under Rafeal Correa, was far more progressive. I can't support the Venezuelan regime, even though I oppose the attempts by the United States to throttle the people of Venezuela and to stop them from making a choice for themselves. To return to the subject of Trump, we are just dusting ourselves off after the complete success of the establishment in imposing Biden as the nominee of the Democrats and snuffing out the Bernie Sanders revolution. The only one who could beat Trump has been defeated by his own party, yet again.

Roger: It is not even a two party system. It is a one party system in which they have given the snake two heads, calling one, Democrat, and one, Republican, where both absolutely, 100 percent, support the prevailing capitalist system.

Yanis: They are both united against having a national healthcare service at a time of a global pandemic!

Roger: How can you reconcile the idea of the providing of healthcare to a nation of people with the fact that it is for profit, and *only* for profit? This is now also being imposed on the National Health Service in England: a completely profit-based model. This is the whole idea of the Friedman school, of Chicago-whatever economics. And it is the whole neoliberal nightmare foisted on us by Reagan, Thatcher, and Blair—let us not forget that the Labour movement joined into this happily and Blair is still a happy perpetrator of the death that it foists on the whole population of the globe. They are trying to kill the whole planet as fast as they can. What do we do? Well, we make as much noise as we can. But how do we, the left, actually create the mass movement? The Socialist Equality Party in the United States, for instance, is actually really bad at selling its "product," which, of course, is not a product but a political philosophy, and it is one to which I absolutely subscribe. I believe in socialism. "Socialism" is a dirty word where I live, in America, but it is not a dirty idea. It is the *only* idea, in my view, that can find a way through the darkness of the world that we live in, to the possible light at the possible end of a possible tunnel that *might* allow our children and grandchildren to live.

Yanis: You have reminded me of something Rosa Luxemburg once said: "It's socialism or barbarism." Unfortunately, those who spoke in the name of socialism proved quite barbaric as well, even the Labour Party, or the Trade Union Council in Britain. A great deal of authoritarianism rises up within our own ranks. That is why I have a soft spot for the Spanish anarcho-syndicalists during the civil war, who had black and red in their flag: red to signify revolution and black to signify the darkness in the soul of each one of us, which we must always be aware of because it can rise up and put us in our own gulags, as has happened so many times. Going back to Thatcher, who you mentioned: I moved to England as a seventeen-year-old in 1978 and left in 1988, so I experienced the whole thrust of Thatcherism. Allow me to ask you a personal question, if I may, about Thatcher. It seems to me, judging by your work, that the postwar consensus that you grew up in, the "postwar dream," made you, personally, as Roger Waters, feel deeply alienated. And yet, when Maggie Thatcher came and shattered that postwar dream, taking that aspiration that was part and parcel of English life before 1979 and replacing it with the cacophony of money making, suddenly, you seem to miss the dream that alienated you? Am I completely wrong here?

Roger: Missed the dream? No, I never missed the dream. We never let go of the dream, of the idea that we might discover a more ecumenical and fairer world, a world where we human beings cooperate with one another and, in consequence, provide ourselves with a future—because the current model is unsustainable and unworkable. Any economist will tell you that we cannot go on expanding. Margaret Thatcher was a product of the times, and what happened in the '70s and '80s was that we started to come up against some of the harsh realities of the divisions that were always there and that survived the revolution after the Second World War. There was something of a revolution after the Second World War in England, with the creation of the welfare state and so on, but, little by little, neoliberal propaganda managed to sell the idea that cooperating with one another in a social way, and acting as civilized society, was not the way for *their* lives to get better. The way for *their* lives to improve, so they could afford more McDonald's and reruns of *Bonanza* (I assume that is what people wanted) was actually to hand over the reins of power to venture capitalists. Give the world to Gordon Gekko and suddenly the cake will expand to the extent that even the crumbs will feel like we're living in luxury. That was the idea.

Yanis: Maybe I shouldn't have used the word dream, but there was a postwar consensus in the '60s, one of a mixed economy, free education, and the welfare state, and yet—from the way I approach your work—that was a consensus that was quite oppressive and alienating for you? Of course, you missed it when Thatcher replaced the consensus with this situation you describe, where you can't even imagine that anyone can do something for nothing, where nobody is taken seriously unless they have money. Nevertheless (and maybe I'm completely wrong), looking at your music, your lyrics, there was an alienation that you seemed to feel that preceded Thatcher.

Roger: I am only who I am, and I don't react well to errant authority. I do not react well to seeing really stupid people doing really stupid things that cause real fucking pain to my brothers and sisters all over the world. I will always respond to that. It may be that if the dream had continued and the gap between the rich and poor had narrowed in England and we had turned into a cross between Sweden and Denmark and Bolivia, I might still find things to rail against. For instance, I would probably find myself fighting against political correctness. But that is a cross that I would far rather bear than the cross that I do bear, which is seeing the human race of which I am a part being killed faster rather than slower. A couple of weeks ago, I watched the DiEM TV conversation with Noam Chomsky, and I was struck by the fact that it doesn't matter how far you go back, nuclear war and climate change are the key issues—he almost stops there. He goes on to talk about democracy, freedom of the press, and other things, but basically he says that war and climate change are killing us faster than anything else. We know that the oligarchs and plutocrats make money out of nuclear weapons, oil, and the fossil fuel industry, and that they won't let any of it go so long as they can make a profit out of it. They love war; war is the most profitable thing. And Chomsky says, "That's all very well, but you are committing suicide, that is what you are doing." I don't think he's wrong. Part of our job is to keep going back to Chomsky's two primary issues. Chomsky also mentioned a risk report presented at the 2020 World Economic Forum in Davos by a major consulting firm, which listed the eighteen biggest threats facing the world today, as ranked by over 2,000 CEOs.[1] Climate change and nuclear war were not included, they didn't make it into the eighteen. What was number one? Regulation.

Yanis: The minimum wage! This is going to destroy the world!

Roger: The question is: How do we arrive at a place where we can make even a small amount of progress? Where we can implement even something as simple as a nuclear arms reduction deal—something you would think anybody with an IQ above room temperature would immediately agree with? If Bernie Sanders [were] to become president of the United States, perhaps he would do that. But he won't because, as you rightly point out, he's been railroaded by the Democratic National Committee for the second time— the only viable candidate who might have made any impression upon the Trump voting base has been wiped out because he doesn't represent the plutocracy that is the United States. Biden obviously does. Biden is perfect:

---

1 https://www.fticonsulting.com/~/media/Files/emea--files/insights/reports/2020/jan/resilience-barometer-2020.pdf.

he's got the false teeth and he has horrible ideas about everything, so he's perfect!

Yanis: Biden has no policies—he is simply the depository of all the policies of the status quo. It is very easy to lose heart, because every time there is a glimmer of hope it is snuffed out, whether it is Jeremy Corbyn or Bernie Sanders. In 2015, once, for five months, the establishment in Europe felt that they were losing control and they went to pieces. They were panicking. But, of course, they managed to turn it all around, with the help of the media. So, what do we do about this? There are two very broad things I think we need to try. Firstly, we have to take a leaf out of the books of the bankers and the fascists. Because the bankers and the fascists understand one thing: that the only way to succeed is through internationalism and solidarity. If you look at Jair Bolsonaro, Donald Trump, Matteo Salvini, Viktor Orbán, and Nigel Farage, you will see that they are mates. They operate like an *internazionale*, right? The same thing with financiers: they know no borders. They have absolutely no *capacity*, even, to discriminate between German bankers and French bankers and Japanese bankers. They are very good at forcing governments, in moments of financial distress, to refloat their banks with public money. We need to learn from this. We need to build a progressive international movement that has one agenda for the world but finds its specializations in different parts of the world. The nation-state–based policies of the UK Labour Party that operates as if there is no world outside, the Greek communist party that is frozen in time and in space, and the German Social Democrats—for them, the rest of the world just doesn't exist. We need to internationalize. The second thing connects to what you said about the corrosive power of money and how we are all committing suicide like a stupid virus that kills too many of its hosts: the planet and society. What is the kernel of that virus of capitalism, that virus of perfect maximization? I think it has to do with shareholding. The one market that is the beginning of all this toxicity is the share market. We have come to accept the idea of the corporation as a given. Lots of people work in it, but none of them own it. The people who own it? We don't even know who they are. There are corporations inside other corporations and shell corporations and so on. How about a very radical idea:

we can have markets and we can have shares, but let's imagine that shares are like library cards in universities. You join the university as a student and you get a library card. If you don't join the university, you can't have one. You can't sell it, you can't buy it. It gives you one vote, let's say, in the corporation. That, to me, is a mental experiment through which to start imagining a world in which money cannot become toxic, it cannot gather sufficient power to mobilize humanity's resources.

Roger: I used to go to the co-op to buy fucking potatoes when I was young. I remember the idea of ownership of the company by the customer and/or by the workers.

Yanis: Do you remember the Trustee Savings Bank in Britain? It used to belong to anyone who had a bank account there. And do you remember what Thatcher did with it? She wanted to privatize it, but it didn't belong to the state, so the state could not sell it. So what she did was she nationalized it in order to privatize it. If we behave like that but in reverse, then we're done.

Roger: What you're suggesting is that if we would cooperate with one another internationally then we would be in a stronger position. But we have to sell this. We have to become such good salesmen that we can persuade people that there is something better than snake oil that actually works—it's called healthcare!—and to persuade the rest of our brothers and sisters all over the world that snake oil is not the answer. Clearly, we all live in communities that have been subsisting on snake oil for a couple of thousand years at least. Today, our leaders, the Jeff Bezoses and Zuckerbergs and neocons, are using their power to kill everyone. They may be starting with the poor—who they are killing happily *just* to make a few quid—but they are going to kill everyone. We have to somehow sell the idea that there is more joy in helping people, in loving one another, than there is in poaching them and killing them to make a few shillings. How do we sell that idea?

Yanis: The DiEM25 movement, with Bernie Sanders and others, is going to put together a manifesto for the world—a socialist, progressive, but very liberal (in the original meaning of the word) manifesto. Speaking of salesmen, though, I can't imagine a better one than Roger Waters! Would you like to share the idea that you had for the tour you were going to do in the United States this summer?

Roger: My idea for the "This Is Not a Drill" tour, that *will*, at some point, go on the road, is that it will be part rock-and-roll show, part cinema that portrays a three-layer society. There is a thing that I call the "i-cloud" in the sky, where the ruling classes live in a sort of weird, white, floaty construct of my imagination. Underneath them, in what I call the Netherworld, is the real world, where the rest of us live in fucking misery. It's the oppressed state that most people live in, where you never have more than $20 in your pocket, and you are desperately wondering what you're going to do at the end of the month. If you are Black in America, it is wondering when they are going to come and put you in prison to work for them for nothing, which is sort of the Thirteenth Amendment, designed to keep slavery going. It's also the wider Southern world, where the colonialists established their proxies, the Modis and others, to take over for them. The Netherworld is pretty grim, in my view. Then there is "the bar," which is a bar, and it is a dream. It is dreamt by the people who are in it and it's where we talk to one another, exchange ideas, and express our love for one another. It's like the little song that I wrote for the end of *The Wall*: "All alone or in twos, the ones who really love you walk up and down outside the wall, some hand in hand, and some gathered together in bands, the bleeding hearts and the artists make their stand, and when they've given you their all, some stagger and fall, after all it's not easy banging your heart against some mad bugger's wall." Well, the bar is where we try to figure out how to make the banging of our hearts against the mad bugger's wall *productive*, which is why I'm speaking about sales and using the salesman analogy. I've actually just finished writing a song in which I try to explain the predicament of those of us who are in the bar. One of the lines is about how we're uncomfortable because we're required to drop napalm on the neighbor's kids—the idea of perpetual warfare being something that's going on in our neighborhoods. Maybe I am a salesman to the extent that I can make that connection and put it in a fucking song and sing about it. People will say, "What are you talking about? We don't drop napalm on the neighbor's kids." Yeah, you do, these are our neighbors; just 'cause they're in Vietnam doesn't mean they're not our neighbors. That old woman who you are killing in Venezuela, or in Iran, or wherever our sanctions are being applied, is just as much your neighbor as your grandmother is.

Yanis: We all live downstream these days; we all receive all the crap that goes into the river. You've reminded me of a moment in *Capital* in which Marx feels for the capitalist. He says, think about it, we live in a system where if the capitalist does not exploit the shit out of the worker, he will go bankrupt, because all the other capitalists will. So what happens? He becomes like his own workers. He sells his soul every day to capital, accumulating it not for himself, but for capital's sake. He becomes enslaved by the machinery that he's created. This is the beauty, for me, of the epic poetry and lyricism of Marx.

Roger: Chomsky makes a similar point about these CEOs of companies like Exxon and Chevron. He points out that these guys have to live a completely schizophrenic life—because how can somebody who is clever enough to become the CEO of Exxon not understand climate change? Particularly someone who is working for a company that spent millions on research to find out if climate change was real and discovered that, in fact, it was, and then took the decision not to tell anyone about it because it was bad for business! If that CEO, when he's at Davos and he's asked, "What's your biggest fear?" replies by saying, "Climate change," he's fired! Immediately!

Yanis: What do you think are some concrete actions we can take to build a global network of solidarity, especially given the present limitations imposed by social distancing?

Roger: We know that the volume of traffic and the exchange of information on social media is beyond our imagination. Unfortunately, 99.9999999 percent of this is entirely vacuous and has nothing to do with the people's struggle against the plutocracies. If, however, we could somehow takeover even 10 percent of the traffic on social media and devote it to the potential that we have for helping one another, then that would be huge.

Yanis: I would like to share an example of how you, Roger, have gone about building solidarity in your own actions. Some time ago, I received an email from Roger regarding a factory near Thessaloniki that went bust in 2013. The owner effectively took a loan and just fled to Switzerland or somewhere and the place went into receivership. The workers occupied the factory and have been working it since 2012, and profitably! They proved that the place was not bust, it was just that the capitalist didn't want to be a capitalist anymore—he wanted to be a rentier. Now, where does Roger come into this? He contacted the workers to give them support and cc'd the message to me and I contacted them immediately. Our right-wing government is trying to shut the factory down out of pure nastiness. What is the point of destroying the livelihood of people who have taken over a failed company? And do you know what they make? They make eco-friendly detergent and handwashing gels—at a time of a global virus outbreak. Two weeks ago, the government switched off the electricity. I contacted the minister of energy and I gave him a scolding—because being a leader of a party I have the right to do this—and he promised me that, within two weeks, the electricity would be back. This is a concrete example of the actions we can and must take. Whether or not they succeed individually, the struggle continues.

Conversation held on April 20, 2020

The Urgent Global Need for Whistleblowers

Daniel Ellsberg and Angela Richter

Angela: Hello, Daniel, how are you coping with the isolation?

Daniel: This week, my wife and I celebrated the fifty-fifth anniversary of our first date, which was the Students for a Democratic Society march against the Vietnam War. At the time, I was working on the war in the Pentagon, but she induced me to come and join her in the march. So I left the Pentagon and marched around the White House protesting the war and, actually, finding that I agreed with most of what I heard.

Angela: It sounds as though falling in love with your wife changed the course of your life, and perhaps influenced you to later become a whistleblower?

Daniel: Yes. We broke up, actually, over the Vietnam War. My role in the Pentagon, I thought, was to moderate the violence in what I saw was a hopeless struggle. But she didn't like what I was doing and asked me, "How can you be part of this?" At that point, I actually broke off our engagement and we were apart for three years. When we got together again in 1969, I had already started copying the Pentagon Papers and expected to go to prison for life when they came out. We spent 1970, the first year of our marriage, putting out the Pentagon Papers. I tried to get them to the United States Senate, which I had already tried in 1969, but they wouldn't accept them because they were afraid of suffering political penalties. Then in 1971, I gave them to the *New York Times*. For the next two years, I was on trial facing a possible 115 years in prison on twelve felony counts. In terms of sentences, that was something like a record at that time, although Julian Assange now faces a possible 175 years. Strictly speaking, it would come to the same thing: life imprisonment. Up until 1973, that was our marriage. It was on August 8, 1973, our third anniversary, that Nixon announced his resignation. This was not really foreseeable and it would not have happened were it not for Nixon's fear that I had other documents that would reveal the nuclear threats he had made against North Vietnam. In order to stop me from putting those documents out, Nixon took the criminal action of sending CIA "assets" into my former psychoanalyst's office to get information that could be used to blackmail me into silence. When there wasn't any such information, he later sent much of the same people to "incapacitate" me totally—which the prosecutor understood to mean "killed"—on the steps of the Capitol on May 3, 1972. These and other crimes were intended to keep me from demonstrating with documents what I was saying: that he was making threats of escalation in Vietnam, including the possibility of nuclear weapons. To this day, most people still don't know about this. They never really believed me, because I didn't have the documents that Nixon feared I had. I should have had them: I knew people who had seen target folders for nuclear weapons on North Vietnam in 1969, Nixon's first year in office. Roger Morris, who resigned from the White House over the invasion of Cambodia, told me that it was the greatest regret of his life that he had not brought out the documents that Nixon feared I had. He said, "We should have thrown open the safes and screamed bloody murder, because that's exactly what it was." The plans for nuclear attack didn't get carried out, and for only one reason: on October 15, 1969, Nixon faced two million people protesting on the streets, on a weekday. This was a general strike, though nobody called it that because it sounded too radical for America. Nixon had scheduled the targets for November 3, one of them only a mile and a half from the Chinese border, and others on the borders of Laos and on the Ho Chi Minh Trail. When two million people abandoned work and school to congregate in public squares and demonstrate against the war, Nixon could not carry out his threat to escalate it. He couldn't give the speech that had been drafted for him, which was to read, "Today, pursuant to my orders . . . bombers are flying." Actually, bombers with nuclear weapons aboard *were* on alert at that time, but Nixon couldn't give the order because of the demonstrations. The next month, indeed, there was an even larger demonstration in Washington itself. Those demonstrators, including myself and my children in Los Angeles, had no idea they were preventing nuclear war. I personally was copying the Pentagon Papers not because I thought there was any chance of an escalation in Nixon's first year, but because I thought that there would be an offensive down the line, within a couple of years, which would cause Nixon to use nuclear weapons. And, indeed, in 1972 Nixon was discussing nuclear weapons with Henry Kissinger, while I was on trial.

Angela: And could you explain why Nixon was so concerned about the Pentagon Papers?

Daniel: The Pentagon Papers were a history, in forty-seven volumes, every page top-secret and sensitive, of our decision-making in Vietnam from 1945 to 1968. That is, they ended before Nixon came into office. They didn't directly threaten Nixon, but what they did show is that the four presidents before him—Eisenhower, Truman, Kennedy, and Johnson—had all lied about their aims and what the consequences were likely to be. They totally misled the public at every stage. And I knew, though I didn't have the documents to prove it, that a fifth president, Nixon, was also lying and making secret threats. And he intended to carry those threats out if the Vietnamese didn't accept his demands, which they never did. I expected the war to escalate and, in an attempt to do what I could to prevent that, I put out this history in the hopes that people would see that yet another president was lying to them. I failed in that. People simply could not believe that having been elected on the promise of ending the war, Nixon would expand it. It was only when word came out, unexpectedly, of the criminal actions Nixon had taken (mainly against me), that he wound up in impeachment hearings that led him to resign.

Angela: And this saved your life?

Daniel: It saved me from prison. And, much more importantly, it made the war endable. I'd understood from '69 onward that the war would not end with Nixon in office. And in November '72, after the revelations of Watergate, he won a landslide election. In October, just before the election, Kissinger appeared on television to impart the message "Peace is at hand." The largest bombing in human history took place in December that year, when the US dropped twenty thousand tons of explosives on North Vietnam. At that point, it had been a year and a half since I'd released the Pentagon Papers, and when people asked me what effect they'd had, the truthful answer was none. And it seemed as though the whole peace movement had had no effect, either. Well, I was wrong, but that's what I thought at the time.

Angela: In the long term, it had a huge effect. One thing that strikes me is that, from what you've said, it sounds as though people were shocked when they discovered that their presidents were lying to them. This seems worlds apart from the situation today.

Daniel: Today, the world has an American president who lies several times a day. Trump has been clocked at an average of about six blatant lies a day, totaling something like thirteen thousand lies. You are absolutely right that the political environment has changed. It is true that when Lyndon B. Johnson, before Nixon, was found to have been lying repeatedly, he couldn't run for office. The fact he kept the war going was the main factor, but his lying shocked people. The people who back Trump pay no attention to his lying. But there is another factor that needs to be taken into account, then and now. The 1972 election was won by Nixon on race. After conducting the war for nearly four years, Nixon was not doing well in the polls, especially when he was faced by George Wallace, an independent. The base for George Wallace were southern racists, mainly, as well as northern racists and blue-collar Catholics who felt displaced, in some cases, by busing and efforts toward civil rights. Had Wallace run, as he was determined to in '72, Nixon would have lost. He wouldn't even have won narrowly. Nixon was working to be number two in the hearts of Wallace voters by promising "law and order," which was code for "keeping Blacks in their place." When George Wallace was shot on May 8, 1972, election year, all of the Wallace vote went to Nixon, giving him a landslide. The Trump base right now, the 32–38 percent of people who will back him despite the lies, or anything else he does, is the Wallace base of support. It is their sons and it is people in the same jobs. It is the people who Hillary Clinton (very fatally and unfairly) called "deplorables." These people are very ordinary, patriotic Americans who are decent in many ways, except that many of them are racist and sexist. For that reason, they are against Hillary, and are very chauvinistic against immigrants, who they feel are taking their jobs, and Jews, who they think are pushing civil rights down their throats. In Charlottesville in 2017, they demonstrated with the slogan: "Jews will not replace us!"[1] A very strange cry. This is the event, remember, which Trump responded to by say-

---

1   https://www.nytimes.com/2017/08/12/us/charlottesville-protest-white-nationalist
    .html.

ing, "There are very good people on both sides." The first time in my life that I saw people openly performing Nazi salutes was the night of Trump's inauguration. That would be forbidden in Germany, if I am not mistaken.

Angela: Yes, it is forbidden in Germany. What you describe is, of course, on one level obvious, but it is also shocking to see that Trump's followers, at least 40 percent of them, behave like a cult, in the sense that they are indifferent to what he does. To them, it is more about what he is, that he is "one of them." They feel that they can be openly racist again, because the president himself is. The cynicism of these people seems very great.

Daniel: Let me give you a slightly different view. When you say cynical, that implies there's no morality involved. I think there is a morality. It is a different morality, a different ethics from what, let's say, you and I are committed to. Were Confederates, the people who fought for slavery in the United States, without morals? Did they have no conscience, no guilt? No, I don't think that's the case. They felt, to their bones, that part of their identity, their moral identity, was white Christian culture. According to this, women must be kept in their place, which is subordinate, and Blacks must be kept in their place, which is subordinate. Confederates aspired to reintroduce slavery to Mexico after it was abolished, and they appropriated a large amount of Mexican land to this end. They didn't succeed in making it all slave territory, but they wanted to. That is a large aspect of what was being fought over in the Civil War: not the existence of slavery, but its expansion. Since Charlottesville, I began delving further into history to understand what had been before, going back as far as the Revolution, which was led, after all, by slave owners. Our most revered icons—Washington, Jefferson, and Madison—were all slave owners, as were nine of the first eleven presidents of the United States. I did not know that until quite recently.

Angela: Neither did I. It is not something that is mentioned or addressed.

Daniel: The slavery of the Civil War has ended, but, in effect, the social and economic aspects of it were reinstituted about ten years later in 1876, the end of Reconstruction, when a century of Jim Crow ensued and the Blacks were not literally enslaved but were subject to what was in effect apartheid.

I've learned about my country in a way that is not reassuring, but explains what is happening today. And sexism is as much a problem as racism. This includes a startling number of women, white women, who don't think their gender is suited to presidency. In 2016, Hillary Clinton lost the votes of a majority of white women. We have major problems here, and not just in America. Very obvious in Europe is the chauvinism against Muslims in particular. Let me move, for a moment, to the major threats that we face as a species, one of which we are seeing now—or at least a hint of it, for Covid-19 is a warning of pandemics to come. At worst, some have said that we can expect a century of pandemics, because of the urbanization occurring with globalization and the expansion of production worldwide. The concentration of populations in major cities makes pandemics almost inevitable, and a pandemic strain more lethal and infectious than Covid-19 is not unlikely.

Angela: Yes, and what will happen when the ice melts with global warming? Will this cause the release of viruses and bacteria that existed millions of years ago and were frozen in the ice? If so, then Covid-19 is only a rehearsal for the pandemics we will face in the future. It is really a wake-up call.

Daniel: My friend Noam Chomsky is one of the few people who really links, in urgency and passion, the problem of climate to that of nuclear weapons. For most people, just one of these issues is enough to keep them occupied. His recent book, *Internationalism or Extinction*, also mentions, toward the end, the pandemic as a third problem. The Covid-19 pandemic doesn't remotely compare to the scale of death and disease possible with nuclear war or climate collapse, but future pandemics? Yes, they may reach that scale. In terms of the climate threat, both drought and rising sea levels will almost certainly cause enormous migrations. We've seen the political response of Europe to efforts such as Angela Merkel's to allow one million refugees to enter Germany. It is not 1 million but tens or hundreds of millions who will be forced to migrate due to climatic changes brought about by human agency, and very specifically by corporations like Exxon and other oil giants. Interestingly, a side effect of the lockdown in America is that oil prices are plummeting. As of today, prices are in the negative, which means that, for the first time in history, oil companies are paying people to take their oil because they don't have anywhere to store it. The world is demanding that what Exxon is pulling out of the ground should be left in the ground. This raises the question: When we go back to work, when we need energy in the factories, what should it be based on? We have months, maybe years, before economic activity is reestablished on a large scale. What should we be doing? Should we be fracking and extracting oil in the Arctic? Absolutely not. We will be told our demands are "unrealistic," that things need to return to "normal," but, if we want human society to remain, then *realistically* we should not go back to building weapons and maintaining the doomsday machine, and we should not be lifting oil out of the ground. We should be building sustainable energy systems, and that means confronting the economic and political power of the strongest institutions in the world, institutions that have co-opted governments. We face an enormous battle in trying to keep the skies as clear as they have become this month. It is unlikely that we will win, but we shouldn't regard it as impossible

Angela: And whistleblowers can greatly increase our chances. Given the impact of Covid-19 on social movements, is there much hope that public pressure will succeed in freeing whistleblowers who are imprisoned?

Daniel: There is some hope. Michael Cohen, the man who was, to some extent, Trump's accomplice, and then, once convicted, turned against him to be almost a whistleblower, has now been released from prison because of the danger of contracting Covid-19.[2] This should be enormously magnified. One person not being released is Julian Assange, despite his immune system being compromised terribly by spending seven years without sunlight in the Ecuadorian Embassy. He is now in prison, and his request for bail due to the grave risk to his health posed by Covid-19 was denied.[3] This cruelty, of course, is intended to send a message to whistleblowers, as was the decision to sentence Chelsea Manning to thirty-five years in prison, and the forcing of Ed Snowden into permanent exile. All of this is intended to silence—just

2   https://www.theguardian.com/us-news/2020/may/20/michael-cohen-to-be-released-from-prison-and-serve-sentence-at-home.

3   https://uk.reuters.com/article/uk-health-coronavirus-britain-assange/wikileaks-founder-julian-assange-denied-bail-by-london-court-idUKKBN21C26G.

as Nixon sought to silence me with his crimes. It takes unusual moral courage, a willingness to sacrifice your freedom, to tell the truth about what
governments are doing. And this is crucial in the present moment. For
what the Covid-19 pandemic has revealed to us is the truth of what Baron
Oxenstierna, a major statesman of Sweden, said to his son: "Do you not
know, my son, with how little wisdom the world is governed?" The message
of my book, *The Doomsday Machine*, is how badly we have all been governed
by nuclear policies which are extraordinarily dangerous and terrible. The
doomsday machines in Russia and the US, and the somewhat smaller ones
in other countries, are all designed to bring about nuclear winter. They are
preparations for the annihilation of most people on Earth. Yet, this isn't
even an issue in the election campaign here in the US or in other countries around the world, every one of which is potential collateral damage
in a war between the US and Russia. The change that we need in the world
will not come from governments or multinational corporations, it will have
to come from the people below. And that will require people to reveal the
truth from inside: we do need more whistleblowers. In addition to the climate and nuclear threats, there is a movement now that Chomsky refers to
as an "ultra-nationalist reactionary international," evident in many parts
of the world, from Brazil to Hungary. And I believe Trump aspires to be like
those he most admires in the world: a president for life. In other words, I
think he is an actual danger to democracy. I am not at all convinced that he
would simply accept an election result against him and step down. It is not
unthinkable that he would take emergency moves to suspend the elections,
dismiss the results as false, or use military means to stay in office, just as
Nixon was feared to be prepared to do in 1974. His defense secretary, James
Schlesinger, was so worried that Nixon would not allow himself to be put
out of office that he gave unconstitutional orders to the Joint Chiefs of Staff
that they must not obey orders from the White House without checking
with him. I believe that measures like that will probably be necessary in
the next nine months, and not only in the US. To return to your question
on whistleblowers, in part, our struggle involves changing the ethics which
condemn whistleblowing on the grounds that the "president knows best,"
that you shouldn't release information that he or she doesn't want released.

One of the most human moral feelings that has ever existed is don't tell outsiders the secrets of "our" group. People who are whistleblowers have promised their corporation or government that they will not tell secrets, and they break that promise when they realize that, as humans, they should (and they find that they do) have a loyalty beyond that promise. In America, we've taken an oath to support the Constitution, and when the Constitution is clearly violated by presidents such as Nixon, Johnson, Bush, and Trump, some people realize that they have a duty to oppose and expose this violation, even at the risk of life imprisonment or possibly death. And the point is: it *is* worth a life. Of course it is worth your life, when you recognize that you were being asked to participate in mass murder or in the destruction of society, as is involved in the climate case. There are loyalties that are more important and should override loyalties to your president, nation, ethnic group, and even family, which is the highest loyalty many people will acknowledge. Such loyalties are important, and to ignore or violate them certainly impacts your social status, career, and freedom. But there is a loyalty higher than them. We have got to develop a loyalty to the human species—and to all life on Earth, actually—that overrides loyalties of nation, religion, corporation, and family. The Covid-19 pandemic, the climate crisis, and the crisis of democracy are showing the urgency of this. We've got to develop a concern for all people on Earth. If we succeed, we might be the first species to have a "species concern" that extends to all of its members. No other species has ever had the capability to destroy itself by its own actions and, along with it, every other large species, as we do in the form of a nuclear winter or climate catastrophe. With our intelligence, technology, language, and ability to collaborate, we have, as the dark side of those abilities, produced (in being, in operation) the ability to wipe out all of human civilization and most other species. And we have a party in power in the US that is built top to bottom on climate change deniers, led by President Trump. That is why Chomsky calls the Republican Party the most dangerous organization in human history.[4] And we now know that, as in the case of every catastrophe known to me, human, social, or otherwise, there were inside warnings of the Covid-19 pandemic. This is always denied—"Who

4 https://www.democracynow.org/2017/4/26/chomsky_on_the_gop_has_any.

could have seen this coming?" But we know that there were the highest level, urgent warnings of this pandemic from late January on (if not earlier), which was two months before Trump actually acted against it. He overrode and ignored the warnings. Humans are capable of changing the policy on all of the key issues that face us today, as we did in 1969 with the general strike against the Vietnam War. The terrible irony is that we are going to be facing decisions, possibly within months, that deserve a general strike, but we can't currently have one! Extinction Rebellion, for instance, can't really continue, responsibly, to hold mass gatherings and carry out acts of civil disobedience. We are already *on* a general strike, in effect, right now!

Angela: So many things are now impossible, but we should never let a good crisis go to waste. As you say, we may not be able to call a general strike, but we are, in effect, having one forced upon us, and this is an opportunity to think about our situation anew. This stoppage of capitalism was unthinkable before the Covid-19 pandemic (although, as you said, there were warnings that went unheeded by our leaders). Before the pandemic, if we had proposed to drastically reduce air travel because of its impact on the climate, everyone would have said, "Impossible! We have to fly!" Now, we can see clear skies in cities around the world, for the first time in decades in some cases. Earlier, you touched on the moral framework of the 50 percent of Trump voters who Hillary Clinton called "deplorables." Could you elaborate more on this?

Daniel: Many Trump voters are influenced by age-old Christian ethical and moral frameworks. Romans 13 in the New Testament says, "Obey your rulers, for they are given by God." This idea that our leaders are divinely authorized is very strong. Bush actually said, as a born-again Christian, "God told me to invade Iraq." I say he should have gotten a second opinion! If somebody told you to invade a country that hasn't threatened us, that wasn't God! And of course, the Bible is also patriarchal. It says, "Wives, submit to your husbands," for men are kings in their households. This is an ethic, and a very strong one. I live in a country that has never had a woman president. And Christians, the Southern evangelicals, definitely point to slavery as an institution that is compatible with the Bible, which it is. Slavery is never condemned in the Bible. In fact, in the Ten Commandments, the command-ment "Thou shalt not covet" includes, in its expanded form, "do not covet your neighbors' slaves." The Bible does not criticize slavery, nor war or gen-ocide. If you look at Exodus or Joshua, you'll find God commanding geno-cide—the killing of every man, woman, child, and animal—in order to make room for the Israelites, for the Hebrews. God reproves those who try and keep some of the women or animals as booty, saying, "You have violated my commandment." God is calling, here, for what we later called "unjust war." He is calling for the "heroes" to do what the US did to Germany and Japan, and what the Nazis did in the blitz of London: indiscriminately bombing men, women, children, and animals. However, what I want to convey is that Hillary Clinton was not only politically mistaken, but was actually wrong to call Trump voters "deplorables." What is deplorable are their ideas—for instance, that it is wrong to participate in elevating women beyond "their place," or to treat Black people as being worthy of respect, as important as white people. That was an ethic and, I would say, a deplorable ethic. And what I am saying is: we have to learn a new ethic. One basis for this ethic is the idea that there are human loyalties that go beyond loyalties to our lead-ers, nations, ethnic groups, and even families. This is not a very common human idea, and the state denies it and punishes it. It is on that basis that Chelsea Manning and Ed Snowden were punished and exiled. Manning very openly said that she thought that the injustice and oppression waged on the Third (or former colonial) World by the First World in general, not only by the US, needed to be exposed. She was acting on a loyalty that went beyond being an American. Similarly, many people thought it was good that Snowden revealed the unconstitutional and criminal surveillance of Americans. However, he also revealed US surveillance occurring all around the world, and people thought that wasn't his business. If the US is trying to get at everybody else's secrets, why should he reveal that? Snowden's atti-tude was that it wasn't wrong to be surveilling Merkel, because that was a targeted surveillance on an individual and that's what intelligence agen-cies are for. He did object, however, to the surveillance of ordinary German citizens and everybody in the world. Was this illegal? No. But he felt it was wrong, and that it threatened democracy everywhere. Snowden is, as many know, an exceptionally patriotic American, as am I. But we are not only loyal to America—we are concerned about what America does to other people. And, beyond this, we have a concern that extends to all humans in the world. That is a new ethic, largely, but it is not newly invented—Gandhi and Martin Luther King talked in this way, precisely, but rather than concern and loyalty they spoke of universal "love." I have never fully accepted that. I think that love is more personal, selective, and subjective. But to extend concern and loyalty beyond the largest groups—national, religious, ethnic—that we identify with, that would be new.

Angela: Despite the fact that you and Snowden both declare yourselves as American patriots, especially in terms of wanting to defend the Constitution, you were considered by many people to be traitors. Today, you are considered as a hero. How long did it take for people to acknowledge that what you did was right, and how long will it take for Chelsea Manning, Edward Snowden, and Julian Assange to also be considered heroes?

Daniel: From the very beginning, there were people who admired and supported what I did, and there were also very many others who thought I was a traitor. This charge, however, went against the Constitution, which defines treason as "making war against the United States or adhering to its enemies, giving them aid and comfort." It is the only felony defined in the Constitution, and it would take a constitutional amendment to broaden it. And that was because, in fact, our country was founded by traitors. Every person who signed the Declaration of Independence in 1776 was liable to be hung as a traitor by King George III. And they understood this. When Benjamin Franklin famously said, "We must all hang together, or we will surely all hang separately," that was not just a metaphor. And several of them were hung, actually. Now, to say that say Chelsea Manning or Edward Snowden adhered to . . . what? the Taliban? some other "enemy" of the United States? That would be absurd. Neither of them, constitutionally, could be charged with treason, and nor could I. I had twelve felony counts, and treason was not one of them. However, the fact that I broke my promise to my party, the Democratic Party, led to the word "betrayal" being used very commonly. I was seen as a traitor to my "group." But of course, exposing the wrongdoings of the "group" to outsiders is often the only way of changing its behavior. I don't know any whistleblowers who are interested in punishment. They are interested in changing and stopping practices that harm others, and for that they are willing to risk their freedom or even their lives. This is an instance, then, of moral courage. It was Bismarck who defined *zivilcourage* (civil courage), which amounts to moral courage. He said that courage on the battlefield is commonplace, but civil courage is very rare, even among otherwise decent people. That is why those people who have attitudes and practices that I deplore are not to be dismissed as less human. They are as human as humans have ever been, actually.

Angela: Li Wenliang, the Chinese doctor who tried to warn people about Covid-19, acted with courage.

Daniel: Yes, he told the truth and was punished for it.[5] He had to retract what he said, and he later died of Covid-19, because he went back (like the hero in Camus's *The Plague*) to do his job and exposed himself to the virus. He did what he could to tell the truth. We are seeing amazing heroism right now. In virtually every country, people are knowingly risking their lives to keep things running in healthcare, transportation, grocery stores, and many other areas. Of course, many of them are doing it because they otherwise couldn't afford to eat in our system. But many of them are not doing it for that reason alone. They are very clearly acting as heroes, as are the US governors who are defying Trump on this issue in order to keep people safe. They are not doing this to keep their jobs, in fact, they are risking their jobs. We are seeing humanity at its best and its worst.

Angela: We in Germany are privileged because we have a very strong health system. Although, it must be said, it used to be better. There have been many cuts in the past few years, especially in employment. We have plenty of equipment and intensive care space—it is yet to reach capacity with the Covid-19 infections—but we have a problem with manpower. But I am positively surprised by the German handling of Covid-19, particularly the

5 https://www.theguardian.com/world/2020/mar/20/chinese-inquiry-exonerates-coronavirus-whistleblower-doctor-li-wenliang.

transparency of officials about the situation. And there are some amazing individuals here among the scientists, like the virologist Christian Drosten, whose lab developed the first test for the SARS virus in 2003.[6] His podcast, *Coronavirus Update*, is very popular. He is not a whistleblower, but someone who is very transparent, which in turn alleviates the need for whistleblowing. For instance, he made his scientific papers on coronaviruses freely available online, which is very unusual. He went against academic protocol in order to inform people and save lives. This gives me some hope. Then there are, as you mentioned, the everyday heroes enabling us to maintain our standard of life, not only medical workers but store clerks, delivery drivers, and waste collectors. We would drown in waste without them!

Daniel: In 2003, I received the biannual German Whistleblower Prize. And while I was waiting to get the award, I asked one of the organizers: "What is the German word for 'whistleblower'?" He replied that there was none, that was why it was called the "whistleblower" prize. Then I asked, "What would be the nearest equivalent in German?" He thought for just a moment and then said, "*Verräter*," which was translated as "traitor." I said, "Is there perhaps a different word?" He thought for another moment and said, "*Petzer*," which translates as "tattletale." And I said, "Yes, it's like that in my country, too." As you said, however, I am now seen, much more commonly, as a patriot and a hero. This is a recent development of the last ten years, and it has served to make a (totally untruthful) distinction between myself and someone like Manning or Snowden. Half a century has gone by, and no harm has ever been attributed to the release of the Pentagon Papers. Therefore, in answer to your earlier question: How long will it take for Manning, Snowden, or Assange to be seen more favorably? I would say that, with each year that goes by, it is increasingly evident that the supposed "blood on their hands" is simply not there, whereas *so much blood* is seen on the hands of the people they exposed. That does have some effect on public opinion. And we want to look forward to a world in which more people put their careers, liberties, and lives at risk to act on a feeling of concern

---

6 https://www.sciencemag.org/news/2020/04/how-pandemic-made-virologist-unlikely-cult-figure.

and loyalty to people everywhere. That can be the miracle that is needed to preserve civilization. And fortunately, miracles do happen: Gorbachev did happen in Russia, and Mandela did come to power in South Africa without a violent revolution. Those were miracles—no one foresaw them. The impossible did happen, and it can again.

Conversation held on April 21, 2020

The Lucrative Lies Underpinning Money and Debt Creation

Stephanie Kelton and Yanis Varoufakis

Yanis: In the midst of the Covid-19 pandemic, with people worldwide in isolation, there is no doubt that many are longing for a return to normality. However, we should desist from this and remember that there was no such thing as normality. I shall quote from the wonderful Arundhati Roy who wrote, in the *Financial Times* of all places, the following words: "Our minds are still racing back and forth, longing for a return to 'normality,' trying to stitch our future to our past and refusing to acknowledge the rupture. But the rupture exists. And in the midst of this terrible despair, it offers us a chance to rethink the doomsday machine we have built for ourselves. Nothing could be worse than a return to normality. Historically, pandemics have forced humans to break with the past and imagine their world anew. This one is no different. It is a portal, a gateway between one world and the next. We can choose to walk through it, dragging the carcasses of our prejudice and hatred, our avarice, our data banks and dead ideas, our dead rivers and smoky skies behind us. Or we can walk through lightly, with little luggage, ready to imagine another world. And ready to fight for it."[1] To help us imagine another world and to be ready to fight for it, I have a remarkable conversation partner, Stephanie Kelton, a comrade and fellow economist who, like me, made the choice to enter into the political sphere, in her case to join Bernie Sanders's campaign as head economic advisor. Why don't you begin, Stephanie, by talking about your early influences in life? What was it in your childhood and teenage years that created the impetus for your work?

Stephanie: Honestly, it was almost a series of accidents. I grew up a military brat. My father was in the Air Force, so we moved around constantly and I never really had time to form attachments. I didn't give much thought to college in advance, so I changed my major seven or eight times. But for one chance encounter in the right economics class while studying something else, I wouldn't have met Professor John Henry, who became so influential in my economic training. He had me begin a reading program on the history of economic thought and that's when economics became something that I had to do.

1   https://www.ft.com/content/10d8f5e8-74eb-11ea-95fe-fcd274e920ca

Yanis: You were lucky, because most economics students have to suffer the dry textbook that condenses five thousand years of knowledge into one aphorism: namely, that to be rational is to maximize utility subject to constraints.

Stephanie: I was very lucky. Studying at Cal State Sacramento was itself an accident. I was going to attend the University of North Carolina, but then my father decided that he was going to retire from the military, and the family would be moving back to California to live. So I ended up at Cal State Sacramento in an economics department where there were conventional, neoclassically trained economists, as well as institutionalists. Mark Tool was there, as well as John Henry, some Marxists and post-Keynesians.

Yanis: Was your family political? Were you?

Stephanie: No.

Yanis: How did that happen?

Stephanie: The history of economic thought. One of the earliest memories I have, which reset my worldview, was sitting in a history of economic thought class when John Henry asked the simplest question I have ever heard: "Can everyone be a capitalist?" Of course you can! That's the American dream: to work and become your own boss and make your own rules. Except that capitalists hire workers, they depend on the existence of workers, so no, not everyone can be a capitalist. That had a real impact on the way I thought about economic and societal outcomes; a whole variety of things were reset in my mind.

Yanis: The answer to that question, really, is yes, but *only* in the kind of models that economists teach, where everybody is a little Robinson Crusoe selling something, whether it is labor tokens or fish. Only in this situation, which is not capitalism but an exchange economy, can you pretend there is a kind of capitalism where everyone is a capitalist. This is why, when I tried to impress upon students the total unrealism and yet beauty of what they were being taught, I would use the 1945 article by Robert A. Radford, where the prisoners of war in Germany trade between themselves the little bits of tea, chocolate, and cigarettes that they get from the Red Cross. That is the kind of economy that students are taught at university, but it's not capitalism: there is no production, there is no labor.

Stephanie: That's exactly right. If everyone is their own petty producer, individually capable of subsisting on their own output, then it's not capitalism as we know it. Economics is taught as if it were a fairy tale: "Once upon a time, man conducted his affairs through barter exchange . . ." It is a stylized abstracting from anything that's historical, ignoring the work of anthropologists, sociologists, and numismatists, that asks us to imagine that, over a period of time, isolated individuals discover that they can trade more efficiently if they invent something to serve as an intermediary in the exchange process. Eventually, they discover that precious metals make a very nice token, because they are portable, durable, and divisible. But all along we are asked to ignore the role of private property or of the state in developing markets and making a monetary system, and told that this all comes about through some spontaneous order as agents look for more efficient ways to carry out exchange.

Yanis: Money is a such a quasi-spiritual commodity or entity, which Marx referred to as the alienated capacity of humans. When did you start wrapping your mind around the concept of money?

Stephanie: I probably started to understand it in 1996, while studying with Randy Wray at the University of Denver, just before heading over to Cambridge. Randy wrote a book called *Money and Credit in Capitalist Economies*, which introduced me to the post-Keynesian way of thinking about money as a credit instrument. When I got to Cambridge, I started reading things like Jeff Ingham's paper on money as a social relation. Similarly, in his discussion of state money in the *Treatise on Money*, Keynes argues that the state has the power to write and rewrite the dictionary, to name the unit in which debts will be denominated and prices will be written, and it can change this at will over time. You, of course, Yanis, are well aware that it takes power to rewrite the dictionary, because the Greek dictionary was rewritten from the drachma to the euro.

Yanis: I was introduced, at a very young age, to the concept of capital as a social relationship by Marx. He tells a true story of an Englishman who made some money on the stock exchange, charted some ships, filled them with proletarians and equipment, and took them to Australia. In Western Australia, however, there was so much land that the workers soon became farmers of their own. The capitalist suddenly realized that his capital was worthless; he had no hold over the workers because there was no social relationship. His monopoly of tools was not sufficient for the capital–labor relationship to exist. Unfortunately, when I went to Cambridge I was stuck with economists, and I didn't meet a single person who had anything interesting to say about money, or economics for that matter. I'd like to read something published a few days ago in the *Financial Times* and ask you to comment on it. It is the conclusion of an article written by Rana Foroohar, titled "We Are Entering the New Age of American Austerity": "Ultimately, debt is a national burden shared by all taxpayers. Policymakers therefore need to think about how to incentivize savings: trimming every unproductive debt and leverage loophole from the tax code is a good place to start. In time, the Fed will also have to explain how it will shrink all that debt off its balance sheet. And everyone will have to think about thrift. Enter the new age of American austerity."[2]

Stephanie: It's obviously very disappointing, from my vantage point. It is full of tropes and misunderstandings and leans very heavily into the austerity direction. It is laying the groundwork for what is inevitable, which is a glance over the shoulder at the accumulated deficits that we will have as a legacy of dealing with the health pandemic and the economic fallout associated with it. I'm working on a piece for the *Financial Times* right now on the question "should we worry about the debt?"[3] I take the position that we should not be wrapping ourselves in knots to try to figure out how best to move forward with an austerity program when we come out the other side of this pandemic. This is because, as I often say, most countries do not have a "debt problem." What we have is a communication or language problem. The fact that we use words like "borrowing," "debt," and "deficit" to describe the

2   https://www.ft.com/content/8b2370be-8092-11ea-8fdb-7ec06edeef84

3   https://www.ft.com/content/53cb3f6a-895d-11ea-a109-483c62d17528

ways in which government spending is financed triggers, for many people, a negative response, as though these things are inherently dangerous, risky, or irresponsible. The Modern Monetary Theory (MMT) position flips all these things around. We claim that there is nothing inherently wrong with governments running a fiscal deficit—this signals nothing more than a financial contribution to some other part of the economy. Right now, the United States government is making a 3- or 4-trillion-dollar financial contribution to some other part of the economy to support it through the pandemic. And governments that issue their own currency, by habit, pair their deficit spending by selling bonds. We've labeled this borrowing, which, to many people, sounds risky, as though the government is dependent on "savers" to finance itself. MMT disagrees with this framing. The deficit has already been financed. The government's trillion-dollar deficit deposits dollars into the economy that are then available to buy the bonds that the government is selling—they are transformed into interest-bearing dollars. I don't look at this as borrowing, but as recycling. The "national debt" is really just part of the net money supply of the country, but this term makes people very agitated with its connotations of a government running its finances imprudently.

Yanis: It is a question of the rhetoric, metaphors, and allegories used. It is really fantastic that when *Financial Times* writers speak of debt, they mean public debt and always ignore private debt. How about worrying about the total amount of debt, private and public? Then, suddenly, it's a question of balancing the two. Now, when I was a young person in Greece, we still had the drachma. This was a small economy that was always deficit-prone and therefore always relying on the kindness of strangers, in the form of capital flows into the country to stabilize the trade deficit, which meant that we couldn't have an industry policy that protected local industry by means of tariffs. I remember governments running around like headless chickens struggling to prevent runs on the drachma, which were quite extraordinary. This was a country that needed to import oil, a dependent country. Trade unions would organize a five-month strike, achieve a 5 percent pay rise, then the drachma would collapse (not because of the strike) and, within five days, they would lose all the gains from the strike. That experience was significant in convincing the Greek working class of the importance of shifting from the drachma to the euro. They were assured that doing so would enable them to at least keep what they earned and not live in fear of a run on the drachma. What would you say to them?

Stephanie: I would say that it is true that if you switch to the euro you won't have to live in fear of a run on the drachma, but you will live in fear of other things! You will live in fear of ending up in a situation where you are forced to borrow to run your policy; to orient your domestic macroeconomic policies in a way that doesn't best serve your people; and to take marching orders from the Troika or whoever is responsible for throwing you a lifeline in times of crisis. On the other hand, the point of MMT is not to say that every country that keeps its own currency can always exercise unilateral authority over its domestic policy agenda. In my new book, I try to make clear that small, open economies, even those that have a floating currency and control their own central bank, can be extremely vulnerable and can be unable to take full advantage of their currency for fear of sharp changes in the exchange rate, for instance.

Yanis: What is your answer to someone who claims that MMT is great only if you live in a country that has the exorbitant power of the dollar to back it up?

Stephanie: I would point toward Japan or Australia, which are not the global reserve currency, but fit the mold well enough to be able to orient their domestic policy agenda around achieving full employment—the most important thing, say, that a government can do. These countries can hire all of those who are seeking paid work in the state's unit of account and put it to work serving the public purpose. You don't have to be the global currency hegemon to run a policy oriented toward, for instance, sustaining full employment domestically.

Yanis: Regarding social policy, MMT advocates for a jobs guarantee program, but can you tell me why there seems to be a certain aversion to the idea of having, in parallel, something like a universal basic income?

Stephanie: I don't think that we view the two as necessarily antagonistic to one another. We are concerned, though, when a universal basic income is offered as preferable to, or instead of, a job guarantee. We think that the job guarantee has a number of advantages, one of the more important being that it is counter cyclical, so that the spending itself is moderating with changing conditions in the underlying economy, whereas the UBI would just layer on the same payment through the business cycle and not have that stabilizing aspect. The other issue is that there isn't a UBI proposal. Every time I am asked to comment on the UBI, I have to immediately ask, "What is your version?" In the United States, the version that got the most attention over the last year was that proposed by presidential candidate Andrew Yang. I personally spoke out very strongly against that version, because it would have required people who are already receiving certain forms of public assistance to "do the math," as Yang put it, and work out whether they would rather keep the assistance they had, or give it up in order to take a monthly UBI disbursement. Somebody like me, who isn't receiving any kind of public assistance, wouldn't have to do the math.

Yanis: DiEM25 would not support that version either. Our position on a universal basic income is that it should not be tax-funded, firstly, because that would be toxic politically as well as unnecessary. Instead, our proposal for Europe—and we ran on this platform last year in the European Parliament elections—is to implement a universal basic dividend, where large companies must give, for instance, 10 percent of their shares to a European equity fund, and the dividends that accumulate are dispersed among the people. The grounds for this is that capital is socially produced, yet companies have a monopoly on the dividends. Therefore, this is a way of redistributing not so much wealth, but property rights or value claims. The money that will trickle down to individuals is very small, but as automation increases, it will too. We also plan to supplement it with helicopter money from the European Central Bank. The proposal is compatible with your notion of automatic stabilizers—a certain amount of money would be added to each person's universal basic dividend, depending on aggregate demand. For instance, during the Covid-19 lockdown, it would be boosted by two or three thousand euros to replace lost incomes and then, when things recover, it would be reduced again.

On another note, what was it like to work with Bernie Sanders during his brilliant but unsuccessful campaign?

Stephanie: It's tough, to be honest. Bernie is, in so many ways, the right man for the moment and we saw it just slip through our fingers. And just weeks after he made the decision to step back and endorse Joe Biden for president, the Covid-19 pandemic unfolded and so many people are now saying that it has revealed all of these vulnerabilities that were at the core of Bernie's campaign—whether it's our healthcare system, inequality, discrimination, or the trade policies that have given rise to the fact that we can't produce facemasks, ventilators, or test kits. The obvious solutions that people are looking to are the very things that he was pushing for all along. It's exhilarating to watch someone capture or recapture people's imaginations in the way that he did. He was able to stand in front of thousands of people and ask them to imagine the world as we could make it together. I'm still inspired by him.

Yanis: We all are. He was the right person to take on Trump. What's next, in terms of the political revolution and what we are up against? We talked about the *Financial Times* article heralding the new age of austerity. The powers that be in Europe are loosening up the purse strings in terms of loans and will be lending money to Italy, Greece, and Spain until the deficit reaches -15 percent and the debt-to-GDP ratio grows to 200 percent. That will be followed by a tremendous wave of austerity in the eurozone, because we don't have sovereign money, as you put it. Where do we go from here? Intellectually, we know what the arguments are. Likewise, economists had many intellectual victories in the controversies of the 1970s. But this wasn't sufficient—we won the argument but we lost the war. How can we win this war? The fascists and the bankers never let a good crisis go to waste.

Stephanie: You are depressing me in a lot of different ways, Yanis, because the problem is the people who are in power, our political leaders. How are we going to change who the decision makers are so that different decisions get made? I don't know that all of the organizing, convincing, and collective action in the world can help us if we have leaders like Boris Johnson, Jair Bolsonaro, and Donald Trump.

Yanis: The simple start of a process leading to an answer must surely be to band together and to learn from the bankers and fascists by not concentrating on our own turf but internationalizing. We must build a transnational political rebellion.

Stephanie: I end my book, *The Deficit Myth: Modern Monetary Theory and the Birth of the People's Economy,* by asking the reader to imagine another, better world, an economy for the people. I want to be able to empower people to fight back against all the things that stand in our way of building a better world. I try to knock down the deficit myths and all the arguments that economists and *Financial Times* writers will use to try and prevent us. I wanted to help readers see that a different world is possible, that many of the obstacles in our way are not legitimate, and that we need to focus on different and real constraints in order to build this world. It is a matter of building power and then being able to transform the world in the way that we want to live.

Yanis: And to return to your earlier point, it is not just a question of language, of metaphors and allegories. Because there are very powerful people and institutions that use those metaphors in order to conceal the extent to which their vested interests are best served by general confusion over the meaning of debt deficit and money in general.

Stephanie: Yes, I do not mean to suggest that changing the world is as simple as changing language or using different framing. It is about building power so that we can take from those who benefit from the current usages and current myths. In my book I discuss Peter G. Peterson, the hedge fund billionaire who spent decades building out an entire infrastructure of think tanks, of ways to popularize and reinforce these myths in the press, at conferences, and with politicians. He dedicated huge amounts of resources to reinforcing myths around the government's finances, for instance, the idea that the debt crisis is being driven by social security and Medicare. It is a power play, and I fully recognize that it is more than a language game.

Yanis: What are your expectations for the euro—do you think it will implode?

Stephanie: Randy Wray and I wrote a paper called "Can Euroland Survive?" about a decade ago and our answer was, "Yes, *if*. . ."[4] That is still the answer. The euro will hold together *if* the currency issuer, the European Central Bank, does what is necessary. I don't think it will. The euro is not sustainable given the current way in which the ECB and the countries all view themselves vis-à-vis one another. The way that certain countries and people have been treated—for instance, the Greeks, Italians, and Spaniards—over many years, and the resulting misery, high rates of poverty, and austerity, is not sustainable.

Yanis: Or, to paraphrase Keynes: the eurozone can stay alive longer than I can stay sane.

Conversation held on April 27, 2020

---

4 http://www.levyinstitute.org/pubs/ppb_106.pdf.

Visible Skies Above, a Tsunami of Banalities Below

Tariq Ali and Maja Pelević

Maja: Tariq, how are you? How are things in London?

Tariq: Things in London are not good, the casualty rate is mounting and there are inequalities between the hospitals. For instance, the richest hospital in Britain, St. Thomas's Hospital, was short of personal protective equipment (PPE), like the whole National Health Service, so it sent two private planes to Eastern Europe to purchase some. That hospital is now fine. Not far from St Thomas's is King's Hospital, which is not such a wealthy hospital, where they have shortages not simply of PPE, but of doctors and nurses and it is completely overcrowded. These issues are now coming to the surface and I hope they will be taken up politically. Apart from that, there is mass unemployment occurring. Some are able to access government furlough payments or benefits, but it is very uneven. Britain's delay in understanding the seriousness and impact of Covid-19 has cost lives. In Greece, by contrast, the mortality rate is incredibly low: at this stage, less than twenty. This is a global crisis, but it hasn't been dealt with globally and that is why many of these failings have arisen.

Maja: I have been thinking a lot about the future of protest, and the civil disobedience that is arising during the pandemic in different parts of the world. Here in Serbia, there is applause each night at eight o'clock for the health workers, as in many countries, but a few days ago, people started protests against the Vučić regime at 8:05 p.m., after the applause, similar to the ones occurring in Brazil against Bolsonaro. We are seeing the emergence of a new form of "balcony protest" in this global lockdown. There are also riots in Paris and protests in Tel Aviv, which have a kind of choreography of social distancing with everyone wearing masks and standing two feet apart. You were a part of two hugely important protests: May '68 and the 2003 protests against the United States invasion of Iraq, one of the largest in human history. You said then, that after the collapse of the Soviet Union, when the US gained world hegemony, was the first time that the world wanted an alternative. The war could have been stopped, but it wasn't, and history took the course that it did. What do you think will happen after the Covid-19 crisis? What is the future for protests and civil disobedience? Do you think that we have an alternative now?

Tariq: Let's start in the following way: There have been many viruses before, including MERS, SARS, and Ebola—what makes this one special? It is not the casualty rates, but the fact that it has hit the West. This has shocked the West into realizing that it isn't immune to the epidemics that it thought were problems of Asia, Africa, and the Middle East. In Africa, there are many viruses at the present time, including malaria, and Asia continues to battle polio. These facts were not newsworthy, but now that the West is hit by a pandemic, it dominates the news. The second question is: What does the pandemic teach us? It teaches us what many have been saying for years now, that prevailing forms of government and economic control are not working. For the first time in three decades, governments from across the political spectrum are beginning to recognize that it is important to invest in creating viable health services. In terms of what will happen after Covid-19 recedes, I'm not optimistic. Everyone thought that the 2008 financial crisis would force serious structural reforms, but it didn't. As we speak, politicians are handing out contracts to their friends to import necessary medical items. Money is being invested in healthcare, but this will only last if there are mass movements. This pandemic has made evident to everyone that state intervention is crucial and neoliberalism has got to go. One positive effect of the pandemic is that, for the first time in years, people can walk out on the streets in huge cities all over the world and see stars in the sky. Pollution levels have plummeted.[1] This is a clear indication that changes in human activity drastically effect air quality and demonstrates what scientists are already aware of: that in order to tackle the climate crisis, we have to abolish the private motorcar. This is not utopian. We have to build up public transport networks to the point that people feel they can exist without a car, except in emergencies. For emergencies, there should be a public ride–hailing service in every city: you press a button and a car comes. There are good and bad possibilities inherent in this crisis, but none of the good ones will come about if protests are silenced and politics restricted to parliament. States of exception are nothing new. We are still living in the state of exception implemented after 9/11, which gives the

---

1   http://www.esa.int/Applications/Observing_the_Earth/Copernicus/Sentinel-5P/Coro-navirus_lockdown_leading_to_drop_in_pollution_across_Europe.

United States power to lift and arrest any citizen suspected of terrorism and detain them, without trial, for months on end. The dishonest and immoral outcomes of this are seen in, for instance, the fact that Julian Assange, a pathbreaking investigative journalist, is rotting in a top-security prison for having defied bail once, which is not even an imprisonable offense, while the United States tries to extradite him. The viciousness of police in many places in the world today, their eagerness to use unnecessary force, is concerning. It is extremely foolish for anyone to imagine that our governments will ensure that the outcomes of the Covid-19 pandemic are in the people's interest. Governments must be pushed. We know that in 2016, for instance, the National Health Service in Britain carried out military-type maneuvers to see how the health system would react if there was a sudden pandemic.[2] The result was that, on the basis of the current organization of the NHS, it would completely collapse. This report was made available to the Conservative government and what did they do? Absolutely nothing. Now, we are faced with a real pandemic. If there are going to be any concessions to workers, to ordinary people, they will have to be fought for. The health workers are suffering more than any other segment of society and are dying all over the world. The recent protests in Quetta, Pakistan, of doctors and nurses who didn't have enough safety clothing to perform their work, were met with the police beating the hell out of them.

Maja: Let's turn to the upcoming elections in the United States. At this point, voters will be choosing between Trump and Biden. Noam Chomsky believes that now is the time for people to vote for the lesser evil and is speaking in favor of Biden. What is your view on this?

Tariq: What the United States needs is a government that can nationalize the fossil fuel industry, which is heavily supported and sustained by government funding, and create a national health service, but neither Biden nor Trump are capable of that, for ideological reasons. The only hope is that there will be mass movements putting pressure on state governments. On the primaries, my view is that there was no shortage of Democratic

2 https://www.theguardian.com/world/2020/apr/02/labour-urges-government-publish-findings-2016-pandemic-drill.

politicians who could have run against Trump, but the Democratic National Committee decided to give Trump a second term and chose Biden to help him. There can be no other basis for this: Biden is a complete imbecile. I don't agree with a single thing he says or does, but one has to feel sorry for him. If this man is beginning to show the signs of incipient dementia, which I think he is, it's better not to expose him to public ridicule. In terms of voting, if the choice is Biden or Trump, I don't accept the argument that a vote for Biden is a vote against fascism and against fascism we defend anything. Trump is, quite openly, a white supremacist—he does believe that white people are superior and it's their right to rule. However, Trump is also one of many eccentric right-wing US presidents who, while he is more open about them, holds very similar views on race to someone like Reagan, the favorite president of Bill Clinton and Obama. *Every four years* we face this problem. Who are we going to choose this time? The one candidate who could have made a difference is Bernie Sanders. If Biden is the Democratic candidate, large numbers of Bernie supporters will not vote, and lots of others won't either. It's not at all certain that Biden will defeat Trump. I disagree with Noam and other friends who say we have to vote for Biden. We did not support voting for Blair after he waged the war in Iraq. The position of myself and many others was: a curse on both your houses. No electoral change could make any real difference.

Maja: Do you think that Trump will be reelected because the radical left will not vote for Biden?

Tariq: Bernie Sanders supporters were not all on the radical left. There were large numbers of commonsense Americans, discerning liberals, who wanted to have at least one president in the twenty-first century who could bring about certain reforms, especially health reforms. They are left with a candidate who doesn't support the idea of a national health service at a time when a pandemic is raging across the United States. The reality of American politics is that the Democrats, as much as the Republicans, are so closely linked to the insurance and pharmaceutical corporations that they dare not to offend them. Almost no politician is prepared to offend Wall Street, as we saw in the aftermath of the 2008 crisis. In short, I don't think it will make much difference whether Trump or Biden is elected—it will be business as usual. The main difference between Trump and others is that he takes the mask off. And Trump's honesty is actually something to be partly grateful for, because it can educate America about who or what it is. In 2017, Trump was asked on public television why he was being friendly with "a killer" like Putin, and Trump's reply was, "There are a lot of killers, you think our country is so innocent?"[3] The liberal press was shocked.

Maja: Recently, wherever we try to implement a truly left government, we fail. What do you think the problem is? Also, you recently published *The Dilemmas of Lenin: War, Empire, Love, Revolution,* and I am interested to know how the dilemmas of Lenin might help us think through the situation today?

Tariq: Lenin's main dilemma, which he faced up to, was what to do in the First World War: whether to follow through with what the Russian people wanted, and what the Bolsheviks campaigned on, which was to end the war as immediately as possible. Many things can be learned from Lenin, including, at the present time, his hard-headed realism. He understood timing and knew exactly when to take a certain action and was not dogmatic on these questions. If, today, we had a social democratic European project, rather than a neoliberal one, we would be much better placed to deal with the Covid-19 pandemic. The Italians were completely isolated; no one in Europe went to their help. The first people to assist Italy were the Chinese and then the hundreds of doctors who came from Cuba. That is genuine internationalism. Germany and France were concerned only with themselves, when the whole point of the EU is supposedly to act in unity. One effect of the pandemic has been the reassertion of the nation-state. It became obvious to European nations that if we're to rely solely on the market, casualties would be ten or twenty times higher than what we are witnessing now. There is, of course, still heavy reliance on the market, as is evident in the privatized care homes for the elderly, which have been totally unable to deal with this pandemic. In Britain, fifteen

---

3 https://www.theguardian.com/us-news/2017/feb/05/donald-trump-repeats-his-respect-for-killer-vladimir-putin.

thousand people have died in these care homes. In the United States, horrific casualty rates are occurring in privatized care homes. In countries like India, Pakistan, Malaysia, and Indonesia, the deaths will not even be recorded, because the poor die, they are expected to die. The Indonesian health minister is a third-rate military doctor who makes money from crazy inventions such as a machine that stops strokes by flushing the brain with water. You want to laugh, but you have to cry. He recently made a public statement stating he was completely sure the pandemic would not come to Indonesia. At the same time, you have Indonesian religious leaders saying that those who get Covid-19 are all *haram* or sinful, they've been breaking the laws, fornicating too much, and so on. When Covid-19 broke out in Malaysia, Indonesia, and Pakistan, governments did not prevent large religious gatherings by born-again Muslim organizations from taking place. These then became clusters from which the disease spread all over the countries. One reason that the Chinese were able to control Covid-19 was that, once they recovered from the huge mistake of not listening to the doctor who alerted them to the virus, they acted with amazing zeal.

Maja: Another issue is the level of state control and regulations that are being implemented in China, which may remain after the pandemic.

Tariq: There is a very interesting diary just published in *New Left Review* written by a documentary filmmaker, Ai Xiaoming, who went to Wuhan in January to see her father.[4] When Covid-19 hit, she got stuck there, so she saw the whole arc. Her diary shows that it is not simply the dominance of the state that is the issue, because there is a lot of hostility among neighbors also. She volunteered, along with many young students, to help nurses in the hospitals, but she writes that when she returned to her neighborhood, she would stand outside, remove her medical clothing, put it in a bag and then enter very calmly. She was scared that if she didn't, she'd be attacked by her neighbors. Western media simplifies the situation and I think what is preoccupying it is not how China dealt with Covid-19, but the worry that

4 https://newleftreview.org/issues/II122/articles/xiaoming-ai-wuhan-diary

China's measures will allow it to recover quickly, resume production, and get a lead on the capitalist countries of the West. One result of the pandemic will be a new Cold War against China.

Maja: Yes, I wanted to ask you about the wars of the future. Do you really think that they will be cold? Presently, there are many wars happening in the world, but there is very little media coverage as the pandemic rages. From the moment Covid-19 arrived on the media scene, the refugee crisis completely vanished, as though it never existed. This virus arrived as a new "other," a new, unknown, and invisible enemy that we must fight. What do you think will happen when the borders open in Europe—that is, if they open at all? Many countries in Fortress Europe wanted to close their borders prior to the Covid-19 pandemic, and now they've got an opportunity to do so, maybe forever.

Tariq: That is not impossible, though I must point out that Europe's borders, while open to European citizens, have always been pretty firmly closed. The whole concept of Fortress Europe is that those on the outside must meet rigorous rules and criteria in order to enter. Economic refugees find it very difficult to enter Europe, while some refugees fleeing war have been permitted, especially by the Germans. These refugees are the consequence of Western wars against the so-called Third World, wars initiated by the United States and backed by Europeans. The Germans and the French did not send troops to Iraq, but they voted for the occupation of Iraq at the United Nations. The world of NATO is their world: a world in which "we" have the right to invade countries, to change regimes. These countries accept, then, as part of the deal, that they have to accommodate the refugees that result from those wars. If states communicated this directly to the people of their countries: that if we wage war against a new country, we must be prepared to take half a million refugees each, the anti-war movement would grow phenomenally. Previously uninterested people would insist, "No, we don't want a war." That of course is why states don't make explicit what has been, historically, the outcome of every war. At the end of the Korean War and Vietnam War, the United States had to permit large numbers of Koreans and Vietnamese to enter. And we shouldn't forget that as a result of the Iraq War, millions of Iraqis became refugees in the neighboring countries of Syria, Lebanon, Jordan, and some of the Gulf states. In 2016, the EU made a deal with Turkey, which promised Erdoğan €6 billion in exchange for keeping Syrian refugees contained in his country, where they live in miserable conditions. Europe is increasingly become a continent without a conscience. Angela Merkel, when she attempted to help the situation by accepting 1 million refugees into Germany, was virtually destroyed as a politician, with the result being a split in the social democratic party and the emergence of very strong parliamentary representation of the far-right AfD party. The combination of wars and neoliberalism is poisonous, it's like a virus. So, what will happen after Covid-19 recedes? I think many of the measures implemented will be retained on the statute books "for exceptional circumstances," and states will use them whenever necessary. I think that refugees will not be accepted, in any large numbers, into any of the major European countries. Long before the Covid-19 pandemic, the Italian government made it illegal for Italians to rescue refugees drowning in the Mediterranean. On the other hand, it is interesting to note that in Britain, hostility to immigrants is decreasing due to the effects of the pandemic. One reason for this is that farmers are desperate for labor, as many of the fields aren't being worked. The larger reason, though, is that large numbers of people now realize that without immigrant workers, the National Health Service would collapse. Most of the doctors and many of the nurses who have died are people of color, and their pictures are published in the newspapers every day. It is not being stated as such, but the hostility to migration is declining. As to the wars of the future, the issue that is now obsessing the West is China, and particularly the economic position of the Chinese which is seen to threaten US dominance. For the time being, the West has decided to frame the issue of China as one of security, despite the fact that most of the top technological companies are not owned by China, but by the United States and Germany, and that the Chinese military does not have the capacity to launch huge wars. Who is China going to attack? The military spending of the United States is equal to the next seven countries combined.

Maja: We are not, then, on the verge of nuclear war?

Tariq: No, because nuclear war is totally destructive. There has only been one big nuclear attack and that was against Japan when the Japanese were on the verge of surrendering. Many of us have pointed this out: peace talks were underway when the United States decided to use nuclear weapons on Hiroshima and Nagasaki, killing civilians. The States wanted to show the Soviet Union what they were capable of, and the Japanese were used as scapegoats. But have they used nuclear weapons against Vietnam? They couldn't, because the Soviet Union and China existed. Have they used them against Iraq? They used depleted uranium against Iraq in the Gulf Wars, leaving a huge number of casualties and deformations, but they did not launch a direct nuclear attack. They would be crazy to do so. If Trump ever decided to do that, he would be removed by the Pentagon without much delay. I doubt very much that the United States will use nuclear weapons in upcoming wars, and so far no other country has shown any interest in doing so. Were they to do so, the Covid-19 pandemic would be nothing; the world would be destroyed.

Maja: The world would be left without humans and, who knows, it might be a better place?

Tariq: It is tempting to think that, given that it has taken a pandemic to force cars off the streets, spend more money on health, and make sure no one is without a wage—all this is now being done by the state, so why the hell can't they do it when there is no virus? That is the question.

Maja: That is the question. On another note, it is known that you were in favor of Brexit. Do you think that the Covid-19 crisis proves that reverting to nation states is not the solution for transnational problems, be it climate change, a pandemic, or austerity?

Tariq: Yes, I was in favor of Brexit, and my position was very clear. I thought that the European Union deserved a very strong kick in the pants in order to come to its senses and realize that it couldn't behave the way it did, for instance, in relation to Greece after the 2008 financial crisis. The EU allowed the Troika's demands to wreck the Greek economy and put intolerable pressure on Greek politicians so that some capitulated, with the result that Greece now has an extreme right-wing government. My vote was not against internationalism, but against the way the European Union was functioning. Not just Britain, but every state in the EU has reacted to Covid-19 nationalistically and this illustrates, again, that the Union isn't functioning properly because of its social and economic priorities. If there was a European Union with a meaningful social democratic plan that marked a sharp break with neoliberalism, I would be strongly for it, obviously. Serious issues like climate change cannot be solved by the free market but only with a global planning agreement. I'm not in favor of eliminating growth or even "degrowth"—that is a luxury for kids in Scandinavia to think about. In the United States, or even the former Yugoslav states, degrowth is not an option; we actually need to have more people in work. What sort of work is, of course, another question. The pandemic has raised this debate, and it will continue afterward.

Maja: A mass movement on the left will require broad-based public support, a populist uprising, even—how do we achieve this?

Tariq: There is no single formula for mass movements and uprising. Every uprising depends on local traditions, histories, and modes of organization. But that they can arise—that is also unpredictable. As Chairman Mao said, "A single spark can start a prairie fire." That is absolutely true, and you can never tell where the spark is going to come from. Will it be some war that has gone out of control? Or will it be something more trivial, someone killed on the streets by the cops? We don't know. However it arises, it's not impossible. It is also necessary for the parliamentary left, where it exists, to develop a common program of basic social and climate measures that can be universalized and fought for globally.

Conversation held on April 28, 2020

Language Is a Virus: On the Avant-Garde and Archiving

Kenneth Goldsmith and Srećko Horvat

Srećko: Often, in our efforts to understand the current Covid-19 pandemic, we start with a virus and end up in semiotics. Such a shift should not be seen as detracting from the very material effects of Covid-19, the illness and deaths it is causing, but rather as a recognition that the virus itself is already a semiotic machine, the virus itself generates meaning. As humans, we can no more escape meaning as we can the archive. When Jacques Derrida talks about the archive, he refers not simply to a place where artifacts, feelings, and signs are stored, but also, necessarily, something oriented toward the future, an arc through which things are transmitted into the future. In the Covid-19 pandemic, we have seen how one country's past suddenly becomes another's future. At the beginning, China was in the future, and now that the virus has arrived in Europe, the United States remains in the past. Kenneth, perhaps you can say a few words on the situation in the US at the moment, before we return to the question of the archive?

Kenneth: I live in Manhattan and it is strange, because I'm told I'm in the epicenter of an epidemic and yet I can't feel it, because I can't leave my house. It is a sort of strange distancing, where I know the virus is all around me, affecting people I know, but I can't see or help those people. The streets of New York are desolate, empty, bereft of energy, and dangerous. The privileges that we've enjoyed, such as being able to take a walk after dark, are no longer available to us. I'm looking out on a brick wall of some empty offices that are usually buzzing with people and have been empty, now, for a month. It is isolation, truly.

Srećko: If a worker from Arizona or Texas was watching us, in the past or in the future, they would likely think that the two of us, isolated indoors, talking about the avant-garde, art, and archiving, are very privileged. As someone who has spent decades curating, archiving, thinking and writing about it, perhaps you can tell us why is it important, precisely at the time of a pandemic, to return to the avant-garde?

Kenneth: Education is a privilege. And most people are educated for practical necessities, which calls into question the entire purpose of a liberal arts education. Why would someone study English when they could be study-ing business or science? The traditional answer to that is that the liberal arts make you a deeper and better person. We don't expect most arts students to remain poets their whole lives. It reminds me of my grandfather, who was an alcoholic and a failed lawyer, but what he lived for was books. His work as a lawyer supported him financially, but he thought of himself as an intellec-tual. He would come home from work and spend the evenings in his library, which he really felt to be his real life. It is the life of the soul, isn't it? Without that, what really is the point?

Srećko: In your most recent book, *Duchamp Is My Lawyer: The Polemics, Pragmatics, and Poetics of UbuWeb,* you tell the history not just of UbuWeb, but the whole scene surrounding it, including so-called shadow libraries and other co-conspirators of a free culture, which still exists but, with the surveillance state, is on the margins. You discuss autodidacts, people like your grandfather, and document these kinds of creative processes that are not necessarily imposed by the discourse of the university and are more creative than it. Founded in 1996, UbuWeb remains today one of the most influential archives for avant-garde art, music, and video—from Ulrike Meinhof's radio plays to Jean-Michel Basquiat's hip hop and more. How did it all begin and develop?

Kenneth: The avant-garde gives us a sense of the future and various futurisms—with all their problems, political, colonialist, antisemitic, and others. The avant-garde, and in particular certain strains of modern-ism, show us how we were going to live in the twenty-first century. They offer us clues as to how to understand the digital through the refracted and shattered surfaces of modernism. One of the problems people find with the internet is that everybody is trying to make what is *essentially* a shattered and fractured medium into something singular: it's either good or it's bad; we are being surveilled or we are not; it's free or it's paid. What modernism asked us to do was to embrace these contradictions, to embrace the fact that there will never be a resolution, nor will there be singularity, and, in fact, that our state of being is a shattered state. Think of the many windows that are currently open on your computer screen: it has the same multi-perspectival context as cubism. Cubism showed many shattered surfaces, many things going on in one window at one time. We sometimes get upset that we are all walking through the streets like zombies on our cellphones, but, of course, a surrealist would see that as a walking dream state: you're both here and you're not here. I think Breton would be delighted to see masses of people dreaming on the street, being elsewhere, speaking to themselves, these sort of mad soliloquies that we are all constantly doing. Even the network seems to be anticipated by the canvases of abstract expressionism. What is a Jackson Pollock but an image of a wireless nodal network of equal distribution where there is no center, no focus, and where everything is simply a point contingent upon other points? This is a very idealized version of modernism, and many will be familiar with its problems, but I actually want to misread modernism as a way of understanding our digital age. To that end, I built an archive of the avant-garde, which made beautiful sense on the web, because the artifacts of the avant-garde have very little economic value, but great historical value. It is possible to create a vast archive of non-permissioned, important artifacts, because nobody is going to come after you. The site has run for twenty-five years now with no money. Despite what we are told, it is possible to do things on the internet with no money. You can write HTML, own and control your own servers, and give your money to ISPs that are benevolent and politically attuned friends and allies. Not everything has to be outsourced. Facebook and Google want you to think that they *are* the internet, but the other internet that always existed, still exists. This is something that many have forgotten.

Srećko: You raise an interesting point about the archive and institutionalization, wherein meaning is ascribed by those who have the power to classify. UbuWeb, in contrast, is organized alphabetically, you do not curate certain artists to appear front and center, and, since the beginning, has been connected to "open-source" culture.

Kenneth: Many people don't know what UbuWeb is, because we've removed ourselves from Google's search engine. As opposed to trying to get UbuWeb to rank higher in searches, we want it to rank lower, so that it disappears to become something that is only "among friends."

Srećko: In *Duchamp Is My Lawyer,* you argue that the DNA of the web is embedded in the art movements of the twentieth century, from surrealism to cubism. And if there is one proof of that, I think it is the 1973 situationist film *Can Dialectics Break Bricks?* Why are the situationists so prevalent on UbuWeb?

Kenneth: Situationism, in many respects, predicted the way that we would be on the web. In the early days of the internet, we would talk about "surfing the web," not knowing where we are going, getting lost on the internet. There used to be something called "webrings," a collection of websites around a certain theme that were circularly linked together. You never really knew where you were going. Many people considered surfing randomly on the web to be a dangerous activity, but it is still possible and still fun to do. As a matter of fact, the algorithm of randomness was so hard-wired into the DNA of the web that, up until a few years ago, the Google homepage had the "I'm feeling lucky" button that would take you to an unknown website. The problem with the algorithmic culture of today is that it reinforces more of what you know. It reifies your taste instead of exposing you to something new. One thing the situationists loved to do was what they called a *dérive,* which was a way of defamiliarizing the city. If you were to map your daily movements, you'd see that you take the same trails every day: from home to work, to the gym, to the restaurant, and back home. The situationists would get blindingly drunk on a Friday night and stumble around Paris not knowing where they were going, just for the sake of defamiliarizing that normal routine, to imbue some mystery and the magic of the urban experience. This was, of course, before Google Maps. Now, we can't get lost. All of us, I hope, have experienced the joy of walking into the library with no specific book in mind, and just starting to pull random books off the shelves. This is a whole different way of learning—no syllabus is ever constructed around randomness. The situationist approach defamiliarizes objects and routines, imbuing them not only with a sense of wonder but of political possibility:

imagine if we could always be unconstrained in our lives, without fear of otherness.

Srećko: In your book, you mention your daily practice of going to the archive in the evening and adding artifacts, which you've done for more than twenty-five years. At one point, you mention Samuel Beckett, who famously said, "You must go on, I can't go on, I'll go on." Many times, you wanted to withdraw from the project, but some "shadow librarians," so-called custodians, convinced you otherwise.

Kenneth: Culture is built upon previous culture, and the problem is that this is mostly unnoticed. Take the Bruno Ganz "Hitler bunker" video: most people think it's very funny and cute and it's got great use-value as a meme, but its historical connections with notions of subtitling and false subtitles are often missed. Sometimes when you pirate a video, you download subtitles and they are slightly off—the translations are bad or the special characters aren't rendered properly. And all of these beautiful errors actually make for new experiences. The notion of the perfect artifact is a fallacy. It is something Hollywood attains toward, an unrealistic perfection. The beauty of the weak artifact, as Hito Steyerl or Boris Groys might say, is in its ability to be remixed, reconfigured, and to be *had*. The art market is based upon singular artifacts in a time when the artifact's value is determined not by its singularity, its scarcity, but by how many people can actually have it. The art world is increasingly beginning to resemble the antiques market and is becoming so marginalized that I think, soon, it will not really matter. The shitty artifact is now standard, people have stopped complaining about resolutions of video, for instance, and accept a fifteenth generation rip as normal. I think Groys and Steyerl are right: the weak image is now the strong image, the democratic image. And I think that we have to begin to embrace the democracy of distribution as opposed to the fetishization of quality. We need to relinquish control, and this includes relinquishing control of copyright. People sometimes complain that they've been bootlegged on UbuWeb, but I would encourage them to take this as a sign that they've made it as an artist. The overwhelming majority of artists never get that recognition. They can't give their work away! Most artists do not want money, first and foremost, but love, recognition, and history. If you are fortunate enough to have somebody pirate your work, you should thank them, because it means you are loved as an artist, and no amount of money can buy that.

Srećko: I really love what you said, but the *advocatus diaboli* is sitting here on my shoulder. And when the *advocatus diaboli* hears that sharing is love and love is sharing, I immediately think of *The Circle*, the dystopian novel in which "sharing" is imposed upon people by the Silicon Valley ideology and hegemony, and not in the sense that you or Aaron Swartz understand it, but as a new form of commodification. On the subject of copyright, in your book you quote Guy Debord, one of the founders of the situationist international, who encouraged people to use materials without regard for property rights, without even acknowledging the "source." Today this sounds like blasphemy, considering the commodification of the art world. I would love for you to talk about "shadow libraries," which is connected to this. UbuWeb is part of a sort of "shadow movement" that is trying to preserve a memory of the world, a movement that also includes Monoskop, Memory of the World, and similar "custodians" around the world. I come from ex-Yugoslavia and, in the 1990s, most of the books not only directly about communism but anything connected to Russia, such as Tolstoy or Dostoevsky, were thrown out of public libraries. The ruling ideology lumped all these books into the same category, classified them as "communist," and threw them away. But the shadow librarians saved the books by digitalizing them. And this brings us to the concept of "open-source" and the fight against copyright. As someone involved in this struggle from the very start, could you perhaps comment on whether there is still a "free internet," and how shadow libraries might resist the universe of surveillance capitalism?

Kenneth: It exists, but it is not theorized, it is not known. And this is one of the problems we have with digital culture: we use it very well, but it's very under theorized and, therefore, we are quite ignorant about it. In theorizing surveillance capitalism, Shoshana Zuboff articulates things about our digital culture that we take for granted and have, now, begun to push back against. "Shadow libraries" is a term that emerged a couple of years ago to describe libraries that build themselves independently in the shadow of regular libraries. When students leave university, they lose access to their university library immediately. And since public libraries, particularly in the US, are being shelled, where do you go when you need a book? You can buy them on Amazon, which will cost you a fortune, or you can go to Google Books, but after three pages the "preview" allowance expires. Next, you might try some of the more mainstream file sharing sites, but you won't find many critical theory and philosophy texts there. In response to this gap of knowledge, a number of people over the past decade have built open-source, often user contributed, libraries. Databases like JSTOR, these aggregators of academic material, are hording knowledge for profit, and much of it is out of copyright and should be free to the public. UbuWeb is a shadow library but it is never password-protected, and there is never a donation box. The knowledge that it all takes place without money, without ads, without grants, is one of the things that makes the site work.

Srećko: Have you ever had any legal issues?

Kenneth: I've got a couple of great stories. My favorite one is that somebody from a very powerful literary agency made a cease and desist claim on us for William S. Burroughs. Of course, according to William S. Burroughs, "language is a virus," and words want to be free. Suddenly, this literary agency wants us to remove every single work by William S. Burroughs, and every single mention of him. I pushed back. I said, "Look, I know where you make your money, and UbuWeb will never share *Naked Lunch*." I'm not going to fuck with that. I deal with out of print and obscure things, things that shed light on the more marginal parts of artistic practice. So I asked them to please narrow their criteria and to let me know if there was really anything on UbuWeb that was costing them a lot of money. But they simply repeated the same thing, sending a list of everything on UbuWeb that was by, or even mentioned, William S. Burroughs and requesting a cease and desist. So I said to them, "Please tell the literary estate that, in the spirit of William S. Burroughs, words want to be free." A little bit of discourse goes a long way. A similar thing happened with Yoko Ono, whose lawyers asked us to remove everything of hers from the site. We had these MP3s of her doing Japanese folk songs from a little magazine from the '60s called *Aspen*. They are really important to the archive, but you couldn't sell them if you wanted to. So I said to the lawyers that to take these artifacts down would be to shred a historical archive which situates them in a historical way that's very flattering and important. I asked them for permission to host the MP3s and, when Yoko Ono understood that I wasn't trying to profit from them, she agreed. Cease and desist letters are designed to scare the shit out of you, but most of the time they are just a warning or an invitation to discourse. They are not a legal document, anybody can draw one up without any of the bulk of a real threat. This is what I call "folk law."

Srećko: In *Duchamp Is My Lawyer*, you mention Foucault's comparison of the archive to geological strata. And this not something new. Freud, who became important for Derrida's conception of the archive, was influenced by archeology and geology. This is seen in Freud's interest in Pompeii, for instance, and his theory of the unconscious itself, which is a kind of geological strata. The point of this comparison, if I am correct, is that the archive is always open to destruction, to a catastrophe. Whether it is the Library of Babel or a virus on a computer, it can disappear. To go a step further, can you imagine a situation in which the archive as such and language would completely disappear? What would happen to the archive if there is no longer language, if there is no witness who can go into the archive? Is your compulsion to archive things accompanied, as with many collectors, by an urge to preserve them from final destruction? And how is this possible if, for instance, the climate crisis and nuclear crisis collide in a hundred years, and there is no archive except radioactive waste?

Kenneth: People assume that the internet is a permanent situation, that because something is on the web, it will be there forever. That is not true at all. Think of the flotsam and jetsam that appear on Netflix and then vanish, or the things on YouTube that you can't watch because they are "not available in your territory due to licensing restrictions," or the pirate sites that continually go down. The entire MP3 blogosphere was ripped down in 2009 by the US Department of Justice following the Megaupload debacle. We should all become our own archivists in a very conscious way, building robust local libraries on hard drives, for instance. We are already doing this in an unconscious way, for instance, when we download MP3s, which many of us still do because streaming services don't offer the music we love. I have far more music than I could listen to in the next ten lifetimes, because I want my library to be robust and vast. And we can't always trust that there will be a Wi-Fi connection or even a cellphone signal available. I've been to conferences in China where everybody brought their papers on Google Docs and were shit outta luck because there is no Google there. Using a VPN is one way around this particular problem, but, still, this assumption of stability is a fallacy. If you love it, download it.

Srećko: Your admission to downloading more music than you could ever consume reminds me of Robert Pfaller's theory of interpassivity, which refers to the delegation of consumption and enjoyment and the ways in which media seem to provide their own reception. It is as though your computer is listening to the music rather than yourself. But what if all of this disappears?

Kenneth: I think that archiving is a folk art now. And I think that we are all unconsciously archivists. Take anyone's download folder: Do we ever get around to cleaning it out? No. It's an accrual and, in a way, it becomes autobiographical. You can go back and trace the waves of thought, the manners, and the paths that your mind took and that your life took by reading through almost a sedimentation, an archeological literary document, of that which you have downloaded. And this is not to mention all the archiving we do when, for example, we send emails. All of this accrual is happening, but not in a conscious way. It is just a big mess that most people don't want to deal with. But if we can theorize this work as being personal, poetic, and autobiographical then we can actually situate the archive as a work of art. We are all keeping time capsules like Andy Warhol, who kept a box by the side of his desk and threw anything that he received into it. All sorts of mundane and amazing things went in, there was no discrimination. And when the fucking thing filled up, he would seal it up and sign it as a work of art. He made hundreds and hundreds of these works which were, in essence, archiving as an artistic practice. Today, these boxes are all sitting in the Andy Warhol Museum up on shelves and to open one of them takes months. Three people with gloves on have to take out the McDonald's wrapper, name it, describe it, and archive it, then they take out the nude photo of Bianca Jagger and repeat the process. Warhol knew that he was so important that all of his trash would end up being valuable to people. It was a trap, but it was also about posterity and the future, and the importance of accrual and archiving. Why can't we look at every activity that we do on the web in the way that Warhol looked at his accrual? We may not receive signed records from Mick Jagger, but on a very personal, local level, it actually is a history.

Srećko: You mentioned email, which also appears in Derrida's 1995 *Archive Fever*. And, when I look at my email inbox or download folder, it is really a sort of geology, made up of different levels. At the same time, it offers a form of psychoanalysis; it can tell you something about yourself. Everything is archived in emails, from a business deal to a fight with a friend. You and I are already, now, part of an archive, as is this conversation, so let's imagine that this is a time capsule like Warhol's. What would be your message to a person watching this in 2025?

Kenneth: I think that the future is in the past. What was possible then, is possible now. The utopianism embedded in the nascent web is still possible today. We've just been brainwashed to think it isn't possible, that it is naïve. It can happen and it continues to happen. The spirits of Aaron Swartz, of shadow libraries, and of keeping things simple remain alive. UbuWeb was built in 1996 on the same templates that I used last night to upload films. I'm not much of a programmer and I've never kept up with technology. What I did was basic, and basic continues to work. Let's also acknowledge the digital divide, the fact that a lot of folks don't have access to high bandwidth. What made the web great in the beginning were people and communities, and supporting those communities as opposed to outsourcing to entities that are in it for profit. I think that the message for 2025 is the same as that for 2020, which is the same as that for 2005.

Conversation held on May 8, 2020

Afterword

By Renata Ávila

"The duty of a revolutionary is always to struggle, to struggle no matter what, to struggle to extinction."

— Auguste Blanqui, *Instructions for an Armed Uprising*, 1868

"I recognized us."

— Michael Ende, *Momo*, 1973

It is the summer of 2020 in the northern hemisphere. We are still in the midst of a pandemic, with record deaths and a stagnated global economy. Our gutted health systems are unable to cope. The middle classes are spiraling into poverty and young workers into further precarity. And yet we are the relatively privileged, with the situation becoming increasingly desperate in the South. We are exhausted, but the Covid-19 pandemic will not give us even a moment to breathe. We face states of exception, militarization, suspended elections, and, even worse, elections proceeding with suppressed opposition in Bolivia, Ecuador, and elsewhere. We face the abuse of our irresponsible leaders, and narratives of fear and hate are driving the polls.

Many of the early predictions that appear in this book are now a reality. Poor countries cannot cope; their peoples are being allowed to die. International financial institutions are pushing them to sign debt deals that will destroy their futures. Hunger on an unprecedented scale is imminent,[1] and it will be followed by exacerbated violence. The UN Secretary General's call for a global ceasefire has failed, despite the initial positive response of warring parties in eleven different countries.[2] Big tech and big pharma are marching triumphantly out of the crisis, richer than ever before. The streets of cities around the world are crowded by people protesting in anger, an anger that is not new but that has been accumulated over decades of austerity and structural inequalities. After weeks and months of confinement,

---

1 https://insight.wfp.org/covid-19-will-almost-double-people-in-acute-hunger-by-end-of-2020-59df0c4a8072

2 https://abcnews.go.com/US/wireStory/chief-cease-fire-appeal-backed-parties-11-nations-69961494

millions are taking to the streets to topple pillars of racism, defiant in the face of police forces that pose more danger to dissenters than Covid-19 itself.

The elites, however, appear to have moved on from the Covid-19 crisis quickly. It seems that they spent their spring "seizing the moment," twisting and crafting it so as to enforce a particular idea of the "new normal" that aligns with their interests. When you visit the websites of those responsible for the human tragedy we are living in, from financial institutions to powerful corporations, the prevalent narrative is one of "restarting" or "rebooting" the system, this time with "sustainability." This is the rhetoric in which the enemy resides. We know this story all too well, and we know how it ends: bailout for the few, austerity and despair for the many. We need to challenge the narrative, respond with solutions, prevail in debates, and defeat the Trojan-horse of capitalism's "great reset."

And we can, because this time is different. We too kept busy over spring, and this book is one of the products of our collective activity. We are certain that, in the hands of readers worldwide, it will be transformed into a decentralized, multidisciplinary action plan for building a better future. The beauty of this collection of conversations is that it does not prescribe a unique formula; there are no definite answers. As Richard Sennett highlights in these pages, difference and disagreement are not a weakness of our struggle, but a strength, together with the ability to listen and debate with one another. This book is a compilation of ideas and suggestions for our next steps. And we are sure that you, having read this, will know how to act, when and where to strike.

The global oligarchy is presently mobilizing all its vast resources and political power to take full advantage of the aftermath of the Covid-19 pandemic. But, this time, we are two steps ahead and we greatly outnumber them: from the International Assembly of the Peoples and its seven hundred organizations in eighty countries, to the emerging Progressive International and DiEM25, we have a broad active network that is creative, thriving, and able not only, as Brian Eno suggests, to imagine alternative futures, but to pilot them. As many of the contributors to this book highlight, we are working to reclaim public life and politics from privatization by the small number of firms that comprise big tech. We are working for a world with more peoples' armies of doctors such as that in Cuba and with less undermining of public healthcare, education, housing, and labor. We are working for future social and natural worlds that are not premised on rampant exploitation. The upcoming months will test our communities and organizational spaces in unprecedented ways, requiring us to put all our knowledge, time, and expertise at the service of the moment. It is the duty of the revolutionary to struggle: Join us in our struggle for another now.

Join DiEM25: https://diem25.org

Join the Progressive International: https://progressive.international/

The Editors and the Contributors

THE EDITORS

Renata Ávila is a Guatemalan international human rights lawyer and author. She co-founded and is a Council member of the Progressive International and is a member of DiEM25's Coordinating Collective. She also co-founded the <A+> Alliance for Inclusive Algorithms. An expert in digital rights, she studies the politics of data, the evolution of transparency, and their implications for trade, democracy, and society, highlighting a phenomenon she describes as digital colonialism.

Srećko Horvat is a philosopher born in Croatia (former Yugoslavia) in 1983. He has published over a dozen books, most recently *After the Apocalypse* (Polity Press, 2020) and *Poetry from the Future* (Penguin, 2019) and has been active in various social movements. He was one of the founders of the Subversive Festival in Zagreb and is a co-founder of DiEM25.

DiEM25 is a pan-European movement that aims to democratise the European Union, in the knowledge that it will only survive if it is radically transformed.

Despite the promise of the European Union, today, a common bureaucracy and common currency divide the peoples of Europe. We, the peoples of Europe, have a duty to regain control over our union from unaccountable technocrats, myopic politicians, and shadowy institutions. Against the non-choice of retreating to nationalism or surrendering to Brussels, there is another course of action, and it is the only one that can save the EU from disintegration: Democratise Europe!

THE CONTRIBUTORS

David Adler is General Coordinator of the Progressive International. Previously, he was the Policy Director of the Democracy in Europe Movement (DiEM25), and the coordinator of its Green New Deal for Europe campaign. His research and writing have been featured in the *New York Times*, the *Washington Post*, and the *Guardian*, among others.

Tariq Ali is a writer, filmmaker, and longstanding editor of *New Left Review*. He has written more than two dozen books on world history and politics, and seven novels as well as scripts for the stage and screen. He is the co-editor of *In Defense of Julian Assange*.

Gael García Bernal is an actor and producer known for his performances in the films *The Science of Sleep; Amores perros* and *Babel,* both directed by Alejandro González Iñárritu; and his portrayal of Che Guevara in *The Motorcycle Diaries,* for which he was nominated for a BAFTA. In 2010, he co-directed *Los Invisibles,* a series of short films about migrants from Central America in Mexico, made in collaboration with Amnesty International. He engages in activism on issues of migration, environment, and human rights, and is the co-founder of Documental Ambulante, a non-profit organization that brings documentary films and training programs to diverse areas across Mexico with the aim of generating social change.

Larry Charles has directed films including *Borat, Bruno, The Dictator, Religulous,* and *Masked and Anonymous,* written with and starring Bob Dylan, as well as numerous TV shows including *Curb Your Enthusiasm,* for which he has been nominated for multiple Emmys. He was also an Emmy winning writer-producer on *Seinfeld.* He most recently created, directed, and wrote a four-part limited series for Netflix, titled *Larry Charles' Dangerous World of Comedy.*

Noam Chomsky is one of the most influential and cited scholars in modern history. He has authored more than 100 books on linguistics, philosophy, history, and politics, and is an ally of anarcho-syndicalists around the world. He is Institute Professor (emeritus) in the Department of Linguistics and Philosophy at MIT, where he has taught since 1955. He is Laureate Professor of Linguistics and Agnese Nelms Haury Chair at the University of Arizona.

Daniel Ellsberg is an economist, activist, and former US military analyst who in 1971 leaked the Pentagon Papers, which revealed how the US public had been misled about the Vietnam war.

Brian Eno is an English musician, composer, producer, theorist, and visual artist known for his pioneering work in ambient music and contributions to rock, pop, and electronica. He is an activist known for his progressive politics and a member of the Advisory Panel for DiEM25.

Kenneth Goldsmith is the author and editor of over 30 books. He teaches writing at the University of Pennsylvania. His most recent book is *Duchamp Is My Lawyer: The Polemics, Pragmatics, and Poetics of UbuWeb.*

David Graeber was a professor of anthropology at the London School of Economics and the author of *Debt: The First 5000 Years* and *Bullshit Jobs.* As a political activist he was involved in the Global Justice Movement and Occupy Wall Street.

Johann Hari is the author of two *New York Times* best-selling books. His first, *Chasing the Scream: the First and Last Days of the War on Drugs*, is being adapted into a major film and a non-fiction documentary series. His most recent book, *Lost Connections: Uncovering The Real Causes of Depression – and the Unexpected Solutions,* was shortlisted for an award by the British Medical Association and is being translated into 28 languages. His TED talks on addiction and depression have been widely viewed and his articles have featured in many of the world's leading newspapers.

Maja Kantar is a researcher currently living and working in London. She studied political science and peace studies in Serbia and postcolonial theory in the UK. Current research interests combine political and cultural theory, philosophy of nihilism, and utopian studies.

Stephanie Kelton is a professor of economics and public policy at Stony Brook University and a leading expert on Modern Monetary Theory. She served as chief economist on the U.S. Senate Budget Committee (Democratic staff) in 2015 and served as a senior economic adviser to Bernie Sanders's 2016 and 2020 presidential campaigns. She was named by Politico as one of the 50 most influential people on the policy debate in America. She is the author of the *New York Times* bestseller *The Deficit Myth: Modern Monetary Theory and the Birth of the People's Economy.*

Stefania Maurizi is an investigative journalist currently working for the major Italian daily *Il Fatto Quotidiano* and previously for *la Repubblica,* one of the top Italian newspapers, and the news magazine *l'Espresso.* She has worked on all WikiLeaks document releases since 2009, and partnered with Glenn Greenwald to reveal the Snowden files about Italy. Stefania has started a multi-jurisdictional freedom of information litigation effort to defend the right of the press to access the full set of documents on the Julian Assange and WikiLeaks case. She is the author of two books: *Dossier WikiLeaks: Segreti Italiani* and *Una Bomba: Dieci Storie*.

Evgeny Morozov is a contributing editor at *The New Republic* and the author of *The Net Delusion: The Dark Side of Internet Freedom* and *To Save Everything, Click Here: The Folly of Technological Solutionism*. He is a former visiting scholar at Stanford University and a Schwartz fellow at the New America Foundation. He is the founder of the Syllabus website, which publishes curated syllabi combining text, audio, and video content with an aim of salvaging what is important from the masses of information we encounter online. He has contributed to the *New York Times*, the *Economist*, the *Financial Times*, the *London Review of Books*, and other publications.

Ivana Nenadović is a theater producer and grassroots activist. She coordinates the Belgrade DiEM25 Spontaneous Collective (DSC) and is a president of the Trade Union of Actors at the National Theater of Belgrade.

Maja Pelević is a playwright and director whose plays have been produced around Europe, translated into several languages, and published in anthologies of contemporary drama. She has worked on more than 20 shows, dramatized novels, and written songs for four musicals. She is the main scriptwriter and dramaturge for the TV series *Morning Changes Everything* and has won many major awards including the Borislav Mihajlovic Mihiz award for achievement in playwriting and the Sterija award for best contemporary play.

Vijay Prashad is the executive director of Tricontinental: Institute for Social Research. He is the author or editor of several books, including *The Darker Nations: A Biography of the Short-Lived Third World* and *The Poorer Nations: A Possible History of the Global South*. He is the editor of *Strongmen*, which analyses the dictatorial politics of Putin, Erdoğan, Duterte, Trump, and Modi. He writes regularly for *Frontline, The Hindu, Alternet, and BirGun*.

Angela Richter is an acclaimed Croatian–German theatre director, activist, and author. She founded Fleetstreet Theater in Hamburg and is a former house director at the Cologne National Theatre Schauspiel Köln.

Richter's recent work, including her 2015 transmedia project 'Supernerds', explore digital mass surveillance, whistleblowing, and digital dissidents, drawing on conversations with Edward Snowden, Daniel Ellsberg, and Julian Assange.

Saskia Sassen is the Robert S. Lynd Professor of Sociology at Columbia University and a Member of its Committee on Global Thought, which she chaired till 2015. Her work focuses on cities, immigration, and states in the world economy, with inequality, gendering, and digitization three key variables running throughout. She is the author of eight books and has received many awards and honors, including the 2020 Edgar de Picciotto Prize from The Graduate Institute, Geneva.

Saša Savanović is a writer and political theorist who works as a researcher and editor. Her interests are at the intersection of politics, economy and technology. She has published several short stories and a number of articles. Her first novel *Deseti život (Life no. 10)*, was shortlisted for the 2018 NIN award, the most prestigious literary award in Serbia.

Jeremy Scahill is an investigative reporter, writer, and a founding editor of *The Intercept*, a news organization dedicated to holding the powerful to account and exposing corruption and injustice. He has reported from Afghanistan, Iraq, Somalia, Yemen, Nigeria, and the former Yugoslavia, among other places. He is the author of *Dirty Wars: The World is a Battlefield* and *Blackwater: The Rise of the World's Most Powerful Mercenary Army*, which won the George Polk Book Award.

Richard Sennett serves as Senior Advisor to the United Nations on its program on Climate Change and Cities. He is a Senior Fellow of the Center on Capitalism and Society at Columbia University. He founded the New York Institute for the Humanities and previously taught at New York University and at the London School of Economics. His works include *The Fall of Public Man, The Culture of the New Capitalism,* and *Building and Dwelling: Ethics for the City.*

John Shipton is an Australian activist and builder, and the father of Wikileaks founder Julian Assange.

Astra Taylor is a filmmaker, author, and activist. She is the author of *The People's Platform: Taking Back Power and Culture in the Digital*

Age and *Democracy May Not Exist, But We'll Miss It When It's Gone.* She is a founder of the Debt Collective.

Ece Temelkuran is a Turkish journalist, novelist, and political commentator. She has contributed to the *Guardian, Newstatesman, New Left Review, Der Spiegel,* and the *New York Times.* She is the author of multiple books including *How to Lose a Country: The 7 Steps from Democracy to Dictatorship.*

Yanis Varoufakis is an economist and politician. He is the founder and secretary of the left wing Greek political party MeRA25, which is part of DiEM 25. A former member of Syriza, he served as the Greek finance minister from January to July 2015 under Prime Minister Alexis Tsipras.

Roger Waters is an English songwriter, singer, bassist, and composer who co-founded the progressive rock band Pink Floyd. He is known for his activism, including raising awareness on issues of climate change, global poverty, and freedom of the press, and supporting the BDS movement in solidarity with Palestinians against the Israeli occupation.

Slavoj Žižek is one of the most prolific and well-known philosophers and cultural theorists in the world today. His inventive, provocative body of work mixes Hegelian metaphysics, Lacanian psychoanalysis, and Marxist dialectic in order to challenge conventional wisdom and accepted verities on both the left and the right.

Shoshana Zuboff is the author of *The Age of Surveillance Capitalism: The Fight for a Human Future at the New Frontier of Power,* a bestselling sociological analysis of the digital era and the expropriation of data and privacy rights from technology users. She is the Charles Edward Wilson Professor Emerita at Harvard Business School and a former Faculty Associate at the Berkman Klein Center for Internet and Society at Harvard Law School.